FULHAM

FOOTBALL CLUB OFFICIAL SEASON REVIEW 2005/06

Editorial
Tim Beynon, Tom Rowland

Sidan Press Team
Simon Rosen, Julian Hill-Wood, Marc Fiszman, Mark Peters, Karim Biria, Rob Cubbon, Anette Lundebye, Marina Kravchenko, Gareth Peters, Janet Calcott, Trevor Scimes, John Fitzroy, Jenny Middlemarch, Anders Rasmussen, Lim Wai-Lee, Emma Turner, Charles Grove, Tim Ryman, Ronen Dorfan

Photography
Action Images

Sidan Press, 63-64 Margaret St, London W1W 8SW
Tel: 020 7580 0200
Email: info@sidanpress.com

sidanpress.com

Club Directory

Chairman and Directors

Chairman
Mohamed Al Fayed

Managing Director
David McNally

Directors
Omar Fayed, Karim Fayed, Mark Collins, Stuart Benson, Ian McLeod

Football Management

Team Manager
Chris Coleman

Assistant Manager
Steve Kean

Reserve Team Managers
Billy McKinlay, Ray Lewington

Goalkeeper Coach
Dave Beasant

Head of Domestic Scouting
Ewan Chester

Sports Physicians
Chris Bradshaw
Steve Lewis

Head Physiotherapist
Jason Palmer

Head of Youth
John Murtough

Management Board

Head of Communications
Sarah Brookes

Head of Commercial Operations
Olly Dale

Head of Business Operations
Harley Evans

Head of Community
Simon Morgan

Head of Finance
Darren Preston

Head of Marketing
Emma Taylor

Club Secretary
Zoe Ward

Contacts

Fulham Football Club Training Ground
Motspur Park
New Malden
Surrey
KT3 6PT

Main Tel: 0870 442 1222
Fax (Motspur Park): 020 8336 0514
FFC Ticket Line: 0870 442 1234
Club FFC: 0870 442 1221
Fulham Direct: 0870 442 1223
Community: 0870 442 5432
Commercial Enquiries: 020 8336 7555
Club Email: enquiries@fulhamfc.com
Web: www.fulhamfc.com

Contents

 # Partner Directory

Official Main Team Sponsor

For the latest offers visit: www.pipex.com

Official Technical Kit Supplier

For the latest Airness Fulham gear visit: www.shop.fulhamfc.com/shop/

Official Cable Partner

For the latest products visit
www.monstercable.com/europe

**Official Mobile Handset & Consumer
Electronics Partner**

For all your LG mobile technology visit: www.wowlg.com
For all the latest products visit: www.lge.com

FULHAM

FOOTBALL CLUB OFFICIAL SEASON REVIEW 2005/06

www.fulhamfc.com

Follow the action all the way to the net!

Chris Coleman
Manager

2005/06 was a tough old season again as I knew it would be, but I am more than pleased with the final finishing position of 12th.

I made some changes in the summer which I had decided on towards the end of the previous season, with the intention of shaking things up a bit and moving us in a different direction behind the scenes. In the summer we lost three key players in Edwin van der Sar, Lee Clark and Andy Cole, and replacing the spine of the team on a limited budget was always going to be a challenge, so I ensured we had the best possible structure in place to get more out of the players we had, and those we brought in.

We introduced a new fitness regime by recruiting Steve Nance, who offered a different perspective on a footballer's performance level. We also added *prozone* to monitor the effectiveness of performances. I knew that it was going to be challenging so it was vital that we got a little bit more from everybody, and on the whole I'm pleased with the way things went, and I fully intend to make sure we take another step forward next season.

In terms of the play, obviously our home performances, with only a few exceptions, were very pleasing. We were great value for money to watch at the Cottage playing really good attacking football, we purposely made our game more open and where at times we were accused of being negative in our play the previous season, we couldn't be accused of that last term.

The away record speaks for itself with only one win on our travels during the whole campaign. This isn't something that any of us are proud of I can assure you, and I can make all the excuses in the world about bad decisions and results not being a fair reflection of the play but at the end of the day we are

in a results business and the stats don't lie. What is more disappointing is that our home form was top eight and if we had combined that with more consistency on our travels, we could have finished there. But it's my job to make sure we make our performances and results consistent next season, and that we push on up the table.

Without doubt the best high of the season was beating Chelsea at home. It was a fantastic performance from every one of the players involved and there was a tremendous atmosphere at the ground – as there was at almost every game - but it was also special because it ended a really tough period of games and run of bad results, and to do it against the Champions was very special.

Inside the camp we had great belief all season and even when things got tough around March with a run of bad results the spirit stayed positive. It's easy having a good spirit when you're winning, it's when the going gets difficult that it really counts, and we proved that we've got a strong group of individuals that make a really good team. I personally, and some of my backroom staff, took some stick. I was given two games by some factions of the press but that didn't worry me. I have great belief in what we have achieved here and great passion for the future, so in some ways I think it's made me even stronger because that sense of belief never dwindled during that period, it just made me more determined.

The Chairman and the Board have been fully supportive of the signings we have made starting with Heidar Helguson and Phillippe Christanval in the summer and through to Antti Niemi, Michael Brown and Simon Elliott in January, and we achieved a real coup in getting Wayne Bridge on loan from Chelsea, who made a valuable contribution for us in the latter part of the campaign.

The business through these summer months looks very promising too, agreeing a deal with Jimmy Bullard before the window even opened was a good bit of business for us and proves that we have ambition to achieve. The Chairman is desperate for us to be a top 10 club and his financial commitment proves that. Let's not forget how much money he has ploughed into this Club already and for him to invest even more so we can push on, is a really exciting step for us and I'm delighted to be part of the next stage of Fulham's future.

The aim is to build and keeping hold of our best players is part of that, but sometimes you don't always get what you want, but if we lose any of our top boys, it won't be because I haven't tried my hardest to get them to stay.

2006/07 is full of promise, and I for one am really looking forward to it.

Chris Coleman, Manager

How to Read the Stats

This year's review is better than ever, packed with the sort of in-depth stats which really get you close to the action. If you'd like to know why a particular match turned out the way it did, how a player's form varied over the course of the season, or how Fulham have fared against their biggest rivals, you'll find all the info inside.

To make sure you're getting the most out of the stats, we're including this section to highlight the information presented by some of the charts and tables.

Colours

Fulham vs Opposition

There are lots of comparisons between Fulham and our opponents throughout the book. Fulham stats are shown in red; opponents are shown in grey:

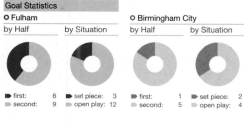

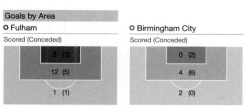

Figure 1: Fulham stats are in red; opposition stats are grey.

WDL, Scored, Conceded

When reviewing match results, wins, draws and losses are indicated by green, grey and orange blocks, respectively. For goals, green blocks indicate goals scored; orange blocks show goals conceded:

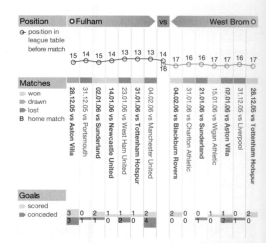

Figure 2: Wins, draws, losses and goals are clearly colour-coded.

Match Reports

The Match Report section contains reports, quotes, facts and stats from every Fulham match of the 2005/06 season.

Stats Order (Home and Away)

The order of the stats varies depending on whether a match was home or away: for home matches, Fulham stats are shown on the left, for away matches they're on the right:

Premiership Totals	Fulham	Man City
Premiership Appearances	937	1,812
Team Appearances	717	685
Goals Scored	123	252
Assists	107	166
Clean Sheets (goalkeepers)	2	127
Yellow Cards	122	209
Red Cards	9	14
Full Internationals	9	6

Figure 3: For home matches, Fulham stats appear on the left.

Premiership Totals	West Brom	Fulham
Premiership Appearances	1,144	1,346
Team Appearances	411	974
Goals Scored	112	137
Assists	94	122
Clean Sheets (goalkeepers)	2	49
Yellow Cards	106	155
Red Cards	4	13
Full Internationals	5	10

Figure 4: For away matches, Fulham stats appear on the right.

Form Coming into Fixture

Stats are from the previous seven league games. For the first few matches, these stats include games from the end of the previous season.

Team Statistics

Stats are for starters and playing subs. The "Premiership Totals" chart measures performance within the Premiership (with the exception of "Full Internationals").

Premiership Totals	Fulham	Portsmouth
Premiership Appearances	1,828	1,094
Team Appearances	855	477
Goals Scored	173	63
Assists	184	52
Clean Sheets (goalkeepers)	52	52
Yellow Cards	163	96
Red Cards	12	7
Full Internationals	10	10

Age/Height	
Fulham Age	Portsmouth Age
▶ 29 yrs	▶ 27 yrs, 7 mo
Fulham Height	Portsmouth Height
▶ 5'11"	▶ 5'11"

Figure 5: Team statistics are for starters and playing subs.

Player Profiles

The Player Profile section provides season reviews and comprehensive stats for Fulham's players. The section is organised by position, starting with goalkeepers.

Pitch Diagram

The diagram shows all positions the player played during 2005/06. The main position is denoted by a dark red circle; alternative positions are denoted by light red circles:

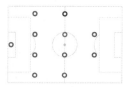

Figure 6: Major positions are shown in dark red; minor positions are shown in light red.

Player Performance

All stats show league performance, with the exception of the "Cup Games" table. The "League Performance" chart provides an excellent overview of the player's performance over the course of the season. At a glance, you can see when and how much he played, and see how he contributed to the team's overall performance at different stages of the season.

Career History

Due to the difficulties involved in obtaining reliable stats for international clubs, the "Clubs" table is incomplete for players who have played for non-English clubs. The names of all clubs have been included for the reader's interest, but international stats have been left blank.

The Opposition

The Opposition section shows how Fulham sizes up against the other 19 teams in the Premiership. Also included are season reviews, stadium diagrams and seating plans, stadium histories, stadium stats, and maps and directions.

Points / Position

The points / position chart is a snapshot of the last 10 years' league performance of Fulham and the opponent. For any season when the two teams met in the league, the results of their clashes are shown at the bottom of the chart.

Premiership Head-to-Head

Stats are only for the two teams' meetings in the Premiership.

Season Review 2005/06

Fulham 0
Birmingham City 0

▶ Steed Malbranque squeezes between Jamie Clapham and Stephen Clemence

Event Line

36 O ▢	Legwinski	
37 O ▢	Clemence	
Half time 0-0		
46 O ⇄	John	> Radzinski
68 O ▢	Upson	
71 O ⇄	Forssell	> Pandiani
87 O ⇄	Morrison	> Heskey
90 O ⇄	Elrich	> Legwinski
Full time 0-0		

Not the usual August sunshine for this opening game of the 05/06 Premiership season but the weather was befitting of a somewhat dour opening salvo.

The game got off to a cagey opening as both sides tentatively weighed each other up. Fulham made the first real opening after some good work by Claus Jensen released Luis Boa Morte down the left hand channel, his teasing cross was met by Tomasz Radzinski but Maik Taylor gathered the shot easily.

With half-time looming Steed Malbranque broke clear of the Birmingham back line and a slick interchange between Boa Morte and McBride saw the Captain with a clear chance. Once again, however, Taylor came to the rescue to block the shot. Boa Morte was alert though and got to the rebound but could only steer his shot against the bar.

The second half proved to be much the same as the first with neither side making the most of their chances. Claus Jensen failed to trouble Taylor with a free kick during the half and Malbranque blazed high over the bar following good work by Collins John and Jensen. A disappointing afternoon all round but the first point of the season.

'Monster' Player of the Match	Quote	Premiership Milestone
8 Claus Jensen	⚽ **Chris Coleman**	▶ **Debut**

There were incidents at both ends and I thoroughly enjoyed the game.

Both Tony Warner and Ahmad Elrich made their Premiership debuts, while Niclas Jensen made his first Premiership appearance in the colours of Fulham.

Venue:	Craven Cottage	Referee:	R.Styles - 05/06	
Attendance:	16,550	Matches:	1	**Fulham**
Capacity:	22,646	Yellow Cards:	3	**Birmingham City**
Occupancy:	73%	Red Cards:	0	

Form Coming into Fixture

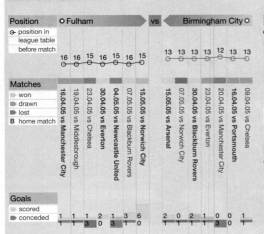

Position
- position in league table before match

Fulham: 16 16 15 16 15 16 15
Birmingham City: 13 13 13 13 12 13 13

Matches
- won
- drawn
- lost
- B home match

Fulham matches:
16.04.05 vs Manchester City
19.04.05 vs Middlesbrough
23.04.05 vs Chelsea
30.04.05 vs Everton
04.05.05 vs Newcastle United
07.05.05 vs Blackburn Rovers
15.05.05 vs Norwich City

Birmingham matches:
15.05.05 vs Arsenal
07.05.05 vs Norwich City
30.04.05 vs Blackburn Rovers
23.04.05 vs Everton
20.04.05 vs Manchester City
16.04.05 vs Portsmouth
09.04.05 vs Chelsea

Goals
scored	1	1	1	2	1	3	6		2	0	2	1	0	0	1
conceded	1	1	3	0	3	1	0		1	1	1	1	3	0	1

Goal Statistics

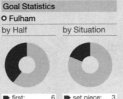

Fulham

by Half | by Situation

| first: | 6 | set piece: | 3 |
| second: | 9 | open play: | 12 |

Birmingham City

by Half | by Situation

| first: | 1 | set piece: | 2 |
| second: | 5 | open play: | 4 |

Goals by Area

Fulham — Scored (Conceded)

2 (9)
12 (5)
1 (1)

Birmingham City — Scored (Conceded)

0 (2)
4 (6)
2 (0)

Team Statistics

Starting Line-Ups

Fulham: Warner; Jensen N, Boa Morte, Rehman, Jensen C, McBride, Knight, Legwinski (Elrich), Radzinski (John), Volz, Malbranque

Birmingham: Pennant, Melchiot, Butt, Cunningham, Heskey (Morrison), Pandiani (Forssell), Clemence, Upson, Taylor Maik, Gray, Clapham

4/4/2 | **4/4/2**

Unused Sub: Batista, Leacock, Helguson
Unused Sub: Vaesen, Lazaridis, Izzet

Premiership Totals

	Fulham	Birmingham
Premiership Appearances	966	1,849
Team Appearances	673	643
Goals Scored	126	169
Assists	124	171
Clean Sheets (goalkeepers)	0	35
Yellow Cards	98	184
Red Cards	9	10
Full Internationals	8	9

Age/Height

	Fulham	Birmingham City
Age	**27 yrs, 3 mo**	**28 yrs, 3 mo**
Height	**6'**	**6'**

Match Statistics

League Table after Fixture

		Played	Won	Drawn	Lost	For	Against	Pts
7	Birmingham	1	0	1	0	0	0	1
8	Fulham	1	0	1	0	0	0	1
9	Liverpool	1	0	1	0	0	0	1
10	Man City	1	0	1	0	0	0	1
11	Middlesbrough	1	0	1	0	0	0	1
12	West Brom	1	0	1	0	0	0	1
13	Arsenal	0	0	0	0	0	0	0
14	Chelsea	0	0	0	0	0	0	0
15	Newcastle	0	0	0	0	0	0	0

Statistics

	Fulham	Birmingham
Goals	0	0
Shots on Target	7	4
Shots off Target	7	3
Hit Woodwork	1	0
Possession %	51	49
Corners	6	6
Offsides	2	6
Fouls	12	13
Disciplinary Points	4	8

Blackburn Rovers 2
Fulham 1

20.08.05

▶ Luis Boa Morte surges down the wing

Event Line

15	⊕	Pedersen / LF / OP / IA
		Assist: Kuqi
Half time 1-0		
49	⊕	McBride / RF / IFK / IA
		Assist: Jensen N
65	▪	Reid
68	▪	Diop
71	⊕	Tugay / RF / C / OA
		Assist: Pedersen
73	▪	Savage
81	⇄	Helguson > McBride
81	⇄	John > Radzinski
89	▪	John
90	⇄	Flitcroft > Emerton
Full time 2-1		

Fulham were undone by a couple of Blackburn wonder goals at Ewood Park in their first away game of the season.

The game started brightly for Fulham, however, with Luis Boa Morte arrowing in an early 30-yard drive that Brad Friedel fumbled but eventually gathered before anyone could pounce on the spillage.

But, as the half progressed, Fulham fell behind to Blackburn's first strike. A fizzing right wing cross – which was over hit by striker Shefki Kuqi and which evaded everyone in the six yard box – fell to Morten Gamst Pedersen who smashed home an unstoppable volley to make it 1-0.

Fulham started the second half well and were awarded an early free kick for a foul on Boa Morte. It was taken quickly and found Niclas Jensen who raced for the by-line before driving in a low cross which Brian McBride prodded home for 1-1.

With both sides battling to take the initiative Blackburn were awarded a corner with 20 minutes to go. Pedersen floated it out to the edge of the box where Tugay was waiting, the Turk unleashed a rocket to seal all three points for Rovers and leave Fulham with just one point from their opening two games.

'Monster' Player of the Match	Quote	Premiership Milestone
30 Tony Warner	❝ **Chris Coleman**	▶ **Debut**

We can't turn up anywhere at only 70 or 80% and expect to get anything.

Heidar Helguson made his first Premiership appearance for Fulham.

Venue:	Ewood Park	Referee:	H.M.Webb - 05/06		**Blackburn Rovers**
Attendance:	16,953	Matches:	2		**Fulham**
Capacity:	31,367	Yellow Cards:	5		
Occupancy:	54%	Red Cards:	1		

Form Coming into Fixture

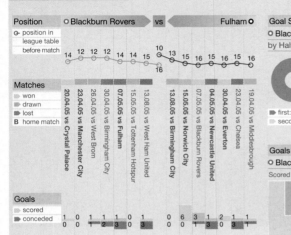

Position
- ○ position in league table before match

○ Blackburn Rovers vs Fulham ○

14 12 12 12 14 14 15 — 10 13 15 16 15 16 15 16 / 16

Matches
- won
- drawn
- lost
- B home match

Blackburn Rovers:
20.04.05 vs Crystal Palace
23.04.05 vs Manchester City
26.04.05 vs West Brom
30.04.05 vs Birmingham City
07.05.05 vs Fulham
15.05.05 vs Tottenham Hotspur

Fulham:
13.08.05 vs West Ham United
13.08.05 vs Birmingham City
15.05.05 vs Norwich City
07.05.05 vs Blackburn Rovers
04.05.05 vs Newcastle United
30.04.05 vs Everton
23.04.05 vs Chelsea
19.04.05 vs Middlesbrough

Goals
- scored
- conceded

| scored | 1 | 0 | 1 | 1 | 1 | 0 | 1 | | 0 | 6 | 3 | 1 | 2 | 1 | 1 |
| conceded | 0 | 0 | | 2 | 3 | 0 | 3 | | 0 | 0 | | 3 | 0 | 3 | 1 |

Goal Statistics

○ Blackburn Rovers

by Half	by Situation
first: 4	set piece: 2
second: 1	open play: 3

○ Fulham

by Half	by Situation
first: 6	set piece: 3
second: 8	open play: 11

Goals by Area

○ Blackburn Rovers

Scored (Conceded)

1 (1)
4 (5)
0 (3)

○ Fulham

Scored (Conceded)

11 (5)
1 (1)

Team Statistics

Starting Line-Ups

Blackburn Rovers:
Friedel
Matteo, Pedersen
Savage
Nelson
Tugay, Kuqi
Todd
Reid
Neill, Emerton
Flitcroft

Fulham:
Malbranque, Volz
Diop, Knight
Radzinski John
Warner
McBride Helguson
Jensen C, Rehman
Boa Morte, Jensen N

▶ 4/5/1   **▶ 4/4/2**

Unused Sub: Enckelman, Gresko, Gallagher, Johnson J
Unused Sub: Batista, Leacock, Elrich

Premiership Totals

	○ Blackburn	Fulham ○
Premiership Appearances	1,554	907
Team Appearances	846	598
Goals Scored	75	130
Assists	111	120
Clean Sheets (goalkeepers)	51	1
Yellow Cards	244	90
Red Cards	12	10
Full Internationals	10	9

Age/Height

Blackburn Rovers Age	Fulham Age
▶ 29 yrs, 6 mo	**▶ 27 yrs, 3 mo**
Blackburn Rovers Height	Fulham Height
▶ 6'	**▶ 6'**

Match Statistics

League Table after Fixture

	Played	Won	Drawn	Lost	For	Against	Pts
↑ 10 Blackburn	2	1	0	1	3	4	3
↓ 11 Bolton	1	0	1	0	2	2	1
↓ 12 Aston Villa	2	0	1	1	2	3	1
↓ 13 Birmingham	2	0	1	1	1	2	1
↓ 14 Fulham	2	0	1	1	1	2	1
↓ 15 Middlesbrough	2	0	1	1	0	2	1
↑ 16 Newcastle	2	0	1	1	0	2	1
↑ 17 Everton	1	0	0	1	0	2	0
↓ 18 Wigan	2	0	0	2	0	2	0

Statistics

	○ Blackburn	Fulham ○
Goals	2	1
Shots on Target	9	4
Shots off Target	7	4
Hit Woodwork	1	0
Possession %	51	49
Corners	8	1
Offsides	3	2
Fouls	26	14
Disciplinary Points	8	8

➤ Claus Jensen is tracked by Aleksandr Hleb

Event Line

22 O ⊕	Jensen C / RF / OP / IA
	Assist: Radzinski
24 O ■	Boa Morte
32 O ⊕	Cygan / H / IFK / IA
	Assist: Bergkamp
35 O ■	Reyes
44 O ■	Bergkamp
45 O ■	Rehman
Half time 1-1	
53 O ⊕	Henry / RF / OP / IA
	Assist: Reyes
56 O ■	Cole
64 O ⇄	John > McBride
72 O ■	Lauren
77 O ⇄	Flamini > Reyes
80 O ■	Flamini
82 O ⊕	Henry / RF / OP / IA
	Assist: Flamini
83 O ⇄	Clichy > Hleb
90 O ⊕	Cygan / LF / IFK / 6Y
	Assist: Toure
Full time 4-1	

The task of upsetting one of the form teams in the Premier League proved just too much for a valiant and attacking Fulham side.

Disaster struck early on when Zat Knight was adjudged to have fouled Thierry Henry and referee Mark Clattenburg had no hesitation in pointing to the spot. Lauren stepped up but Tony Warner guessed correctly and kept the scores level.

Fulham took a surprise lead when Kolo Toure failed to clear and Claus Jensen, on the edge of the box, curled a delicious shot over Lehmann to make it 1-0 to Fulham.

Arsenal took just 10 minutes to get back on level terms, as Pascal Cygan ghosted in to meet a Dennis Bergkamp free kick.

The Gunners stepped it up in the second half and Thierry Henry found himself clear on goal after 54 minutes, he calmly took it around Warner and slotted home for the lead. Two successive goals in the last 10 minutes gave the scoreline an added gloss for Arsenal, with Henry and Cygan both netting braces and leaving an unlucky Fulham side to travel back across London with no points.

'Monster' Player of the Match	Quote	Premiership Milestone
30 Tony Warner	🔒 **Chris Coleman**	▶ **50**
	We created chances and it was a good team effort. The result looks like a hammering, but we gave them a good game.	Brian McBride made his 50th Premiership appearance for the Whites.

Venue:	Highbury	Referee:	M.Clattenburg - 05/06	Arsenal
Attendance:	37,867	Matches:	3	**Fulham**
Capacity:	38,419	Yellow Cards:	8	
Occupancy:	99%	Red Cards:	1	

Form Coming into Fixture

Position

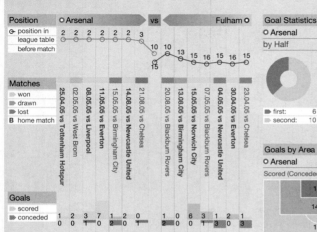

	O Arsenal	vs	Fulham O

position in league table before match

Arsenal: 2 2 2 2 2 2 3
Fulham: 10 10 13 15 16 15 16 15 / 15

Matches
- won
- drawn
- lost
- **B** home match

25.04.05 vs Tottenham Hotspur
02.05.05 vs West Brom
08.05.05 vs Liverpool
11.05.05 vs Birmingham City
15.05.05 vs Everton
14.08.05 vs Newcastle United
21.08.05 vs Chelsea
20.04.05 vs Blackburn Rovers
13.08.05 vs Birmingham City
15.05.05 vs Norwich City
07.05.05 vs Blackburn Rovers
04.05.05 vs Newcastle United
30.04.05 vs Everton
23.04.05 vs Chelsea

Goals
	scored	1 2 3 7 1 2 0	1 0 6 3 1 2 1
	conceded	0 0 1 0 2 0 1	2 0 0 1 3 0 3

Goal Statistics

O Arsenal

by Half	by Situation
first: 6	set piece: 3
second: 10	open play: 13

O Fulham

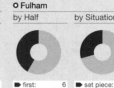

by Half	by Situation
first: 6	set piece: 4
second: 8	open play: 10

Goals by Area

O Arsenal
Scored (Conceded)

1 (0)
14 (3)
1 (1)

O Fulham
Scored (Conceded)

2 (2)
11 (5)
1 (2)

Team Statistics

Starting Line-Ups

Cole, Reyes, Flamini, Malbranque, Volz, Jensen C, Cygan, Gilberto Silva, Henry, Knight, Lehmann, Warner, McBride, John, Diop, Bergkamp, Toure, Fabregas, Rehman, Boa Morte, Lauren, Hleb, Clichy, Radzinski, Jensen N

 4/4/2  4/5/1

Unused Sub: Almunia, Pires, van Persie

Unused Sub: Batista, Leacock, Elrich, Helguson

Premiership Totals

	O Arsenal	Fulham O
Premiership Appearances	1,216	903
Team Appearances	1.216	610
Goals Scored	260	125
Assists	239	118
Clean Sheets (goalkeepers)	27	1
Yellow Cards	144	86
Red Cards	2	10
Full Internationals	9	8

Age/Height

Arsenal Age	Fulham Age
26 yrs, 6 mo	27 yrs, 2 mo
Arsenal Height	Fulham Height
5'11"	6'

Match Statistics

League Table after Fixture

		Played	Won	Drawn	Lost	For	Against	Pts
↑ 4	Arsenal	3	2	0	1	6	2	6
...		...	...	...	...	...	...	...
↓ 14	Aston Villa	3	0	2	1	3	4	2
↑ 15	Portsmouth	3	0	1	2	2	5	1
↓ 16	Fulham	3	0	1	2	2	6	1
↑ 17	Birmingham	3	0	1	2	1	5	1
↓ 18	Newcastle	3	0	1	2	0	4	1
● 19	Wigan	2	0	0	2	0	2	0
● 20	Sunderland	3	0	0	3	2	6	0

Statistics

	O Arsenal	Fulham O
Goals	4	1
Shots on Target	14	4
Shots off Target	6	5
Hit Woodwork	0	0
Possession %	57	43
Corners	6	7
Offsides	3	4
Fouls	16	11
Disciplinary Points	20	8

Fulham 1
Everton 0

  Everton

27.08.05

▶ Brian McBride celebrates his winning goal

Event Line

44 ○ ▨	Weir
Half time 0-0	
57 ○ ⊕	McBride / RF / OP / IA
	Assist: Volz
70 ○ ▨	Neville
75 ○ ⇄	Ferguson > Kilbane
77 ○ ⇄	McFadden > Bent M
77 ○ ⇄	Vaughan > Davies
90 ○ ◢	Neville
	2nd Bookable Offence
90 ○ ▨	Malbranque
Full time 1-0	

A massive win for the Whites as the early season pressure was beginning to mount on the back of a couple of disappointing results.

It was Everton, however, who started the brighter of the two sides, with Mikael Arteta and Kevin Kilbane playing some neat football to create an early chance for Marcus Bent who failed to capitalise on it.

Fulham began to get a foot hold in the game as the half went on and Zat Knight played a 50-yard ball to Tomasz Radzinski. The Canadian found Luis Boa Morte homing in on goal but the Portuguese international squeezed his shot inches wide.

Fulham came out for the second half with renewed vigour. Soon after the re-start Steed Malbranque evaded his marker and played the ball perfectly into the stride of Moritz Volz. The full back spotted the movement of Brian McBride and cut the ball back to the American to steer a shot past the outstretched dive of Nigel Martyn and take the lead.

Fulham continued to pile on the pressure in the closing stages of the game and, apart from a late Duncan Ferguson chance, the Whites looked the more likely to score with good chances for Malbranque and McBride.

'Monster' Player of the Match

20 Brian McBride

Quote

❝ Chris Coleman

I am delighted with the win. This was a game we might have lost last season.

Venue:	Craven Cottage	Referee:	M.A.Riley - 05/06		Fulham
Attendance:	17,169	Matches:	2		Everton
Capacity:	22,646	Yellow Cards:	9		
Occupancy:	76%	Red Cards:	0		

Form Coming into Fixture

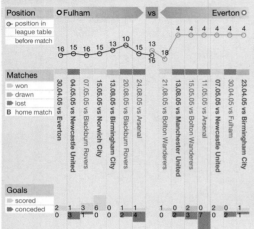

Position

- ⚬ position in league table before match

Matches

- won
- drawn
- lost
- B home match

Fulham: 16 15 16 15 13 15 13 — 30.04.05 vs Everton, 04.05.05 vs Newcastle United, 07.05.05 vs Blackburn Rovers, 15.05.05 vs Norwich City, 13.08.05 vs Birmingham City, 20.08.05 vs Blackburn Rovers, 24.08.05 vs Arsenal

Everton: 10 18 16 — 4 4 4 4 4 4 — 21.08.05 vs Bolton Wanderers, 13.08.05 vs Manchester United, 15.05.05 vs Bolton Wanderers, 11.05.05 vs Arsenal, 07.05.05 vs Newcastle United, 30.04.05 vs Fulham, 23.04.05 vs Birmingham City

Goals

- scored
- conceded

scored	2	1	3	6	0	1	1	1	0	2	0	2	0	1
conceded	0	3	1	0	0	2	4	0	2	3	7	0	2	1

Goal Statistics

○ Fulham

by Half | by Situation

- first: 6
- second: 8
- set piece: 4
- open play: 10

○ Everton

by Half | by Situation

- first: 2
- second: 4
- set piece: 3
- open play: 3

Goals by Area

○ Fulham

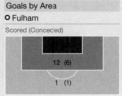

Scored (Conceded)

- 12 (6)
- 1 (1)

○ Everton

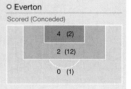

Scored (Conceded)

- 4 (2)
- 2 (12)
- 0 (1)

Team Statistics

Starting Line-Ups

Fulham: Jensen N, Radzinski, Boa Morte, Bocanegra, Warner, Diop, McBride, Knight, Jensen C, Volz, Malbranque

Everton: Davies, Vaughan, Hibbert, Arteta, Yobo, Bent M, McFadden, Neville, Weir, Cahill, Osman, Kilbane, Ferguson, Martyn

▶ 4/5/1 | **▶ 4/5/1**

Unused Sub: Rehman, Batista, Elrich, John, Helguson

Unused Sub: Wright, Ferrari

Premiership Totals

	○ Fulham	Everton ○
Premiership Appearances	899	1,798
Team Appearances	606	908
Goals Scored	119	158
Assists	118	124
Clean Sheets (goalkeepers)	1	131
Yellow Cards	85	181
Red Cards	11	15
Full Internationals	8	9

Age/Height

Fulham Age	Everton Age
▶ 28 yrs, 3 mo	**▶ 27 yrs, 2 mo**
Fulham Height	Everton Height
▶ 6'	**▶ 6'**

Match Statistics

League Table after Fixture

		Played	Won	Drawn	Lost	For	Against	Pts
↓	9 West Ham	3	1	1	1	4	3	4
↓	10 Middlesbrough	3	1	1	1	3	2	4
↓	11 Liverpool	2	1	1	0	1	0	4
↓	12 Blackburn	4	1	1	2	3	5	4
↑	13 Birmingham	4	1	1	2	4	7	4
↑	14 Fulham	4	1	1	2	3	6	4
↓	15 West Brom	4	1	1	2	4	8	4
↑	16 Wigan	3	1	0	2	1	2	3
↓	17 Everton	3	1	0	2	1	3	3

Statistics

	○ Fulham	Everton ○
Goals	1	0
Shots on Target	4	2
Shots off Target	5	4
Hit Woodwork	0	0
Possession %	52	48
Corners	6	2
Offsides	0	4
Fouls	19	25
Disciplinary Points	4	14

▶ Brian McBride fires Fulham in front

Event Line

13 ○ ⊕	McBride / RF / OP / IA
	Assist:: Boa Morte
20 ○ ▪	Bocanegra
35 ○ ⇄	N'Zogbia > Luque
Half time 0-1	
46 ○ ⇄	Bowyer > Taylor
54 ○ ▪	Parker
66 ○ ▪	Faye
70 ○ ⇄	John > Radzinski
72 ○ ⇄	Clark > Faye
78 ○ ⊕	N'Zogbia / LF / DFK / OA
	Assist: Owen
79 ○ ▪	Bowyer
81 ○ ⇄	Helguson > McBride
83 ○ ◢	Parker
	2nd Bookable Offence
86 ○ ▪	Clark
Full time 1-1	

A confident Fulham were unlucky not to get their first away victory of the season as they outplayed Newcastle at St James' with some inventive football.

The Whites couldn't have asked for a better start as they were gifted a glorious opening when Steven Taylor's weak backpass was intercepted by Tomasz Radzinski, who knocked it into the path of Luis Boa Morte. The Captain moved into the box and played a ball to Brian McBride to slot home from eight yards.

Fulham then looked to cement their advantage as they pressed forward in the hope of claiming a second. Papa Bouba Diop unleashed one of his customary exocets in the 35th minute and the ball seemed to momentarily deceive Newcastle keeper Shay Given, but he somehow managed to scramble it behind to safety. After the break McBride retrieved a long pass, on 65 minutes, to set up Radzinski but some agile keeping by Given kept the Canadian off the scoresheet.

With 78 minutes gone and the score still at 1-0, Newcastle were awarded a free kick following a foul on Michael Owen. Charles N'Zogbia stepped up to float over a cross/shot that completely eluded Tony Warner to salvage a point for the Geordies in a game they were lucky not to lose.

'Monster' Player of the Match	Quote
14 Papa Bouba Diop	🔊 **Chris Coleman**

It looked like only one team was going to win until we were caught out by Charles N'Zogbia's wonder strike.

Venue:	St James' Park	Referee:	A.G.Wiley - 05/06	Newcastle United
Attendance:	52,208	Matches:	4	Fulham
Capacity:	52,327	Yellow Cards:	9	
Occupancy:	100%	Red Cards:	1	

Form Coming into Fixture

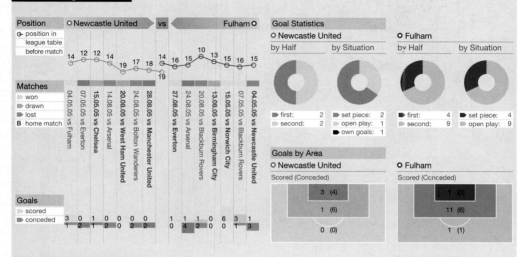

Position

Newcastle United vs Fulham

- position in league table before match

Newcastle: 14 12 12 14 19 17 18 14 16 15 19 13 15 16 15

Fulham: 10 13 15 16 15

Matches
- won
- drawn
- lost

B home match

	04.05.05 vs Fulham	07.05.05 vs Everton	15.05.05 vs Chelsea	14.08.05 vs Arsenal	20.08.05 vs West Ham United	24.08.05 vs Bolton Wanderers	28.08.05 vs Manchester United	27.08.05 vs Everton	24.08.05 vs Arsenal	20.08.05 vs Blackburn Rovers	13.08.05 vs Birmingham City	15.05.05 vs Norwich City	07.05.05 vs Blackburn Rovers	04.05.05 vs Newcastle United

Goals
- scored
- conceded

| scored | 3 | 0 | 1 | 0 | 0 | 0 | 0 | | 1 | 1 | 1 | 0 | 6 | 3 | 1 |
| conceded | 1 | 2 | 1 | 2 | 0 | 2 | 2 | | 0 | 4 | 2 | 0 | 0 | 1 | 3 |

Goal Statistics

Newcastle United

by Half / by Situation

first:	2	set piece:	2
second:	2	open play:	1
		own goals:	1

Fulham

by Half / by Situation

| first: | 4 | set piece: | 4 |
| second: | 9 | open play: | 9 |

Goals by Area

Newcastle United — Scored (Conceded)

3 (4)
1 (6)
0 (0)

Fulham — Scored (Conceded)

1 (3)
11 (6)
1 (1)

Team Statistics

Starting Line-Ups

Babayaro, Luque, N'Zogbia, Malbranque, Volz

Boumsong, Parker, Owen, McBride (Helguson), Diop, Knight

Given, Warner

Bramble, Faye (Clark), Shearer, Radzinski (John), Jensen C, Bocanegra

Taylor (Bowyer), Carr, Boa Morte, Jensen N

▶ 4/4/2   ▶ 4/4/2

Unused Sub: Harper, Elliott

Unused Sub: Batista, Christanval, Elrich

Premiership Totals

	Newcastle	Fulham
Premiership Appearances	2,068	965
Team Appearances	863	656
Goals Scored	446	134
Assists	230	123
Clean Sheets (goalkeepers)	69	2
Yellow Cards	263	96
Red Cards	12	11
Full Internationals	10	10

Age/Height

Newcastle United Age	Fulham Age
▶ 27 yrs	▶ 27 yrs, 8 mo
Newcastle United Height	Fulham Height
▶ 5'11"	▶ 6'

Match Statistics

League Table after Fixture

	Played	Won	Drawn	Lost	For	Against	Pts
↓ 11 Aston Villa	4	1	2	1	4	4	5
↑ 12 Fulham	5	1	2	2	4	7	5
↓ 13 West Ham	3	1	1	1	4	3	4
↓ 14 Blackburn	4	1	1	2	3	5	4
↑ 15 Portsmouth	5	1	1	3	4	7	4
↓ 16 Birmingham	5	1	1	3	4	8	4
↓ 17 West Brom	5	1	1	3	5	10	4
↓ 18 Everton	4	1	0	3	1	4	3
● 19 Newcastle	5	0	2	3	1	7	2

Statistics

	Newcastle	Fulham
Goals	1	1
Shots on Target	10	8
Shots off Target	5	5
Hit Woodwork	1	1
Possession %	57	43
Corners	10	8
Offsides	5	6
Fouls	19	16
Disciplinary Points	22	4

Fulham 1
West Ham United 2

▶ Fapa Bouba Diop goes in hard on Matthew Etherington

Event Line

21 O	▪	Boa Morte
40 O	▪	Reo-Coker
45 O	▪	Bocanegra
Half time 0-0		
46 O	⊕	Harewood / RF / IFK / IA
		Assist: Zamora
52 O	⊕	Warner / H / OG / 6Y
		Assist: Harewood
64 O	⇄	Newton > Zamora
66 O	⊕	Boa Morte / LF / OP / OA
		Assist: Malbranque
67 O	⇄	John > Radzinski
74 O	⇄	Sheringham > Benayoun
80 O	⇄	Christanval > Knight
87 O	⇄	Aliadiere > Harewood
Full time 1-2		

With their first London derby of the season at Craven Cottage the Whites would look back on this game as one where the chances were just not put away.

It didn't take long for them to get their first chance either. With two minutes on the clock Tomasz Radzinski muscled his way through the West Ham back line before laying a neat pass into the feet of Claus Jensen, the Dane's shot forced a fine save from Roy Carroll.

With the score 0-0 at half-time, West Ham didn't take long to open their account after the break. With less than a minute gone Marlon Harewood capitalised on a Zat Knight slip to touch the ball past Warner for the opener.

West Ham added a second six minutes later, and it was the cruellest of goals to concede. Striker Harewood was involved as the ball struck the post before hitting Tony Warner and trickling over the line to make it 2-0.

With a third of the game left Luis Boa Morte scored a fantastic individual goal to pull one back and raise hopes of a fight back. However, they prove to no avail as the Whites slip to their first home loss of the season.

'Monster' Player of the Match	Quote	Premiership Milestone
4 Steed Malbranque	💬 **Chris Coleman**	▶ **Debut**

They started better than us in the second half. The first goal was poor on our behalf and the second one was lucky in that it came off the post.

Phillippe Christanval made his Premiership debut.

Venue:	Craven Cottage	Referee:	G.Poll - 05/06		Fulham
Attendance:	21,907	Matches:	5		West Ham United
Capacity:	22,646	Yellow Cards:	20		
Occupancy:	97%	Red Cards:	1		

Form Coming into Fixture

Position

o Fulham vs West Ham United o

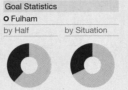
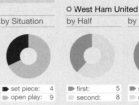

- position in league table before match
- B home match

Matches
- won
- drawn
- lost

16 15 13 10 15 16 14 13 / 13   7 7 2 6 6 6 7

07.05.05 vs Blackburn Rovers
15.06.05 vs Norwich City
13.08.05 vs Birmingham City
20.08.05 vs Blackburn Rovers
24.08.05 vs Arsenal
27.08.05 vs Everton
10.09.05 vs Newcastle United
12.09.05 vs Aston Villa
27.08.05 vs Bolton Wanderers
20.08.05 vs Newcastle United
13.08.05 vs Watford
08.05.05 vs Blackburn Rovers
29.04.05 vs Sunderland
23.04.05 vs Brighton

Goals
- scored
- conceded

| scored | 3 | 6 | 0 | 1 | 1 | 1 | 1 | | 4 | 1 | 0 | 3 | 2 | 1 | 2 |
| conceded | 1 | 0 | 0 | 2 | 4 | 0 | 1 | | 0 | 2 | 0 | 1 | 1 | 2 | 2 |

Goal Statistics

o Fulham

by Half   by Situation

- first: 5   set piece: 4
- second: 8   open play: 9

o West Ham United

by Half   by Situation

- first: 5   set piece: 6
- second: 8   open play: 7

Goals by Area

o Fulham
Scored (Conceded)

1 (1)
11 (5)
1 (2)

o West Ham United
Scored (Conceded)
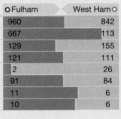
3 (3)
9 (5)
1 (0)

Team Statistics

Starting Line-Ups

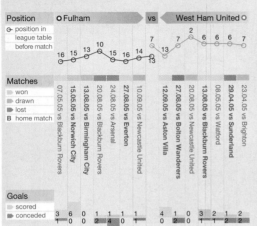

Unused Sub: Batista, Elrich, Helguson   Unused Sub: Hislop, Dailly

▶ 4/4/2   ▶ 4/5/1

Premiership Totals

	o Fulham	West Ham o
Premiership Appearances	960	842
Team Appearances	667	113
Goals Scored	129	155
Assists	121	111
Clean Sheets (goalkeepers)	2	26
Yellow Cards	91	84
Red Cards	11	6
Full Internationals	10	6

Age/Height

Fulham Age   West Ham United Age

▶ **27 yrs, 7 mo**   ▶ **26 yrs, 6 mo**

Fulham Height   West Ham United Height

▶ **6'**   ▶ **5'11"**

Match Statistics

League Table after Fixture

		Played	Won	Drawn	Lost	For	Against	Pts
↑ 4	West Ham	5	3	1	1	10	4	10
...	...	...	...	...	...	...	...	...
↑ 14	Portsmouth	6	1	2	3	5	8	5
↑ 15	Birmingham	6	1	2	3	5	9	5
↓ 16	Fulham	6	1	2	3	5	9	5
• 17	West Brom	6	1	2	3	6	11	5
• 18	Everton	4	1	0	3	1	4	3
• 19	Newcastle	5	0	2	3	1	7	2
• 20	Sunderland	6	0	1	5	3	10	1

Statistics

	o Fulham	West Ham o
Goals	1	2
Shots on Target	6	3
Shots off Target	3	7
Hit Woodwork	0	1
Possession %	43	57
Corners	4	6
Offsides	1	12
Fouls	11	14
Disciplinary Points	8	4

▶ Heidar Helguson is a picture of concentration

Event Line

26 ⊕ Rehman / H / OP / IA	
Assist: Helguson	
31 ⊕ Helguson / H / C / 6Y	
Assist: John	
Half time 2-0	
54 Green	
63 ⇄ Radzinski > Leacock	
70 ⊕ Green / RF / OP / IA	
Assist: Birch	
73 ⇄ McBride > John	
75 ⇄ Robinson M > Beevers	
80 ⇄ Mayo > Keates	
81 ⇄ Volz > Rehman	
82 ⊕ Volz / RF / OG / 6Y	
Assist: Green	
86 Molango	
87 Christanval	
93 ⊕ Rosenior / H / C / 6Y	
Assist: McBride	
95 ⊕ Radzinski / RF / OP / IA	
Assist: Volz	
97 ⇄ Asamoah > Molango	
101 ⊕ Kerr / RF / DFK / OA	
Assist: Asamoah	
115 ⊕ Robinson M / RF / C / 6Y	
Assist: Brown	
120 ⊕ McBride / H / IFK / IA	
Full time 5-4	

When Lincoln were drawn from the hat many assumed that Fulham would establish a Third Round berth at a canter, but it would prove to be anything but as the Imps came close to a classic giant killing.

Fulham opened their account after 26 minutes following good work from Collins John and Heidar Helguson, the latter's cross found Zesh Rehman who nodded Fulham into the lead. Four minutes later the Whites were two up when an Adam Green corner was only half cleared and Helguson rose highest to head home.

Lincoln City hit back in the second half and scored two goals in the space of 10 minutes. The Imps' first glimmer of hope was ignited when Francis Green raced forward to calmly take the ball round Batista before slotting home to make it 2-1. The second goal came from the first touch of substitute Moritz Volz, who managed to get himself on the score sheet at the wrong end of the park.

The game went into extra-time and again Fulham went two goals clear thanks to strikes from Liam Rosenior and a well worked goal from Tomasz Radzinski. The young Englishman was the quickest to react to a goalmouth melee that saw Lincoln unable to clear their lines. Fulham's fourth had a touch of class to it as Radzinski found himself one-on-one with the Lincoln keeper, before coolly chipping it over Marriott in to the back of the net.

Lincoln once again refused to lie down, however, and hit back again to take the score to 4-4. Keen not to be outdone by their Premiership rivals the lower division side scored a sublime free kick which once again gave them a glimmer. The equaliser came through Robinson following a Lincoln onslaught on the Whites'

➡ Liam Rosenior is the centre of attention after making the score 3-2

Match Statistics

Starting Line-Ups

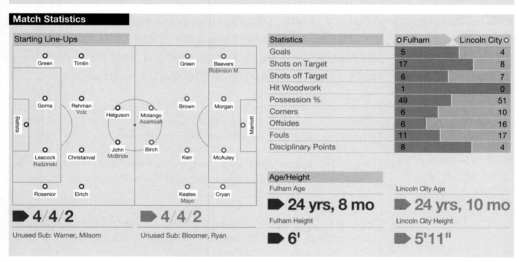

Statistics	o Fulham	Lincoln City o
Goals	5	4
Shots on Target	17	8
Shots off Target	6	7
Hit Woodwork	1	0
Possession %	49	51
Corners	6	10
Offsides	6	16
Fouls	11	17
Disciplinary Points	8	4

Age/Height

Fulham Age	Lincoln City Age
➡ **24 yrs, 8 mo**	➡ **24 yrs, 10 mo**
Fulham Height	Lincoln City Height
➡ **6'**	➡ **5'11"**

Fulham: Green, Timlin, Goma, Rehman (Volz), Helguson, Molango (Asamoah), Batista, Leacock (Radzinski), Christanval, John McBride, Birch, Rosenior, Elrich
4/4/2
Unused Sub: Warner, Milsom

Lincoln City: Green, Beevers (Robinson M), Brown, Morgan, Marriott, Kerr, McAuley, Keates (Mayo), Cryan
4/4/2
Unused Sub: Bloomer, Ryan

goal. With penalties looming Fulham were awarded a free kick which Adam Green swung in and was met by a stooping McBride header to win a pulsating game. It had been action from start to finish and, although Fulham came away as eventual winners, Lincoln were the real headline makers that night.

'Monster' Player of the Match

18 Ahmad Elrich

Quote

❝ Chris Coleman

I thought we were outstanding in the first half, played some great football and created plenty of chances.

Tottenham Hotspur 1
Fulham 0

BARCLAYS PREMIERSHIP

26.09.05

▶ Luis Boa Morte leaves defenders trailing in his wake

Event Line

8 ⭘ ⊕ Defoe / LF / OP / IA		
	Assist: King	
16 ⭘ ▪ Knight		
Half time 1-0		
62 ⭘ ▪ Diop		
71 ⭘ ⇄ Reid > Lennon		
75 ⭘ ⇄ Keane > Defoe		
75 ⭘ ⇄ John > McBride		
87 ⭘ ▪ John		
89 ⭘ ⇄ Rasiak > Mido		
Full time 1-0		

Another disappointing away day for the Whites, who conceded early and faced an uphill struggle, but set about the task with serious effort and were unlucky not to come away from the game with more.

The goal came after just seven minutes of play. Ledley King knocked a long ball beyond the Fulham defence and Spurs striker, Jermaine Defoe, latched on to it before calmly slotting the ball past an advancing Tony Warner.

However, an excellent move on the stroke of half-time almost brought Fulham back into the game. A long Moritz Volz pass found Luis Boa Morte who turned the ball back to Niclas Jensen, but his cross was headed over by Tomasz Radzinski.

Volz turned supplier again in the second half when he sprayed a cross field pass to Brian McBride. The American exchanged passes with Boa Morte before teeing up Steed Malbranque, but the Frenchman's shot flew narrowly over the bar.

Deep into added time, Fulham forced a corner on the right. Claus Jensen swung a menacing delivery into a crowded penalty area – that included keeper Tony Warner – but Volz's goalward header was easily saved by Paul Robinson, thus condemning Fulham to a further away defeat.

'Monster' Player of the Match	Quote	Premiership Milestone
8 Claus Jensen	❝ **Chris Coleman**	▶ **100**
	We've looked really exciting in attack previously, but we were under par. When we got to the final third, we just weren't good enough	Zat Knight made his 100th Premiership appearance.

Venue:	White Hart Lane	Referee:	A.G.Wiley - 05/06	Tottenham Hotspur
Attendance:	35,427	Matches:	7	Fulham
Capacity:	36,247	Yellow Cards:	21	
Occupancy:	98%	Red Cards:	2	

Form Coming into Fixture

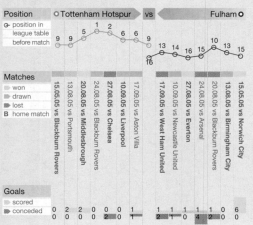

Position

- position in league table before match

Tottenham Hotspur vs Fulham

Matches

- won
- drawn
- lost
- B home match

15.05.05 vs Blackburn Rovers
13.08.05 vs Portsmouth
20.08.05 vs Middlesbrough
24.08.05 vs Blackburn Rovers
27.08.05 vs Chelsea
10.09.05 vs Liverpool
17.09.05 vs Aston Villa
17.09.05 vs West Ham United
10.09.05 vs Newcastle United
27.08.05 vs Everton
24.08.05 vs Arsenal
20.08.05 vs Blackburn Rovers
13.08.05 vs Birmingham City
15.05.05 vs Norwich City

Goals

	scored	0	2	2	0	0	0	1	1	1	1	1	1	0	6
	conceded	0	0	0	0	2	0	1	2	1	0	4	2	0	0

Goal Statistics

Tottenham Hotspur
by Half / by Situation

- first: 1
- second: 4
- set piece: 0
- open play: 4
- own goals: 1

Fulham
by Half / by Situation

- first: 4
- second: 7
- set piece: 3
- open play: 8

Goals by Area

Tottenham Hotspur
Scored (Conceded)

- 0 (0)
- 3 (2)
- 2 (1)

Fulham
Scored (Conceded)

- 8 (5)
- 2 (2)

Team Statistics

Starting Line-Ups

Lee, Davids
King, Mendes
Defoe / Keane, McBride / John
Robinson
Naybet, Jenas, Mido / Raslak, Radzinski
Stalteri, Lennon / Reid

Malbranque, Volz
Diop, Knight
Jensen C, Bocanegra
Warner
Boa Morte, Jensen N

4/4/2 (Tottenham)
4/4/2 (Fulham)

Unused Sub: Cerny, Kelly
Unused Sub: Crossley, Christanval, Leacock, Elrich

Premiership Totals

	Tottenham	Fulham
Premiership Appearances	817	972
Team Appearances	450	679
Goals Scored	124	130
Assists	67	122
Clean Sheets (goalkeepers)	34	2
Yellow Cards	50	93
Red Cards	3	11
Full Internationals	13	9

Age/Height

Tottenham Hotspur Age	Fulham Age
26 yrs	27 yrs, 8 mo

Tottenham Hotspur Height	Fulham Height
5'11"	6'

Match Statistics

League Table after Fixture

		Played	Won	Drawn	Lost	For	Against	Pts
↑ 4	Tottenham	7	3	3	1	6	3	12
...		...	...	...	...	...	...	...
● 14	Birmingham	7	1	3	3	7	11	6
● 15	Aston Villa	7	1	3	3	6	11	6
↑ 16	Portsmouth	7	1	2	4	5	9	5
↓ 17	Fulham	7	1	2	4	5	10	5
● 18	West Brom	7	1	2	4	7	13	5
● 19	Sunderland	7	1	1	5	5	10	4
● 20	Everton	6	1	0	5	1	7	3

Statistics

	Tottenham	Fulham
Goals	1	0
Shots on Target	4	5
Shots off Target	6	4
Hit Woodwork	0	0
Possession %	56	44
Corners	6	6
Offsides	10	8
Fouls	11	9
Disciplinary Points	0	12

► Steed Malbranque only has eyes for the ball

Event Line

2 O ⊕	John / LF / OP / IA	
	Assist: McBride	
17 O ⊕	v. Nistelrooy / RF / P / IA	
	Assist: Park	
18 O ⊕	Rooney / RF / OP / IA	
	Assist: Park	
27 O ▪	Fletcher	
28 O ⊕	Jensen C / RF / DFK / OA	
	Assist: Boa Morte	
45 O ⊕	v. Nistelrooy / RF / OP / IA	
	Assist: Park	

Half time 2-3

51 O ▪	Boa Morte	
57 O ⇄	Bardsley > Richardson	
60 O ▪	Diop	
72 O ⇄	Helguson > McBride	
77 O ⇄	Roraldo > Giggs	
77 O ⇄	Radzinski > John	
84 O ⇄	Scholes > v. Nistelrooy	

Full time 2-3

A day of 'what could have been' for Fulham as they pushed the former champions all the way at the Cottage but were eventually undone by a controversial Ruud van Nistelrooy goal.

It could not have got off to a better start for the Whites as they opened the scoring within two minutes. Brian McBride flicked on a goal kick which Collins John was first to react to. While his initial shot was blocked by Ferdinand, John was alert to the second chance and drilled a deflected shot past van der Sar.

United quickly recovered, equalising through a van Nistelrooy penalty after 16 minutes, before taking the lead two minutes later through Wayne Rooney.

Fulham didn't seem fazed, however, and were on the attack straight away, a surging Boa Morte run was stopped abruptly by Fletcher. From the resulting free kick, Jensen scored having swung in a cross that no one reacted to, leaving van der Sar shocked as it nestled in the net.

United won the game in controversial fashion, with van Nistelrooy seemingly straying offside. Park ran to the by-line and cut back for a now onside van Nistelrooy to tap home.

'Monster' Player of the Match

14 Papa Bouba Diop

Quote

🎙 Chris Coleman

I'm finding it difficult to know what to say to my players, because they are doing really well and not getting points.

Venue:	Craven Cottage	Referee:	H.M.Webb - 05/06	Fulham
Attendance:	21,862	Matches:	7	Manchester United
Capacity:	22,646	Yellow Cards:	21	
Occupancy:	97%	Red Cards:	1	

Form Coming into Fixture

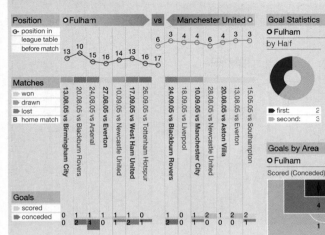

Position

O Fulham vs Manchester United O

- position in league table before match

Matches
- won
- drawn
- lost
- B home match

Goals
- scored
- conceded

Matches listed: 13.08.05 vs Birmingham City, 20.08.05 vs Blackburn Rovers, 24.08.05 vs Arsenal, 27.08.05 vs Everton, 10.09.05 vs Newcastle United, 17.09.05 vs West Ham United, 26.09.05 vs Tottenham Hotspur, 24.09.05 vs Blackburn Rovers, 18.09.05 vs Liverpool, 10.09.05 vs Manchester City, 28.08.05 vs Newcastle United, 20.08.05 vs Aston Villa, 13.08.05 vs Everton, 15.05.05 vs Southampton

Goal Statistics

O Fulham — by Half / by Situation

- first: 2
- second: 3
- set piece: 1
- open play: 4

O Manchester United — by Half / by Situation

- first: 3
- second: 6
- set piece: 1
- open play: 8

Goals by Area

O Fulham — Scored (Conceded)

- 4 (6)
- 1 (2)

O Manchester United — Scored (Conceded)

- 3 (2)
- 6 (1)
- 0 (1)

Team Statistics

Starting Line-Ups

Fulham (4/4/2)

- Crossley (GK)
- Jensen N, Boa Morte
- Bocanegra, Jensen C, John Radzinski, van Nistelrooy Scholes
- Goma, Diop, McBride Helguson, Rooney
- Volz, Malbranque

Unused Sub: Warner, Leacock, Elrich

Manchester United (4/4/2)

- Park, O'Shea
- Fletcher, Ferdinand
- Smith, Silvestre
- Giggs Ronaldo, Richardson Bardsley
- van der Sar (GK)

Unused Sub: Howard, Pique

Premiership Totals

	O Fulham	Man Utd O
Premiership Appearances	1,220	2,015
Team Appearances	693	1,456
Goals Scored	136	352
Assists	125	318
Clean Sheets (goalkeepers)	49	46
Yellow Cards	120	201
Red Cards	11	12
Full Internationals	11	13

Age/Height

Fulham Age	Manchester United Age
28 yrs, 8 mo	25 yrs, 8 mo
Fulham Height	Manchester United Height
5'11"	6'

Match Statistics

League Table after Fixture

		Played	Won	Drawn	Lost	For	Against	Pts
↑ 4	Man Utd	7	4	2	1	10	5	14
...		...	...	...	...	...	...	...
● 14	Birmingham	7	1	3	3	7	11	6
↑ 15	Portsmouth	8	1	3	4	5	9	6
↓ 16	Aston Villa	7	1	3	3	6	11	6
↑ 17	Sunderland	8	1	2	5	6	11	5
↓ 18	Fulham	8	1	2	5	7	13	5
↓ 19	West Brom	8	1	2	5	7	15	5
● 20	Everton	6	1	0	5	1	7	3

Statistics

	O Fulham	Man Utd O
Goals	2	3
Shots on Target	6	8
Shots off Target	5	4
Hit Woodwork	0	0
Possession %	47	53
Corners	3	9
Offsides	1	8
Fouls	20	11
Disciplinary Points	8	4

Charlton Athletic 1
Fulham 1

17.10.05

► Collins John celebrates opening the scoring

Event Line

27	○ ■	Kishishev
28	○ ⊕	John / RF / IFK / IA
		Assist: Malbranque
29	○ ■	Christanval
35	○ ⇄	Radzinski > Christanval
Half time 0-1		
47	○ ⊕	Murphy / RF / OP / IA
		Assist: Rommedahl
59	○ ⇄	Bothroyd > Thomas
68	○ ■	Volz
76	○ ⇄	El Karkouri > Kishishev
78	○ ■	El Karkouri
78	○ ⇄	McBride > John
82	○ ⇄	Hughes > Smertin
87	○ ■	Malbranque
Full time 1-1		

Fulham pick up only their second away point of the season, but it could have been so much more as the Whites dominated long periods of the game.

Collins John continually proved to be the main threat to the Charlton backline as his pace and power brought mistakes from Hreidarsson and Perry. After only 12 minutes some good work from Moritz Volz down the right set up John but his shot was dragged wide.

John made amends for this earlier miss with his second goal of the season after 27 minutes. A quick free-kick was played forward to Steed Malbranque who pulled the ball back for the Dutchman to hammer it low into the corner of the net.

Into the second half and Charlton took just a couple of minutes to grab an equaliser. Dennis Rommedahl jinked his way down the wing before setting up Danny Murphy to strike home from 10 yards.

Fulham piled the pressure on in the closing stages as they searched for that elusive winner. Papa Bouba Diop unleashed a customary thunder bolt but saw it flash just wide. Then, with stoppage time looming, Boa Morte found himself clear but his dipping volley went agonisingly wide.

'Monster' Player of the Match

4 Steed Malbranque

Quote

⑪ Chris Coleman

I was disappointed with the way we conceded the goal so early in the second half.

Venue:	The Valley	Referee:	M.A.Riley - 05/06		**Charlton Athletic**
Attendance:	26,310	Matches:	6		**Fulham**
Capacity:	27,111	Yellow Cards:	24		
Occupancy:	97%	Red Cards:	2		

Form Coming into Fixture

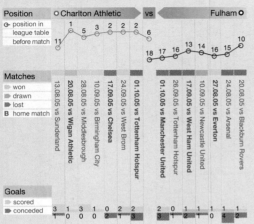

Position

O Charlton Athletic vs Fulham O

- position in league table before match

Matches
- won
- drawn
- lost
- B home match

13.08.05 vs Sunderland
20.08.05 vs Wigan Athletic
28.08.05 vs Middlesbrough
10.09.05 vs Birmingham City
17.09.05 vs Chelsea
24.09.05 vs West Brom
01.10.05 vs Tottenham Hotspur
01.10.05 vs Manchester United
26.09.05 vs Tottenham Hotspur
17.09.05 vs West Ham United
10.09.05 vs Newcastle United
27.08.05 vs Everton
24.08.05 vs Arsenal
20.08.05 vs Blackburn Rovers

Goals
- scored
- conceded

| 3 | 1 | 3 | 1 | 0 | 2 | 2 | | 2 | 0 | 1 | 1 | 1 | 1 | 1 |
| 1 | 0 | 0 | 0 | 2 | 1 | 3 | | 3 | 1 | 2 | 1 | 0 | 4 | 2 |

Goal Statistics

O Charlton Athletic — by Half / by Situation

O Fulham — by Half / by Situation

- first: 7
- second: 5
- set piece: 3
- open play: 9

- first: 4
- second: 3
- set piece: 2
- open play: 5

Goals by Area

O Charlton Athletic — Scored (Conceded)

2 (2)
8 (5)
2 (0)

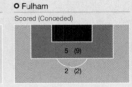

O Fulham — Scored (Conceded)

5 (9)
2 (2)

Team Statistics

Starting Line-Ups

Powell, Thomas Bothroyd, Murphy, Hreidarsson, Andersen, Kishishev El Karkouri, Bent D, Perry, Smertin Hughes, Young, Rommedahl

Malbranque, Volz, Diop, Goma, John McBride, Christanval Radzinski, Crossley, Bocanega, Jensen C, Boa Morte, Jensen N

➤ 4/5/1   ➤ 4/5/1

Unused Sub: Myhre, Spector

Unused Sub: Warner, Rosenior, Helguson

Premiership Totals

	O Charlton	Fulham O
Premiership Appearances	1,585	1,215
Team Appearances	753	704
Goals Scored	79	132
Assists	89	124
Clean Sheets (goalkeepers)	3	49
Yellow Cards	187	116
Red Cards	5	11
Full Internationals	9	11

Age/Height

Charlton Athletic Age	Fulham Age
➤ **28 yrs, 2 mo**	➤ **28 yrs, 8 mo**
Charlton Athletic Height	Fulham Height
➤ **6'**	➤ **6'**

Match Statistics

League Table after Fixture

		Played	Won	Drawn	Lost	For	Against	Pts
↑ 5	Charlton	8	5	1	2	13	8	16
...		...	...	...	...	...	...	...
• 14	Aston Villa	9	2	3	4	9	14	9
• 15	West Brom	9	2	2	5	9	16	8
• 16	Portsmouth	9	1	4	4	6	10	7
↑ 17	Fulham	9	1	3	5	8	14	6
↓ 18	Birmingham	9	1	3	5	7	13	6
• 19	Sunderland	9	1	2	6	7	14	5
• 20	Everton	8	1	0	7	1	11	3

Statistics

	O Charlton	Fulham O
Goals	1	1
Shots on Target	3	2
Shots off Target	13	14
Hit Woodwork	0	0
Possession %	49	51
Corners	6	1
Offsides	4	2
Fouls	18	23
Disciplinary Points	8	12

➡ Goalscorers Collins John and Luis Boa Morte savour a memorable victory

Event Line

30 ⊙ John / RF / OP / IA	
Assist: Jensen C	
Half time 1-0	
53 ⬜ Josemi	
59 ⇄ Garcia > Traore	
63 ⇄ Warner > Crossley	
69 ⇄ Rosenior > Jensen N	
75 ⇄ Crouch > Kewell	
76 ⇄ McBride > Elrich	
86 ⬜ Sissoko	
90 ⊙ Boa Morte / LF / OP / IA	
Assist: Malbranque	
Full time 2-0	

A sombre day at the Cottage as Fulham fans came to pay their respects to the Club's favourite son, Johnny Haynes. On an emotional afternoon, however, it was a triumphant Fulham who paid Haynes the greatest tribute with a fantastic victory over the European Champions.

The match almost started in perfect fashion as Collins John and Steed Malbranque combined excellently to set up Ahmad Elrich, but the Australian blazed over from eight yards out.

On the half-hour mark, Claus Jensen pounced on a loose clearance from Liverpool defender Josemi, threading the ball to John, who took it on his chest before prodding the ball past Jose Reina for his third goal in as many games.

While the game remained at 1-0, Liverpool increased the tempo, but in the dying minutes it was Fulham who got the goal to give the Whites the victory on an unforgettable day for the Club. Malbranque was the provider as he played in Boa Morte to smash the ball past a stranded Reina to make it 2-0, scoring his 50th goal in all competitions in a Fulham shirt in the process.

'Monster' Player of the Match	Quote	Premiership Milestone
11 Luis Boa Morte	🎙 **Chris Coleman**	➡ **22,480**

I'm thrilled with the players. Liverpool had a lot of possession, but we were patient.

The attendance of 22,480 was a Premiership record at Craven Cottage.

Venue:	Craven Cottage	Referee:	M.Atkinson - 05/06
Attendance:	22,480	Matches:	9
Capacity:	22,646	Yellow Cards:	22
Occupancy:	99%	Red Cards:	1

Fulham
Liverpool

Form Coming into Fixture

Position

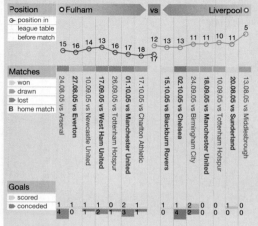

○ Fulham vs Liverpool ○

- position in league table before match

15 16 14 13 16 17 18 17 12 13 13 11 11 10 11 5

Matches
- won
- drawn
- lost
- B home match

24.08.05 vs Arsenal | 27.08.05 vs Everton | 10.09.05 vs Newcastle United | 17.09.05 vs West Ham United | 26.09.05 vs Tottenham Hotspur | 01.10.05 vs Manchester United | 17.10.05 vs Charlton Athletic | 15.10.05 vs Blackburn Rovers | 02.10.05 vs Chelsea | 24.09.05 vs Birmingham City | 18.09.05 vs Manchester United | 10.09.05 vs Tottenham Hotspur | 20.08.05 vs Sunderland | 13.08.05 vs Middlesbrough

Goals
- scored
- conceded

| 1 | 1 | 1 | 1 | 0 | 2 | 1 | | 1 | 1 | 2 | 0 | 0 | 1 | 0 |
| 4 | 0 | 1 | 2 | 1 | 3 | 1 | | 0 | 4 | 2 | 0 | 0 | 0 | 0 |

Goal Statistics

○ Fulham

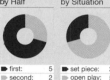

by Half | by Situation

- first: 5
- second: 2
- set piece: 2
- open play: 5

○ Liverpool

by Half | by Situation

- first: 2
- second: 3
- set piece: 4
- open play: 1

Goals by Area

○ Fulham
Scored (Conceded)

0 (2)
5 (9)
2 (1)

○ Liverpool
Scored (Conceded)

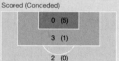

0 (5)
3 (1)
2 (0)

Team Statistics

Starting Line-Ups

Fulham: Warner / Crossley, Rosenior, Jensen N, Malbranque, Boa Morte, Bocanegra, Diop, John, Cisse, Morientes, Goma, Jensen C, Volz, Elrich, McBride

Liverpool: Reina, Kewell, Josemi, Crouch, Alonso, Carragher, Sissoko, Hyypia, Riise, Traore / Garcia

▶ 4/5/1 **▶ 4/4/2**

Unused Sub: Rehman, Helguson

Unused Sub: Carson, Hamann, Warnock

Premiership Totals

	○ Fulham	Liverpool ○
Premiership Appearances	1,116	1,144
Team Appearances	696	899
Goals Scored	102	131
Assists	105	110
Clean Sheets (goalkeepers)	49	5
Yellow Cards	117	103
Red Cards	12	5
Full Internationals	10	12

Age/Height

Fulham Age
▶ 27 yrs, 11 mo

Liverpool Age
▶ 25 yrs, 11 mo

Fulham Height
▶ 6'

Liverpool Height
▶ 6'1"

Match Statistics

League Table after Fixture

	Played	Won	Drawn	Lost	For	Against	Pts
● 12 Liverpool	8	2	4	2	5	8	10
● 13 Newcastle	9	2	3	4	5	8	9
↑ 14 Fulham	10	2	3	5	10	14	9
↓ 15 Aston Villa	10	2	3	5	9	16	9
↓ 16 West Brom	9	2	2	5	9	16	8
↓ 17 Portsmouth	10	1	4	5	7	12	7
● 18 Birmingham	10	1	3	6	7	15	6
● 19 Sunderland	9	1	2	6	7	14	5
● 20 Everton	8	1	0	7	1	11	3

Statistics

	○ Fulham	Liverpool ○
Goals	2	0
Shots on Target	3	6
Shots off Target	3	8
Hit Woodwork	0	0
Possession %	37	63
Corners	3	8
Offsides	3	7
Fouls	9	14
Disciplinary Points	0	8

Fulham 2
West Brom 3

► Steed Malbranque shows off his dribbling skills

Event Line

3	⊕	Earnshaw / LF / OP / IA
		Assist: Inamoto
43	◻	Boa Morte
Half time 0-1		
46	⇄	Diop > Legwinski
54	⇄	Chaplow > Carter
57	⇄	John > Elrich
63	⊕	Boa Morte / LF / OP / IA
		Assist: Malbranque
68	◻	Robinson
73	◻	Diop
85	◻	Pearce
88	⊕	Kanu / RF / OP / IA
90	⇄	Gaardsoe > Kanu
90	⊕	Helguson / H / IFK / IA
		Assist: Boa Morte
93	⇄	Bocanegra > Pearce
99	⊕	Inamoto / RF / OP / OA
		Assist: Wallwork
99	⇄	Campbell > Kamara
120	◼	Robinson
		Violent Conduct
120	◻	Knight
Full time 2-3		

The Whites were paired with West Brom in one of the all-Premiership fixtures in the Third Round of the Carling Cup. Leacock, Elrich and Helguson were brought in to a slightly re-shaped Fulham side for this evening game.

It was the worst of starts for Fulham though as West Brom opened the scoring after just three minutes. Inamoto picked up a loose ball to play in Robert Earnshaw who clipped the ball over Warner.

Fulham managed to net an equaliser out of the blue on the hour mark, Steed Malbranque spotted the smallest of gaps which Luis Boa Morte muscled his way through to find himself with only Kuszczak to beat. The Portugal international had no problem dispatching the ball past the Polish keeper.

With just a couple of minutes left on the clock and the game seemingly heading towards injury time, Bouba Diop played a simple backpass to Warner, but Warner's first touch was heavy and Kanu was alert to steal in to give West Brom what looked like a Fourth Round berth.

With time running out Inamoto conceded a free kick on the edge of the box. Luis Boa Morte swung in a dangerous set piece and Helguson muscled his way past a host of West Brom defenders to nod home for an unlikely equaliser for the Whites.

The game went into extra-time and ex-Fulham midfielder Junichi Inamoto came back to haunt his old side. The Japanese player gathered possession almost 35 yards out and unleashed a howitzer that left Warner with no chance.

Venue:	Craven Cottage	Referee:	A.P.D'Urso - 05/06	
Attendance:	7,373	Matches:	8	
Capacity:	22,646	Yellow Cards:	30	
Occupancy:	33%	Red Cards:	5	

▶ Luis Boa Morte draws Fulham level

Match Statistics

Starting Line-Ups

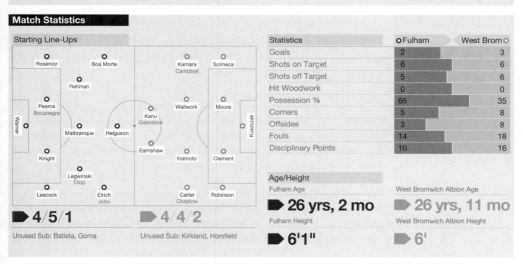

▶ 4/5/1   ▶ 4/4/2

Unused Sub: Batista, Goma   Unused Sub: Kirkland, Horsfield

Statistics	o Fulham	West Brom o
Goals	2	3
Shots on Target	6	6
Shots off Target	5	6
Hit Woodwork	0	0
Possession %	65	35
Corners	5	8
Offsides	3	8
Fouls	14	18
Disciplinary Points	16	16

Age/Height

Fulham Age	West Bromwich Albion Age
▶ **26 yrs, 2 mo**	▶ **26 yrs, 11 mo**
Fulham Height	West Bromwich Albion Height
▶ **6'1"**	▶ **6'**

Fulham refused to lie down though and as time slowly slipped away the Whites threw everything at West Brom in hope of taking the game to penalties. Bouba Diop collected the ball on the edge of the area but Kuszczak was equal to his strike, pulling off a fine save and, in so doing, securing West Brom's passage to the next round.

'Monster' Player of the Match

22 Dean Leacock

Quote

❝ Steve Kean

We're disappointed to go out. We fielded a team we thought could beat West Brom.

BARCLAYS
PREMIERSHIP

29.10.05

▶ Alain Goma prepares to clear the danger

Event Line

30	○ ■	Kavanagh
42	○ ■	Volz
Half time 0-0		
62	○ ⇄	Johansson > Mahon
74	○ ⇄	McMillan > Baines
82	○ ⇄	Elrich > Jensen C
82	○ ⇄	McBride > John
84	○ ⇄	Teale > Bullard
90	○ ⇄	Rosenior > Bocanegra
90	○ ⊕	Chimbonda / H / IFK / IA
		Assist: Kavanagh
Full time 1-0		

A solid performance from Fulham was undone at the last, in the cruellest of fashions, as Wigan Athletic continued their impressive start to the season.

A confident Fulham side looked like they had made the journey to the north-west with only victory in mind and the early stages of the game seemed to suggest just that. Luis Boa Morte was a live wire from the outset and, following some good interchange between the Captain and Collins John, Tomasz Radzinski unleashed a first time shot that whistled narrowly wide.

With just over half an hour of the game gone, controversy struck as a long pass from Diop saw John clean through on goal. Wigan keeper John Filan raced out and seemed to handle the ball but all appeals were waved away. Another contentious incident saw Moritz Volz break into the penalty area, where he seemed to be scythed down, but the referee awarded a free kick the other way and booked Volz for simulation.

With the game seemingly heading for a 0-0 draw, Wigan won a free kick deep into injury time. Graham Kavanagh sent the ball to the far post where Pascal Chimbonda stooped to head home an unlikely winner.

'Monster' Player of the Match	Quote
4 Steed Malbranque	⓯ **Chris Coleman**
	I hope the referee can sleep tonight, because I won't be able to.

Venue:	JJB Stadium	Referee:	A.Marriner - 05/06		**Wigan Athletic**
Attendance:	17,266	Matches:	1		**Fulham**
Capacity:	25,023	Yellow Cards:	3		
Occupancy:	69%	Red Cards:	0		

Form Coming into Fixture

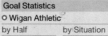

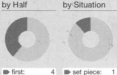

Position

- ⊙ position in league table before match

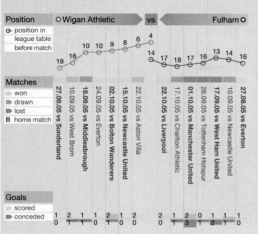

Wigan Athletic vs Fulham

Matches:
- won
- drawn
- lost
- B home match

Goals:
- scored
- conceded

Goal Statistics

Wigan Athletic

by Half		by Situation	
first:	4	set piece:	1
second:	6	open play:	8
		own goals:	1

Fulham

by Half		by Situation	
first:	5	set piece:	2
second:	3	open play:	6

Goals by Area

Wigan Athletic — Scored (Conceded)

- 1 (0)
- 7 (2)
- 2 (1)

Fulham — Scored (Conceded)

- 0 (1)
- 6 (6)
- 2 (1)

Team Statistics

Starting Line-Ups

Wigan Athletic: Baines, McMillan, Mahon, Johansson, De Zeeuw, Kavanagh, Camara, Filan, Henchoz, Francis, Teale, Bullard, John McBride, Chimbonda, Taylor

Fulham: Malbranque, Volz, Jensen C, Elrich, Goma, Diop, Warner, Bocanegra, Rosenior, Boa Morte, Radzinski, Jensen N

4/4/1/1

Unused Sub: Pollitt, Jackson

4/5/1

Unused Sub: Batista, Helguson

Premiership Totals

	Wigan	Fulham
Premiership Appearances	555	1,071
Team Appearances	86	745
Goals Scored	29	135
Assists	22	128
Clean Sheets (goalkeepers)	15	2
Yellow Cards	70	119
Red Cards	0	11
Full Internationals	7	10

Age/Height

Wigan Athletic Age	Fulham Age
28 yrs, 4 mo	**27 yrs, 7 mo**
Wigan Athletic Height	Fulham Height
5'10"	**6'**

Match Statistics

League Table after Fixture

		Played	Won	Drawn	Lost	For	Against	Pts
↑ 2	Wigan	10	7	1	2	11	5	22
...	...	...	...	...	...	...	...	...
↑ 14	Portsmouth	11	2	4	5	11	13	10
↓ 15	Fulham	11	2	3	6	10	15	9
↓ 16	Aston Villa	10	2	3	5	9	16	9
↓ 17	West Brom	10	2	2	6	9	18	8
↑ 18	Everton	10	2	1	7	3	12	7
↓ 19	Birmingham	11	1	3	7	7	16	6
↓ 20	Sunderland	11	1	2	8	10	21	5

Statistics

	Wigan	Fulham
Goals	1	0
Shots on Target	6	1
Shots off Target	6	6
Hit Woodwork	0	0
Possession %	46	54
Corners	6	3
Offsides	7	4
Fouls	11	7
Disciplinary Points	4	4

Fulham 2
Manchester City 1

05.11.05

> Steed Malbranque prepares to take on Danny Mills

Event Line

6 O ⊕ Malbranque / RF / OP / IA	
Assist: Boa Morte	
12 O ▪ Barton	
20 O ⊕ Croft / RF / OP / IA	
Assist: Ireland	
39 O ▪ Boa Morte	
43 O ⇄ Sibierski > Musampa	
45 O ⊕ Malbranque / RF / OP / IA	
Assist: Boa Morte	
Half time 2-1	
66 O ▪ Croft	
68 O ⇄ Jihai > Mills D	
75 O ▪ Jordan	
77 O ⇄ Helguson > McBride	
80 O ⇄ Wright-Phillips > Jordan	
Full time 2-1	

A real cracker of a game that lived up to its bonfire night potential as two of the Premiership's youngest managers were pitted against each other. It was Frenchman Steed Malbranque, however, who grabbed all the plaudits.

With the game just six minutes old, a Bocanegra clearance was not dealt with by City defender Richard Dunne. Luis Boa Morte sprinted past the hapless Dunne and drew David James out of his goal. As James approached Boa Morte slid the ball to Malbranque who had the simple task of tapping home for the opener.

The City equaliser came after 19 minutes when Lee Croft made the most of some good work by Stephen Ireland to notch up his first Premiership goal.

Fulham restored their lead on 44 minutes, Malbranque collecting from Boa Morte before taking the ball around James and grabbing his second of the game.

Late into the match Fulham should have had a third but, with James going walkabout, Radzinski could not capitalise on the open net and Sun Jihai cleared from in front of an open goal.

'Monster' Player of the Match

4 Steed Malbranque

Quote

🄯 **Chris Coleman**

I was delighted for Steed Malbranque to get two goals, because his attitude and performance were excellent.

Premiership Milestone

▶ **150**

Steed Malbranque marked his 150th Premiership appearance with two goals.

Venue:	Craven Cottage	Referee:	R.Styles - 05/06	Fulham
Attendance:	22,241	Matches:	13	Manchester City
Capacity:	22,646	Yellow Cards:	35	
Occupancy:	98%	Red Cards:	2	

Form Coming into Fixture

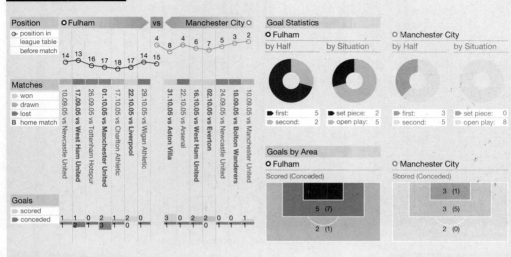

Position

- position in league table before match

Fulham vs **Manchester City**

Fulham: 14, 13, 16, 17, 18, 17, 14, 15
Manchester City: 4, 8, 4, 6, 7, 5, 3, 2

Matches

- won
- drawn
- lost
- B home match

Fulham	
10.09.05 vs Newcastle United	
17.09.05 vs West Ham United	
26.09.05 vs Tottenham Hotspur	
01.10.05 vs Manchester United	
17.10.05 vs Charlton Athletic	
22.10.05 vs Liverpool	
29.10.05 vs Wigan Athletic	

Manchester City	
31.10.05 vs Aston Villa	
22.10.05 vs Arsenal	
16.10.05 vs West Ham United	
02.10.05 vs Everton	
24.09.05 vs Newcastle United	
18.09.05 vs Bolton Wanderers	
10.09.05 vs Manchester United	

Goals

- scored
- conceded

Fulham: scored 1 1 0 2 1 2 0 / conceded 1 2 1 3 1 0 1
Manchester City: scored 3 0 2 2 0 0 1 / conceded 1 1 1 0 1 1 1

Goal Statistics

Fulham

by Half | by Situation
- first: 5 | set piece: 2
- second: 2 | open play: 5

Manchester City

by Half | by Situation
- first: 3 | set piece: 0
- second: 5 | open play: 8

Goals by Area

Fulham
Scored (Conceded)
5 (7)
2 (1)

Manchester City
Scored (Conceded)
3 (1)
3 (5)
2 (0)

Team Statistics

Starting Line-Ups

Fulham: Jensen N, Radzinski, Boa Morte, Bocanegra, Warner, Diop, McBride, Halgúson, Cole, Goma, Malbranque, Volz, John

Manchester City: Croft, Mills D, Jihai, Barton, Dunne, James, Vassell, Ireland, Distin, Musampa, Jordan Sibierski, Wright-Phillips

4/5/1   **4/4/2**

Unused Sub: Batista, Knight, Rosenior, Elrich

Unused Sub: De Vlieger, Thatcher

Premiership Totals	Fulham	Man City
Premiership Appearances	937	1,812
Team Appearances	717	685
Goals Scored	123	252
Assists	107	166
Clean Sheets (goalkeepers)	2	127
Yellow Cards	122	209
Red Cards	9	14
Full Internationals	9	6

Age/Height

Fulham Age	Manchester City Age
28 yrs, 4 mo	**26 yrs, 7 mo**
Fulham Height	Manchester City Height
6'	**5'11"**

Match Statistics

League Table after Fixture

		Played	Won	Drawn	Lost	For	Against	Pts
↓ 5	Man City	12	6	2	4	15	11	20
...	...	...	...	...	...	...	...	...
↑ 14	Fulham	12	3	3	6	12	16	12
↓ 15	Portsmouth	12	2	4	6	11	15	10
• 16	Aston Villa	12	2	3	7	10	21	9
• 17	West Brom	12	2	2	8	9	22	8
• 18	Everton	10	2	1	7	3	12	7
• 19	Birmingham	12	1	3	8	7	17	6
• 20	Sunderland	12	1	2	9	11	24	5

Statistics	Fulham	Man City
Goals	2	1
Shots on Target	5	2
Shots off Target	4	2
Hit Woodwork	0	0
Possession %	55	45
Corners	4	2
Offsides	3	12
Fouls	10	16
Disciplinary Points	4	12

▶ Brian McBride sets his sights for a volley at goal

Event Line

9 ○ ⊕	John	/ LF / OP / IA
	Assist: Legwinski	
31 ○ ■	Jensen N	
Half time 0-1		
46 ○ ⇄	Nemeth > Pogatetz	
64 ○ ⊕	Morrison	/ RF / OP / 6Y
	Assist: Yakubu	
70 ○ ⊕	Diop	/ H / C / IA
	Assist: John	
76 ○ ⊕	Yakubu	/ RF / OP / 6Y
	Assist: Hasselbaink	
78 ○ ⇄	Helguson > John	
84 ○ ⊕	Hasselbaink	/ RF / OP / IA
	Assist: Nemeth	
86 ○ ⇄	Doriva > Hasselbaink	
Full time 3-2		

Two late goals from Boro compounded Fulham's away travel woes, as Chris Coleman's men returned empty handed from the Riverside.

Fulham were the first to find the back of the net, however, and it came in spectacular circumstances. A Niclas Jensen throw-in on the left was flicked on by Sylvain Legwinski, Collins John then controlled it neatly before swivelling and dispatching a superb dipping volley over the outstretched arm of Brad Jones in the Boro goal, without question one of the goals of the season.

Boro managed to get back on level terms midway through the second half through James Morrison who capitalized on some slack Fulham defending.

Fulham regained their lead within five minutes though as Papa Bouba Diop climbed to power home a header from a Collins John corner.

A controversial equaliser followed for Boro. As Yakubu seemed to be in an offside position he touched in Jimmy Hasselbaink's goalbound shot. It then went from bad to worse eight minutes later as Hasselbaink picked up a pass from Nemeth to rifle an unstoppable shot past Warner to confine Fulham to a cruelly disappointing 3-2 reverse.

'Monster' Player of the Match

15 Collins John

Quote

❛❛ **Chris Coleman**

Yakubu's goal was very dubious and that was disappointing, but I'm not going to make excuses.

Venue:	Riverside Staduim	Referee:	U.D.Rennie - 05/06
Attendance:	27,599	Matches:	13
Capacity:	35,100	Yellow Cards:	24
Occupancy:	79%	Red Cards:	2

Middlesbrough
Fulham

Form Coming into Fixture

Position

O Middlesbrough vs Fulham O

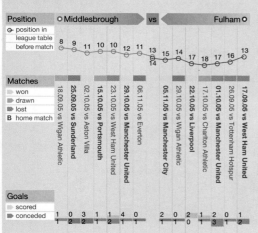

- position in league table before match

8 9 11 10 10 12 11 13 15 14 14 17 18 17 16 13

Matches
- won
- drawn
- lost
- B home match

18.09.05 vs Wigan Athletic
25.09.05 vs Sunderland
02.10.05 vs Aston Villa
15.10.05 vs Portsmouth
23.10.05 vs West Ham United
29.10.05 vs Manchester United
06.11.05 vs Everton
05.11.05 vs Manchester City
29.10.05 vs Wigan Athletic
22.10.05 vs Liverpool
17.10.05 vs Charlton Athletic
01.10.05 vs Manchester United
26.09.05 vs Tottenham Hotspur
17.09.05 vs West Ham United

Goals
- scored
- conceded

| scored | 1 | 0 | 3 | 1 | 1 | 4 | 0 | | 2 | 0 | 2 | 1 | 2 | 0 | 1 |
| conceded | 1 | 2 | 2 | 1 | 2 | 1 | 1 | | 1 | 1 | 0 | 1 | 3 | 1 | 2 |

Goal Statistics

O Middlesbrough

by Half | by Situation

- first: 5
- second: 5
- set piece: 6
- open play: 4

O Fulham

by Half | by Situation

- first: 6
- second: 2
- set piece: 2
- open play: 6

Goals by Area

O Middlesbrough
Scored (Conceded)

| 2 (1) |
| 7 (7) |
| 1 (2) |

O Fulham
Scored (Conceded)

| 0 (1) |
| 6 (8) |
| 2 (0) |

Team Statistics

Starting Line-Ups

Pogatetz
Nemeth
Queudrue
Rochemback
Yakubu
Jones
Southgate
Boateng
Hasselbaink
Doriva
Riggott
Morrison
Parnaby

John
Helguson
Volz
Legwinski
Knight
McBride
Malbranque
Warner
Goma
Diop
Radzinski
Jensen N

5/3/2

Unused Sub: Knight, Bates, Maccarone

4/5/1

Unused Sub: Batista, Pearce, Rehman, Rosenior

Premiership Totals

	O Boro	Fulham O
Premiership Appearances	1,518	946
Team Appearances	761	765
Goals Scored	222	110
Assists	162	86
Clean Sheets (goalkeepers)	2	2
Yellow Cards	202	107
Red Cards	9	7
Full Internationals	8	8

Age/Height

Middlesbrough Age

26 yrs, 11 mo

Fulham Age

28 yrs, 8 mo

Middlesbrough Height

6'

Fulham Height

6'

Match Statistics

League Table after Fixture

		Played	Won	Drawn	Lost	For	Against	Pts
↑	11 Middlesbrough	13	5	3	5	18	18	18
↓	12 Blackburn	13	5	3	5	15	15	18
↓	13 Newcastle	13	5	3	5	12	13	18
•	14 Fulham	13	3	3	7	14	19	12
•	15 Aston Villa	13	3	3	7	13	22	12
•	16 West Brom	13	3	2	8	13	22	11
•	17 Portsmouth	13	2	4	7	11	18	10
•	18 Everton	12	3	1	8	4	16	10
•	19 Birmingham	12	1	3	8	7	17	6

Statistics

	O Boro	Fulham O
Goals	3	2
Shots on Target	11	6
Shots off Target	9	3
Hit Woodwork	0	1
Possession %	57	43
Corners	9	4
Offsides	6	2
Fouls	9	16
Disciplinary Points	0	4

Fulham 2
Bolton Wanderers 1

▶ Luis Boa Morte is on hand to congratulate Brian McBride

Event Line

4 ⊙ ⊕	McBride / RF / OP / IA
	Assist: Radzinski
18 ⊙ ⊕	McBride / RF / OP / IA
	Assist: Crossley
32 ⊙ ⇄	N'Gotty > Jaidi
38 ⊙ ■	Speed
42 ⊙ ■	Ben Haim
45 ⊙ ■	Davies
Half time 2-0	
51 ⊙ ■	Rosenior
53 ⊙ ⇄	Okocha > Nakata
59 ⊙ ⇄	Djetou > Diagne-Faye
61 ⊙ ⇄	Legwinski > Boa Morte
68 ⊙ ■	Okocha
83 ⊙ ■	Nolan
86 ⊙ ■	O'Brien
88 ⊙ ■	Bocanegra
89 ⊙ ⇄	Helguson > John
90 ⊙ ◪	Diouf
	2nd Bookable Offence
90 ⊙ ⊕	Legwinski / RF / OG / IA
	Assist: Nolan

Full time 2-1

The day belonged to Brian McBride as Fulham's American international stole the show with a two goal salvo against Sam Allardyce's gritty Bolton side.

Again it was an early goal that got the Whites off to a flyer with just four minutes on the clock. Liam Rosenior, on the left, threw in field to Brian McBride who headed the ball wide into space behind O'Brien. Radzinski saw the gap and sprinted forward to send a low, teasing cross into the box where McBride, who had continued his run, arrived between Jaidi and Jaaskelainen to stab home.

A second goal soon followed after 20 minutes, when McBride once again got on the score sheet. Crossley thumped a long clearance upfield, McBride challenged Jaidi, who failed to clear the bouncing ball and McBride lashed a sweet volley past the despairing dive of Jaaskelainen.

With the match coming to an end, Bolton attempted to make a game of it when Nolan bustled his way into the penalty area. As he was about to shoot, Sylvain Legwinski slid in, in an attempt to clear, but only succeeded in prodding the ball past his own keeper, thus making the last few minutes quite nervy for Fulham.

'Monster' Player of the Match

20 Brian McBride

Quote

❝ Chris Coleman

I thought we played very well in the first half and we could have gone in more than 2-0 up. We deserved the three points on the overall performance.

Venue:	Craven Cottage	Referee:	G.Poll - 05/06		Fulham
Attendance:	19,768	Matches:	15		Bolton Wanderers
Capacity:	22,646	Yellow Cards:	57		
Occupancy:	87%	Red Cards:	2		

Form Coming into Fixture

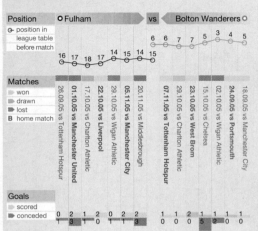

Position

○ Fulham vs ◁ Bolton Wanderers ○

- position in league table before match

Fulham: 16 17 18 17 14 15 14 15
Bolton: 6 6 7 7 5 3 4 5

Matches
- won
- drawn
- lost
- B home match

26.09.05 vs Tottenham Hotspur	01.10.05 vs Manchester United	17.10.05 vs Charlton Athletic	22.10.05 vs Wigan Athletic	29.10.05 vs Manchester City	05.11.05 vs Middlesbrough	20.11.05 vs Tottenham Hotspur	07.11.05 vs Charlton Athletic	29.10.05 vs West Brom	23.10.05 vs Chelsea	15.10.05 vs Wigan Athletic	02.10.05 vs Portsmouth	24.09.05 vs Manchester City	18.09.05 vs

Goals
- scored
- conceded

scored: 0 2 1 2 0 2 2 | 1 1 2 1 1 1 1
conceded: 1 3 1 0 1 3 | 0 0 0 5 2 0 0

Goal Statistics

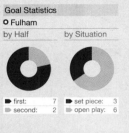

○ Fulham — by Half / by Situation

- first: 7
- second: 2
- set piece: 3
- open play: 6

○ Bolton Wanderers — by Half / by Situation

- first: 3
- second: 5
- set piece: 2
- open play: 6

Goals by Area

○ Fulham — Scored (Conceded)

- 8 (8)
- 1 (0)

○ Bolton Wanderers — Scored (Conceded)

- 1 (0)
- 4 (6)
- 3 (1)

Team Statistics

Starting Line-Ups

Fulham:
- Rosenior
- Radzinski
- Boa Morte / Legwinski
- Bocanegra
- Crossley
- Diop
- McBride
- Goma
- Malbranque
- Volz
- John / Helguson

Bolton:
- Nolan
- O'Brien
- Nakata / Okocha
- Ben Haim
- Davies
- Diagne-Faye / Djetou
- Jaaskelainen
- Jaidi / N'Gotty
- Speed
- Diouf
- Gardner

Fulham: ▶ 4/5/1
Bolton: ▶ 4/5/1

Unused Sub: Warner, Knight, Pearce
Unused Sub: Walker, Vaz Te

Premiership Totals

	○ Fulham	Bolton ○
Premiership Appearances	1,232	1,579
Team Appearances	860	931
Goals Scored	134	179
Assists	118	149
Clean Sheets (goalkeepers)	49	42
Yellow Cards	145	209
Red Cards	11	11
Full Internationals	9	11

Age/Height

Fulham Age: ▶ 28 yrs, 4 mo
Bolton Wanderers Age: ▶ 28 yrs, 6 mo
Fulham Height: ▶ 5'11"
Bolton Wanderers Height: ▶ 5'11"

Match Statistics

League Table after Fixture

		Played	Won	Drawn	Lost	For	Against	Pts
● 6	Bolton	13	7	2	4	15	13	23
● 7	Liverpool	12	6	4	2	13	8	22
● 8	Man City	14	6	3	5	15	12	21
● 9	West Ham	13	5	4	4	17	13	19
↑ 10	Middlesbrough	14	5	4	5	20	20	19
↓ 11	Charlton	13	6	1	6	17	18	19
● 12	Newcastle	14	5	3	6	12	14	18
● 13	Blackburn	14	5	3	6	15	18	18
↑ 14	Fulham	14	4	3	7	16	20	15

Statistics

	○ Fulham	Bolton ○
Goals	2	1
Shots on Target	7	3
Shots off Target	3	2
Hit Woodwork	0	0
Possession %	45	55
Corners	3	6
Offsides	1	6
Fouls	17	18
Disciplinary Points	8	34

West Brom 0
Fulham 0

▶ Luis Boa Morte shields the ball from Curtis Davies

Event Line

10 O	■	Watson
45 O	◢	Boa Morte
		2nd Bookable Offence

Half time 0-0

51 O	■	McBride
67 O	⇄	Carter > Kamara
70 O	⇄	Knight > Volz
71 O	⇄	Legwinski > John
72 O	⇄	Horsfield > Kanu
82 O	⇄	Earnshaw > Greening
82 O		Diop
83 O	⇄	Helguson > McBride

Full time 0-0

Looking to make amends for their Carling Cup exit, Fulham came to the Midlands with hope. However, with four defeats and four victories at home by this stage of the season it was difficult to assess which Baggies side would turn up.

An open first half saw both sides struggling to stamp their authority on the game. An early Nathan Ellington free kick saw Mark Crossley at his acrobatic best and Brian McBride watched a looping header well saved by Albion keeper Kuszczak.

The fixture erupted on the stroke of half time when Luis Boa Morte was harshly dismissed for picking up a second booking for a challenge on Steve Watson.

The second half looked like it would be a struggle for the Whites with their numerical disadvantage but they set about the task with great endeavour. A corner just after 70 minutes saw a goalbound Brian McBride header cleared to safety.

Fulham almost snatched a dramatic winner deep into stoppage time when substitute Sylvain Legwinski arrived to meet a Malbranque pass on the edge of the box, only for a Junichi Inamoto tackle to deny him at the last.

'Monster' Player of the Match

3 Carlos Bocanegra

Quote

🔊 **Chris Coleman**

When you get a man sent off it changes things. At half-time we told the players to keep their composure, and I thought they did that very well.

Venue:	The Hawthorns	Referee:	S.G.Bennett - 05/06	**West Bromwich Albion**
Attendance:	23,144	Matches:	16	**Fulham**
Capacity:	28,003	Yellow Cards:	61	
Occupancy:	83%	Red Cards:	3	

Form Coming into Fixture

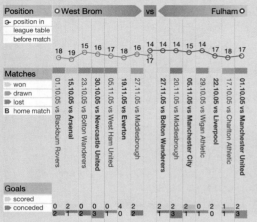

Position

- position in league table before match

O West Brom vs Fulham O

Matches	won	drawn	lost	B home match

Goals: scored / conceded

01.10.05 vs Blackburn Rovers — 2 (scored) / 2 (conceded)
15.10.05 vs Arsenal — 0 / 1
23.10.05 vs Bolton Wanderers — 2 / 2
30.10.05 vs Newcastle United — 0 / 3
05.11.05 vs West Ham United — 0 / 1
19.11.05 vs Everton — 4 / 0
27.11.05 vs Middlesbrough — 2 / 2
27.11.05 vs Bolton Wanderers — 2 / 1
20.11.05 vs Middlesbrough — 2 / 3
05.11.05 vs Wigan Athletic — 2 / 1
22.10.05 vs Manchester City — 0 / 1
17.10.05 vs Charlton Athletic — 1 / 0
01.10.05 vs Manchester United — 2 / 3

Goal Statistics

O West Bromwich Albion

by Half	by Situation
first: 3	set piece: 2
second: 5	open play: 6

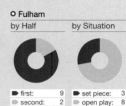

O Fulham

by Half	by Situation
first: 9	set piece: 3
second: 2	open play: 8

Goals by Area

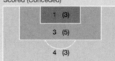

O West Bromwich Albion
Scored (Conceded)
1 (3)
3 (5)
4 (3)

O Fulham
Scored (Conceded)
0 (2)
10 (8)
1 (0)

Team Statistics

Starting Line-Ups

West Brom
Kuszczak
Robinson, Kamara, Carter, John, Volz
Clement, Inamoto, Legwinski, Knight
Ellington, Malbranque, Goma
McBride, Helgusón, Diop
Kanu, Horsfield, Crossley
Davies C, Wallwork, Bocanegra
Boa Morte
Watson, Greening, Earnshaw, Radzinski, Rosenior

4/4/2 **4/5/1**

Unused Sub: Hoult, Albrechtsen   Unused Sub: Warner, Pearce

Premiership Totals

	O West Brom	Fulham O
Premiership Appearances	1,144	1,346
Team Appearances	411	974
Goals Scored	112	137
Assists	94	122
Clean Sheets (goalkeepers)	2	49
Yellow Cards	106	155
Red Cards	4	13
Full Internationals	5	10

Age/Height

West Bromwich Albion Age	Fulham Age
26 yrs, 4 mo	**28 yrs, 2 mo**
West Bromwich Albion Height	Fulham Height
6'	**6'**

Match Statistics

League Table after Fixture

		Played	Won	Drawn	Lost	For	Against	Pts
9	West Ham	13	5	4	4	17	13	19
10	Middlesbrough	15	5	4	6	20	21	19
11	Charlton	13	6	1	6	17	18	19
12	Newcastle	15	5	4	6	13	15	19
13	Blackburn	15	5	3	7	15	20	18
14	Fulham	15	4	4	7	16	20	16
15	Aston Villa	15	4	4	7	15	23	16
16	Everton	14	5	1	8	7	16	16
17	West Brom	15	3	4	8	15	24	13

Statistics

	O West Brom	Fulham O
Goals	0	0
Shots on Target	4	1
Shots off Target	1	7
Hit Woodwork	0	0
Possession %	49	51
Corners	1	3
Offsides	12	4
Fouls	8	15
Disciplinary Points	4	18

▶ Phillippe Christanval in midfield action

Event Line

Half time 0-0

53	⇄ Pennant > Lazaridis
69	⇄ Jarosik > Tebily
74	⇄ Clapham > Dunn
84	⊕ Butt / H / OP / IA
	Assist: Heskey

Full time 1-0

It was a less than satisfactory return to the Midlands as Fulham succumbed to yet another late goal, this time at the hands of Birmingham City.

A dour opening exchange saw little in the way of creativity from either side. If anything it was Birmingham who had the better of the half with David Dunn an industrious figure throughout. It was his free kick after just six minutes that Crossley had to move over smartly to, to deal with.

Fulham's best chance of the half fell to Brian McBride. Tomasz Radzinski outpaced Olivier Tebily down the right flank before delivering a pinpoint centre, McBride rose to meet it but his header flew just over the bar.

Into the second half and it was much the same as the first, Fulham continued to create half chances and David Dunn was still the man most likely to find the openings for City. With 50 minutes gone a tantalising cross from Steed Malbranque just evaded the darting runs of McBride and John.

With six minutes remaining ex-Manchester United midfielder Nicky Butt delivered a hammer blow. A long ball from Clapham was knocked down by Emile Heskey, Butt saw his chance and bundled the ball past the stranded Crossley.

'Monster' Player of the Match	Quote	Premiership Milestone
1 Mark Crossley	❝ **Chris Coleman**	**50**

I was bitterly disappointed with us going forward, because we didn't offer anything.

Collins John made his 50th Premiership appearance.

Venue:	St Andrew's	Referee:	U.D.Rennie - 05/06		Birmingham City
Attendance:	27,597	Matches:	16		Fulham
Capacity:	30,016	Yellow Cards:	28		
Occupancy:	92%	Red Cards:	2		

Form Coming into Fixture

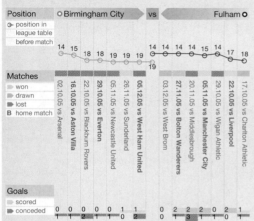

Position
- ○ position in league table before match

Birmingham City vs **Fulham** ○

Birmingham City positions: 14 15 18 18 19 19 19 19

Fulham positions: 14 14 14 14 15 14 17 18

Matches
- won
- drawn
- lost
- B home match

Birmingham City matches:
02.10.05 vs Arsenal
16.10.05 vs Aston Villa
22.10.05 vs Blackburn Rovers
29.10.05 vs Everton
05.11.05 vs Newcastle United
26.11.05 vs Sunderland
05.12.05 vs West Ham United
03.12.05 vs West Brom

Fulham matches:
27.11.05 vs Bolton Wanderers
20.11.05 vs Middlesbrough
05.11.05 vs Wigan Athletic
29.10.05 vs Manchester City
22.10.05 vs Liverpool
17.10.05 vs Charlton Athletic

Goals
- scored
- conceded

Birmingham City Goals scored: 0 0 0 0 0 1 1
Birmingham City Goals conceded: 1 1 2 1 1 0 2

Fulham Goals scored: 0 2 2 2 0 2 1
Fulham Goals conceded: 0 1 3 1 1 0 1

Goal Statistics

○ **Birmingham City**

by Half	by Situation
first: 1	set piece: 0
second: 1	open play: 2

○ **Fulham**

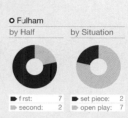

by Half	by Situation
first: 7	set piece: 2
second: 2	open play: 7

Goals by Area

○ **Birmingham City**
Scored (Conceded)

1 (2)
1 (3)
0 (3)

○ **Fulham**
Scored (Conceded)

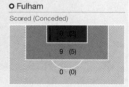

9 (5)
0 (0)

Team Statistics

Starting Line-Ups

Birmingham City: Painter, Lazaridis (Pennant), Upson, Clemence, Heskey, Vaesen, Cunningham, Butt, Dunn (Clapham), Tebily (Jarosik), Johnson

Fulham: John, Rosenior, Malbranque, Knight, McBride, Christanval, Crossley, Goma, Legwinski, Radzinski, Bocanegra

4/4/1/1

4/5/1

Unused Sub: Taylor Maik, Pandiani

Unused Sub: Warner, Jensen N, Pearce, Elrich, Helguson

Premiership Totals	○ Birmingham	Fulham ○
Premiership Appearances	1,965	1,048
Team Appearances	778	731
Goals Scored	158	101
Assists	203	85
Clear Sheets (goalkeepers)	6	50
Yellow Cards	227	91
Red Cards	12	7
Full Internationals	9	8

Age/Height

Birmingham City Age	Fulham Age
28 yrs, 7 mo	**28 yrs, 7 mo**
Birmingham City Height	Fulham Height
5'11"	**6'**

Match Statistics

League Table after Fixture

		Played	Won	Drawn	Lost	For	Against	Pts
↑	10 Newcastle	16	6	4	6	14	15	22
↑	11 Charlton	15	7	1	7	21	23	22
↑	12 Blackburn	16	6	3	7	18	22	21
↓	13 Middlesbrough	16	5	4	7	20	23	19
↑	14 Aston Villa	16	4	5	7	16	24	17
↓	15 Fulham	16	4	4	8	16	21	16
↑	16 West Brom	16	4	4	8	17	24	16
↓	17 Everton	14	5	1	8	7	16	16
↓	18 Birmingham	15	3	3	9	10	19	12

Statistics	○ Birmingham	Fulham ○
Goals	1	0
Shots on Target	7	3
Shots off Target	4	4
Hit Woodwork	0	0
Possession %	43	57
Corners	2	2
Offsides	9	4
Fouls	12	10
Disciplinary Points	0	0

Fulham 2
Blackburn Rovers 1

► Luis Boa Morte gets away from Brett Emerton

Event Line

35 ○ ⇄	Helguson > John	
42 ○ ▪	Helguson	
45 ○ ⊕	Diop / LF / IFK / 6Y	
	Assist: Boa Morte	
Half time 1-0		
49 ○ ⇄	Legwinski > Diop	
52 ○ ⊕	Boa Morte / RF / OP / IA	
	Assist: Helguson	
57 ○ ⇄	Kuqi > Emerton	
61 ○ ▪	Bentley	
63 ○ ▪	Dickov	
67 ○ ▪	Knight	
71 ○ ▪	Radzinski	
76 ○ ⇄	Thompson > Pedersen	
80 ○ ▪	McBride	
83 ○ ▪	Tugay	
84 ○ ▪	Neill	
90 ○ ⊕	Knight / H / OG / IA	
	Assist: Dickov	
90 ○ ⇄	Elrich > Boa Morte	
Full time 2-1		

With only a point from the last two games on the road, Fulham were keen to make amends at the Cottage and overcoming a solid Blackburn side was the perfect tonic.

Brad Friedel was the busier of the two keepers from the start. Luis Boa Morte slipped away from Tugay and sent over a cross which was met by the head of Collins John, only to see Friedel fling an arm out to deflect the ball over the bar.

The Fulham breakthrough arrived on the stroke of half time, Boa Morte delivering a wicked cross into the middle of the box for Papa Bouba Diop, who evaded his marker to side-foot the ball into the corner of the net.

Fulham extended their lead seven minutes after the break through a Boa Morte goal to cap what was a wonderful individual performance. Helguson powered down the right flank and cut the ball back to Boa. He sidestepped his marker before planting the ball home with a confident right foot finish.

A nervous end again for the Whites as Blackburn pulled one back late on through a Zat Knight own goal.

'Monster' Player of the Match

11 Luis Boa Morte

Quote

❛❛ **Chris Coleman**

When Luis Boa Morte and Papa Bouba Diop are in the team, we have got a bit more purpose, pace and strength about us.

Venue:	Craven Cottage	Referee:	M.Clattenburg - 05/06		Fulham
Attendance:	20,138	Matches:	18		Blackburn Rovers
Capacity:	22,646	Yellow Cards:	62		
Occupancy:	89%	Red Cards:	4		

Form Coming into Fixture

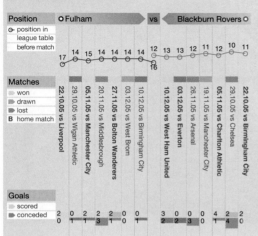

Position ○ Fulham vs Blackburn Rovers ○

- position in league table before match

17 14 15 14 14 14 14 / 16 12 13 13 12 11 12 10 11

Matches
- won
- drawn
- lost
- B home match

22.10.05 vs Liverpool
29.10.05 vs Wigan Athletic
05.11.05 vs Manchester City
20.11.05 vs Middlesbrough
27.11.05 vs Bolton Wanderers
03.12.05 vs West Brom
10.12.05 vs Birmingham City
10.12.05 vs West Ham United
03.12.05 vs Everton
26.11.05 vs Arsenal
19.11.05 vs Manchester City
05.11.05 vs Charlton Athletic
29.10.05 vs Chelsea
22.10.05 vs Birmingham City

Goals
- scored
- conceded

scored: 2 0 2 2 2 0 0 | 3 0 0 0 4 2 2
conceded: 0 1 1 3 1 0 1 | 2 2 3 0 1 4 0

Goal Statistics

○ Fulham — by Half / by Situation

first:	6	set piece:	1
second:	2	open play:	7

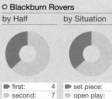

○ Blackburn Rovers — by Half / by Situation

first:	4	set piece:	4
second:	7	open play:	7

Goals by Area

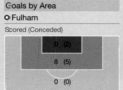

○ Fulham — Scored (Conceded)

0 (2)
8 (5)
0 (0)

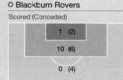

○ Blackburn Rovers — Scored (Conceded)

1 (2)
10 (6)
0 (4)

Team Statistics

Starting Line-Ups

Fulham: Rosenior, Radzinski, Boa Morte (Elrich), Goma, Crossley, Christanval, McBride, Dickov, Knight, Diop (Legwinski), Leacock, John (Helguson)

Blackburn: Emerton (Kuqi), Neill, Savage, Todd, Bentley, Tugay, Khizanishvili, Friedel, Pedersen (Thompson), Gray

4/5/1

Unused Sub: Warner, Pearce

4/4/1/1

Unused Sub: Enckelman, Mokoena, Reid

Premiership Totals	○ Fulham	Blackburn ○
Premiership Appearances	1,092	1,534
Team Appearances	720	831
Goals Scored	108	108
Assists	81	139
Clean Sheets (goalkeepers)	50	56
Yellow Cards	128	250
Red Cards	13	15
Full Internationals	11	10

Age/Height

Fulham Age	Blackburn Rovers Age
28 yrs	**29 yrs, 1 mo**
Fulham Height	Blackburn Rovers Height
6'	**5'11"**

Match Statistics

League Table after Fixture

	Played	Won	Drawn	Lost	For	Against	Pts
● 12 Blackburn	17	6	3	8	19	24	21
● 13 Middlesbrough	16	5	4	7	20	23	19
↑ 14 Fulham	17	5	4	8	18	22	19
↓ 15 Aston Villa	17	4	5	8	16	26	17
↓ 16 Everton	17	5	2	10	9	23	17
● 17 West Brom	17	4	4	9	17	25	16
↑ 18 Portsmouth	17	3	4	10	13	26	13
↓ 19 Birmingham	16	3	3	10	11	23	12
● 20 Sunderland	17	1	2	14	14	35	5

Statistics	○ Fulham	Blackburn ○
Goals	2	1
Shots on Target	5	4
Shots off Target	3	7
Hit Woodwork	0	1
Possession %	46	54
Corners	8	12
Offsides	1	7
Fouls	12	13
Disciplinary Points	16	16

49

▶ Brian McBride celebrates his goal at Stamford Bridge

Event Line

3 ○ ⊕	Gallas / RF / C / 6Y
	Assist: Huth
24 ○ ⊕	Lampard / RF / OP / OA
	Assist: Robben
29 ○ ⊕	McBride / RF / IFK / 6Y
	Assist: Knight
Half time 2-1	
46 ○ ⇄	Gudjohnsen > W-Phillips
56 ○ ▪	Cole J
56 ○ ⊕	Helguson / RF / P / IA
	Assist: McBride
57 ○ ⇄	Drogba > Huth
62 ○ ▪	Christanval
65 ○ ▪	Legwinski
69 ○ ⇄	John > Helguson
71 ○ ⇄	Warner > Crossley
74 ○ ⊕	Crespo / LF / OP / IA
	Assist: Cole J
76 ○ ⇄	Geremi > Crespo
89 ○ ▪	John
Full time 3-2	

The first of a two part mini-drama as Fulham pushed the Champions all the way at Stamford Bridge. Although Round One would end in defeat, revenge would come in Round Two.

There were just three minutes on the clock as Chelsea opened their account, a corner from the left was not cleared and William Gallas was on hand to pounce. With just over a quarter of the game gone, Chelsea midfielder Frank Lampard tried from 25 yards out and it took a fortuitous deflection off Sylvain Legwinski leaving Mark Crossley with no chance to make it 2-0.

Fulham took just four minutes to strike back, as Brian McBride, who seconds before had been receiving treatment for a nasty head wound, turned in a swinging Luis Boa Morte free kick which had eluded Petr Cech in the Chelsea goal.

With 10 minutes gone in the second half Fulham grabbed an equaliser! Having been brought down in the area McBride handed the ball to Helguson who calmly stepped up to cheekily stroke the ball past Cech.

Fulham hearts were broken though as Hernan Crespo picked up a Joe Cole pass before lashing it past Tony Warner for an eventual 3-2 win.

'Monster' Player of the Match	Quote	Premiership Milestone
20 Brian McBride	**⑰ Chris Coleman**	**▶ 200**
	When we got an equaliser, we looked to win it. Overall, it was a great display.	Brian McBride's goal was the 200th scored by Fulham in the Premiership.

Venue:	Stamford Bridge	Referee:	G.Poll - 05/06	Chelsea
Attendance:	42,313	Matches:	17	Fulham
Capacity:	42,449	Yellow Cards:	71	
Occupancy:	100%	Red Cards:	3	

Form Coming into Fixture

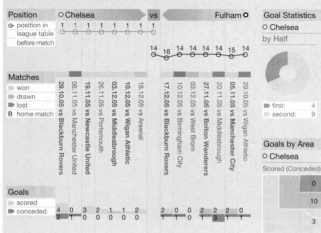

Position
o Chelsea vs Fulham o

position in league table before match

Chelsea: 1 1 1 1 1 1 1 1
Fulham: 14 16 14 14 14 14 15 14

Matches
- won
- drawn
- lost
- B home match

29.10.05 vs Blackburn Rovers
06.11.05 vs Manchester United
19.11.05 vs Newcastle United
26.11.05 vs Portsmouth
03.12.05 vs Middlesbrough
10.12.05 vs Wigan Athletic
18.12.05 vs Arsenal
17.12.05 vs Blackburn Rovers
10.12.05 vs Birmingham City
03.12.05 vs West Brom
27.11.05 vs Bolton Wanderers
20.11.05 vs Middlesbrough
05.11.05 vs Manchester City
29.10.05 vs Wigan Athletic

Goals
- scored: 4 0 3 2 1 1 2 | 2 0 0 2 2 2 0
- conceded: 2 1 0 0 0 0 0 | 1 1 0 1 3 1 1

Goal Statistics

o Chelsea
by Half   by Situation

first:	4	set piece:	6
second:	9	open play:	6
		own goals:	1

o Fulham
by Half   by Situation

| first: | 6 | set piece: | 2 |
| second: | 2 | open play: | 6 |

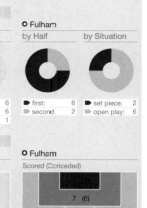

Goals by Area

o Chelsea
Scored (Conceded)

0 (1)
10 (2)
3 (0)

o Fulham
Scored (Conceded)

7 (6)
0 (0)

Team Statistics

Starting Line-Ups

Gallas, Robben, Leacock, Lampard, Legwinski, Terry, Knight, Cech, Makelele, Crespo (Garemi), McBride, Radzinski, Christanval, Crossley, Huth (Drogba), Helguson (John), Goma, Warner (Kuyt), Cole J, Boa Morte, Ferreira, Wright-Phillips (Gudjohnsen), Rosenior

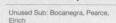

4/3/3   **4/4/2** (Diamond)

Unused Sub: Cucicini, Bridge

Unused Sub: Bocanegra, Pearce, Elrich

Premiership Totals

	o Chelsea	Fulham o
Premiership Appearances	1,505	1,069
Team Appearances	1,084	697
Goals Scored	231	102
Assists	193	83
Clean Sheets (goalkeepers)	33	50
Yellow Cards	152	121
Red Cards	7	11
Full Internationals	14	9

Age/Height

Chelsea Age
26 yrs, 4 mo

Fulham Age
28 yrs, 7 mo

Chelsea Height
6'

Fulham Height
6'1"

Match Statistics

League Table after Fixture

	Played	Won	Drawn	Lost	For	Against	Pts
• 1 Chelsea	18	16	1	1	40	9	49
...	...	...	...	...	...	...	...
↑ 14 Aston Villa	18	5	5	8	20	26	20
↓ 15 Fulham	18	5	4	9	20	25	19
• 16 Everton	18	5	2	11	9	27	17
• 17 West Brom	18	4	4	10	17	28	16
• 18 Portsmouth	18	3	5	10	14	27	14
• 19 Birmingham	17	3	3	11	11	25	12
• 20 Sunderland	18	1	3	14	14	35	6

Statistics

	o Chelsea	Fulham o
Goals	3	2
Shots on Target	11	5
Shots off Target	4	5
Hit Woodwork	0	0
Possession %	54	46
Corners	10	4
Offsides	3	2
Fouls	16	16
Disciplinary Points	4	12

Fulham 3
Aston Villa 3

BARCLAYS PREMIERSHIP

28.12.05

▶ Heidar Helguson nonchalantly scores from the spot

Event Line

13 O ⊕	McBride / H / OP / IA
	Assist: Radzinski
29 O ⊕	Moore / RF / OP / IA
	Assist: Baros
32 O	Baros
32 O ⊕	Helguson / RF / P / IA
	Assist: Radzinski
Half time 2-1	
57 O ⇄	Jensen N > Leacock
60 O ⊕	Ridgewell / LF / C / 6Y
	Assist: Milner
61 O ⊕	McBride / H / OP / IA
	Assist: Boa Morte
67 O	Moore
70 O ⇄	Angel > Moore
76 O ⊕	Ridgewell / LF / OP / 6Y
	Assist: Milner
76 O ⇄	Bakke > Bouma
78 O ⇄	Elrich > Legwinski
81 O	Hughes
84 O ⇄	John > Helguson
86 O	Ridgewell
Full time 3-3	

Those who braved the freezing conditions were rewarded with a feast of goals as this six goal thriller was a nail biter from start to finish.

The goal fest got under way within 13 minutes when a long Crossley clearance eventually made its way out to Tomasz Radzinski on the left. He sped to the by-line before crossing for Brian McBride to head home the opener.

Villa replied just shy of the half hour mark when Moore latched on to a Baros pass to drive the ball past Crossley. The Whites, however, took just three minutes to regain their lead as Tomasz Radzinski was bundled over in the area and Helguson stepped up to confidently knock home the spot kick.

Fulham started the second half intent on increasing their lead but it was Villa who hit back to equalise, a Milner cross was somehow not cleared and Liam Ridgewell bundled it into the goal. Fulham replied in lightening quick time as McBride, unmarked, steered a header past Sorensen for 3-2.

Refusing to lay down Villa scored the game's last goal to level the match at 3-3, again it was Ridgewell who popped up to ruin Fulham fans' festive cheer.

'Monster' Player of the Match

20 Brian McBride

Quote

🔢 **Steve Kean**

If you score five goals in two games, you should have more than one point – so we're disappointed.

Premiership Milestone

▶ **200**

Mark Crossley made his 200th Premiership appearance.

Venue:	Craven Cottage	Referee:	A.P.D'Urso - 05/06		Fulham
Attendance:	20,446	Matches:	16		Aston Villa
Capacity:	22,646	Yellow Cards:	61		
Occupancy:	90%	Red Cards:	7		

Form Coming into Fixture

Position

O Fulham vs Aston Villa O

- position in league table before match

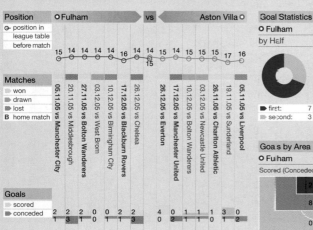

Matches
- won
- drawn
- lost
- B home match

	05.11.05 vs Manchester City	20.11.05 vs Middlesbrough	27.11.05 vs Bolton Wanderers	03.12.05 vs West Brom	10.12.05 vs Birmingham City	17.12.05 vs Blackburn Rovers	26.12.05 vs Chelsea	26.12.05 vs Everton	17.12.05 vs Manchester United	10.12.05 vs Bolton Wanderers	03.12.05 vs Newcastle United	26.11.05 vs Charlton Athletic	19.11.05 vs Sunderland	05.11.05 vs Liverpool
Position	15	14	14	14	14	16 15	14	14	15	14	15	15	15	17	16

Goals
- scored
- conceded

| scored | 2 | 2 | 2 | 0 | 0 | 2 | 2 | 4 | 0 | 1 | 1 | 1 | 3 | 0 |
| conceded | 1 | 3 | 1 | 0 | 1 | 1 | 3 | 0 | 2 | 1 | 1 | 0 | 1 | 2 |

Goal Statistics

O Fulham

by Half | by Situation

first: 7
second: 3
set piece: 4
open play: 6

O Aston Villa

by Half | by Situation

first: 1
second: 9
set piece: 2
open play: 8

Goals by Area

O Fulham
Scored (Conceded)

2 (0)
8 (6)
0 (1)

O Aston Villa
Scored (Conceded)

5 (0)
4 (6)
1 (1)

Team Statistics

Starting Line-Ups

Rosenior, Boa Morte, Bocanegra, McBride, Baros, Christanval, Radzinski, Crossley, Knight, Helguson / John, Moore / Angel, Legwinski / Elrich, Leacock / Jensen N, Milner, Hughes, McCann, Delaney, Sorensen, Davis, Ridgewell, Barry, Bouma / Bakke

4/4/2 (Diamond) | **4/4/2**

Unused Sub: Warner, Pearce

Unused Sub: Taylor, Gardner, Whittingham

Premiership Totals	O Fulham	Aston Villa O
Premiership Appearances	1,030	1,585
Team Appearances	658	866
Goals Scored	105	118
Assists	84	113
Clean Sheets (goalkeepers)	50	63
Yellow Cards	115	170
Red Cards	12	4
Full Internationals	11	10

Age/Height

Fulham Age	Aston Villa Age
27 yrs, 10 mo	**25 yrs, 5 mo**
Fulham Height	Aston Villa Height
6'	**5'11"**

Match Statistics

League Table after Fixture

		Played	Won	Drawn	Lost	For	Against	Pts
●	12 Charlton	17	7	1	9	21	27	22
↑	13 Aston Villa	19	5	6	8	23	29	21
↑	14 Fulham	19	5	5	9	23	28	20
↓	15 Middlesbrough	18	5	5	8	23	28	20
↑	16 West Brom	19	5	4	10	19	28	19
↓	17 Everton	19	5	2	12	10	30	17
●	18 Portsmouth	19	3	5	11	14	31	14
●	19 Birmingham	18	3	4	11	13	27	13
●	20 Sunderland	18	1	3	14	14	35	6

Statistics	O Fulham	Aston Villa O
Goals	3	3
Shots on Target	4	4
Shots off Target	3	5
Hit Woodwork	0	0
Possession %	43	57
Corners	6	10
Offsides	3	4
Fouls	13	12
Disciplinary Points	0	16

Portsmouth 1
Fulham 0

31.12.05

▶ Brian McBride battles for possession

Event Line

28 ⊙ ⇄	John > Helguson	
41 ⊙ ■	Rosenior	
43 ⊙ ⊕	O'Neil / LF / OP / IA	
	Assist: Silva	
Half time 1-0		
59 ⊙ ⇄	Bocanegra > Elrich	
85 ⊙ ■	Bocanegra	
86 ⊙ ⇄	Karadas > Silva	
87 ⊙ ■	Karadas	
90 ⊙ ⇄	Cisse > Robert	
Full time 1-0		

With 2006 looming, Fulham tried desperately to break their duck on the road but, as the hectic festive schedule took its toll, Pompey snuck a desperately needed victory.

With seven goals scored in the last three games the Whites' confidence was understandably high going in to the game. After only five minutes an Ahmad Elrich corner was whipped in and flicked on by Heidar Helguson, the ball eventually landed at the feet of Radzinski but his shot whistled narrowly over the bar.

A long ball from Zat Knight, with quarter of the game gone, saw Helguson race clear of the Pompey backline, but his quick thinking was matched by that of Portsmouth keeper Sander Westerveld who rushed out to smother the danger.

Portsmouth struck the controversial winner with half time approaching, Gary O'Neil seeming to control with his hand before scoring past Warner from close range.

The second half was a scrappy affair with both sets of players looking jaded. With chances few and far between the only glimpses on goal came in the last 10 minutes as Radzinski had a stinging volley deflected for a corner by Stefanovic and O'Neil came close to adding a second for Pompey.

'Monster' Player of the Match

13 Tomasz Radzinski

Quote

🔾 **Chris Coleman**

Portsmouth coped better with the heavy pitch and they were the better team on the day.

Venue:	Fratton Park	Referee:	M.A.Riley - 05/06		Portsmouth
Attendance:	19,101	Matches:	19		Fulham
Capacity:	20,288	Yellow Cards:	67		
Occupancy:	94%	Red Cards:	4		

Form Coming into Fixture

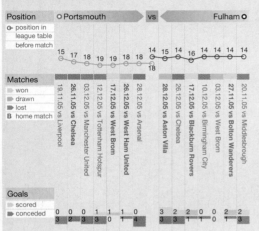

Position

- ⊙ position in league table before match

Portsmouth vs Fulham

15 17 18 19 19 18 18 18 14 15 14 16 14 14 14 14

Matches
- won
- drawn
- lost
- B home match

19.11.05 vs Liverpool
26.11.05 vs Chelsea
03.12.05 vs Manchester United
12.12.05 vs Tottenham Hotspur
17.12.05 vs West Brom
26.12.05 vs West Ham United
28.12.05 vs Arsenal
28.12.05 vs Aston Villa
26.12.05 vs Chelsea
17.12.05 vs Blackburn Rovers
10.12.05 vs Birmingham City
03.12.05 vs West Brom
27.11.05 vs Bolton Wanderers
20.11.05 vs Middlesbrough

Goals
- scored
- conceded

| 0 | 0 | 0 | 1 | 1 | 1 | 0 | | 3 | 2 | 2 | 0 | 0 | 2 | 2 |
| 3 | 2 | 3 | 3 | 0 | 1 | 4 | | 3 | 3 | 1 | 1 | 0 | 1 | 3 |

Goal Statistics

○ Portsmouth

by Half | by Situation

- first: 2
- second: 1
- set piece: 0
- open play: 3

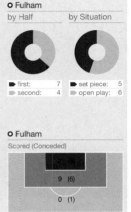

○ Fulham

by Half | by Situation

- first: 7
- second: 4
- set piece: 5
- open play: 6

Goals by Area

○ Portsmouth
Scored (Conceded)

0 (0)
2 (15)
1 (1)

○ Fulham
Scored (Conceded)

9 (6)
0 (1)

Team Statistics

Starting Line-Ups

Griffin, Taylor, Elrich, Leacock (Bocanegra)

Stefanovic, Hughes, Silva (Karadas), Helguson (John), Legwinski, Knight

Westerveld, Warner

O'Brien, O'Neil, Lua Lua, McBride, Boa Morte, Goma

Priske, Robert (Cisse), Radzinski, Rosenior

▶ 4/4/2   ▶ 4/4/2

Unused Sub: Guatelli, Viafara, Todorov

Unused Sub: Drobny, Jensen N, Pearce

Premiership Totals

	○ Portsmouth	Fulham ○
Premiership Appearances	1,043	948
Team Appearances	427	761
Goals Scored	68	108
Assists	83	87
Clean Sheets (goalkeepers)	28	2
Yellow Cards	124	129
Red Cards	12	11
Full Internationals	10	9

Age/Height

Portsmouth Age	Fulham Age
▶ 27 yrs, 9 mo	▶ 27 yrs, 8 mo
Portsmouth Height	Fulham Height
▶ 5'11"	▶ 6'

Match Statistics

League Table after Fixture

		Played	Won	Drawn	Lost	For	Against	Pts
↓	10 West Ham	20	7	5	8	26	27	26
↓	11 Newcastle	19	7	4	8	18	21	25
●	12 Charlton	18	8	1	9	23	27	25
↓	13 Aston Villa	20	5	7	8	23	29	22
↑	14 Middlesbrough	19	5	6	8	23	28	21
↓	15 Fulham	20	5	5	10	23	29	20
↑	16 Everton	20	6	2	12	11	30	20
↓	17 West Brom	20	5	4	11	19	29	19
●	18 Portsmouth	20	4	5	11	15	31	17

Statistics

	○ Portsmouth	Fulham ○
Goals	1	0
Shots on Target	7	4
Shots off Target	10	5
Hit Woodwork	0	0
Possession %	54	46
Corners	8	8
Offsides	5	2
Fouls	14	7
Disciplinary Points	4	8

Fulham 2
Sunderland 1

02.01.06

▶ Liam Rosenior utilises his pace

Event Line

7 ○ ⊕	Lawrence / LF / OP / OA	
40 ○ ⇄	Helguson > Diop	
43 ○ ⊕	John / H / OP / IA	
	Assist: McBride	
45 ○ ■	Leacock	
Half time 1-1		
57 ○ ■	Caldwell	
	Foul	
59 ○ ■	Legwinski	
61 ○ ⊕	John / H / OP / IA	
	Assist: Helguson	
64 ○ ⇄	Murphy D > Hoyte	
64 ○ ⇄	Nosworthy > Le Tallec	
65 ○ ⇄	Gray > Stead	
69 ○ ⇄	Malbranque > John	
75 ○ ⇄	Jensen N > Rosenior	
76 ○ ■	Miller	
90 ○ ■	Arca	
Full time 2-1		

Mick McCarthy's Premiership basement boys gave Fulham an early scare before the Whites eventually came through for their first win of the New Year.

Sunderland's lively early attacking play was rewarded in only the seventh minute. A half headed clearance from Zat Knight was controlled on the edge of the area by Liam Lawrence, who then converted a perfect left foot volley.

Fulham were fired into action and their response created some serious questions for the Sunderland defence but no goal was forthcoming for the Whites.

The equaliser arrived with half time approaching, Brian McBride teeing up Collins John to divert past Sunderland keeper Kelvin Davis.

It was John who struck again on the hour mark to give Fulham the lead, Heidar Helguson made space for himself down the left before delivering a delicious cross with the outside of his right foot for John to simply head home.

Sunderland had Caldwell sent off and with this numerical advantage Fulham never looked in danger of losing their lead.

'Monster' Player of the Match

10 Heidar Helguson

Quote

🄯 **Chris Coleman**

I dont thin k it was a great performance from us in terms of quality of possession, but we showed courage.

56

Venue:	Craven Cottage	Referee:	D.J.Gallagher - 05/06		Fulham
Attendance:	19,372	Matches:	22		Sunderland
Capacity:	22,646	Yellow Cards:	52		
Occupancy:	86%	Red Cards:	5		

Form Coming into Fixture

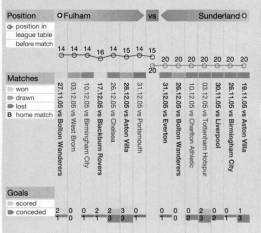

Position

- position in league table before match

Fulham vs **Sunderland**

Fulham: 14 14 14 16 14 15 14 15
Sunderland: 20 20 20 20 20 20 20 20 / 20

Matches:
- won
- drawn
- lost
- B home match

Fulham matches:
27.11.05 vs Bolton Wanderers
03.12.05 vs West Brom
10.12.05 vs Birmingham City
17.12.05 vs Blackburn Rovers
26.12.05 vs Chelsea
28.12.05 vs Aston Villa
31.12.05 vs Portsmouth

Sunderland matches:
31.12.05 vs Everton
26.12.05 vs Bolton Wanderers
10.12.05 vs Charlton Athletic
03.12.05 vs Tottenham Hotspur
30.11.05 vs Liverpool
26.11.05 vs Birmingham City
19.11.05 vs Aston Villa

Goals:
- scored
- conceded

Fulham scored/conceded: 2/1 0/0 0/1 2/1 2/3 3/3 0/1
Sunderland scored/conceded: 0/1 0/0 0/2 2/3 0/2 0/1 1/3

Goal Statistics

Fulham

by Half | by Situation
- first: 6
- second: 3
- set piece: 4
- open play: 5

Sunderland

by Half | by Situation
- first: 1
- second: 2
- set piece: 2
- open play: 1

Goals by Area

Fulham — Scored (Conceded)
2 (3)
7 (6)
0 (1)

Sunderland — Scored (Conceded)
0 (6)
2 (5)
1 (1)

Team Statistics

Starting Line-Ups

Fulham (4/5/1)

Warner
Rosenior, Jensen N, Radzinski
Boa Morte
Pearce
Legwinski, McBride
Knight
Diop, Helguson
Leacock, John Malbranque

Unused Sub: Drobny, Rehman

Sunderland (4/4/2)

Davis
Lawrence, Hoyte, Murphy D
Stead, Gray
Whitehead, Breen
Le Tallec, Nosworthy
Miller, Caldwell
Arca, Collins D

Unused Sub: Alnwick, Woods

Premiership Totals

	Fulham	Sunderland
Premiership Appearances	1,201	530
Team Appearances	834	256
Goals Scored	153	26
Assists	129	28
Clean Sheets (goalkeepers)	2	2
Yellow Cards	140	59
Red Cards	15	1
Full Internationals	8	4

Age/Height

Fulham Age	Sunderland Age
28 yrs	25 yrs, 3 mo
Fulham Height	Sunderland Height
6'1"	6'

Match Statistics

League Table after Fixture

	Played	Won	Drawn	Lost	For	Against	Pts
↑ 12 Aston Villa	21	6	7	8	25	30	25
↓ 13 Charlton	19	8	1	10	24	30	25
↑ 14 Fulham	21	6	5	10	25	30	23
↑ 15 Everton	21	7	2	12	14	31	23
↓ 16 Middlesbrough	20	5	7	8	25	30	22
● 17 West Brom	21	5	4	12	20	31	19
● 18 Portsmouth	21	4	5	12	16	33	17
● 19 Birmingham	20	4	4	12	15	29	16
● 20 Sunderland	20	1	3	16	14	38	6

Statistics

	Fulham	Sunderland
Goals	2	1
Shots on Target	9	7
Shots off Target	3	3
Hit Woodwork	0	0
Possession %	44	56
Corners	6	6
Offsides	3	1
Fouls	9	14
Disciplinary Points	8	20

Fulham 1
Leyton Orient 2

08.01.06

➡ Simon Elliott gets to grips with English football

Event Line

17 ⊙ ⊕ Easton / RF / OP / IA	
Assist: Keith	
18 ⊙ ■ Rosenior	
24 ⊙ ■ Tudor	
44 ⊙ ⊕ Keith / LF / OP / IA	
Assist: Easton	
Half time 0-2	
50 ⊙ ⊕ John / RF / OP / OA	
Assist: Radzinski	
62 ⊙ ⇄ Timlin > Elrich	
71 ⊙ ■ Pearce	
72 ⊙ ⇄ McMahon > Tudor	
85 ⊙ ⇄ Carlisle > Keith	
86 ⊙ ⇄ Goma > Pearce	
90 ⊙ ⇄ Barnard > Alexander	
Full time 1-2	

Arguably the lowest point of Fulham's season so far as the Whites were unceremoniously dumped out of the FA Cup by League Two side, Leyton Orient.

However, it took just nine minutes for the Whites to register their first serious threat on the Orient goal. Fulham broke quickly from midfield and Luis Boa Morte's precision pass was gladly picked up by Canada international Tomasz Radzinski who coolly finished past Garner. The goal was chalked off, however, as Radzinski deserved to be offside.

But, after a bright start, the Whites were left shocked as Orient opened the scoring. A heavy first touch on the edge of the area by debutant Simon Elliott fell to Orient midfielder Easton whose shot ricocheted off Elliott and looped over Tony Warner for the opener.

Orient doubled their lead after 44 minutes as Fulham were undone by another deflection, this time Keith's strike hit the foot of Rosenior, again wrong footing Warner in the Fulham goal.

The perfect repost came after half-time as Fulham pulled an early goal back. Some good work down the right flank from Radzinski saw his well weighted pass allow John to race through the middle and score with an emphatic drive.

Fulham piled the pressure on in the second half in attempt to find an equaliser. John smashed a 50 yard cross-field pass to Boa Morte who in turn carried the ball down the left flank. His whipped delivery was inches in front of the despairing lunge of Radzinski.

➤ Michael Timlin gets stuck in

Match Statistics

Starting Line-Ups

Jensen N, Boa Morte, Tudor, McMahon, Miller
Pearce (Goma), Elliott, Radzinski, Ibehre, Simpson, Zakuani
Warner, Garner
Knight, Legwinski, John, Alexander (Barnard), Easton, Mackie
Rosenior, Elrich (Timlin), Keith (Carlisle), Lockwood

➤ 4/4/2   ➤ 4/4/2

Unused Sub: Drobny, Milsom, Rehman

Unused Sub: Morris, Saah

Statistics	○ Fulham	Orient ○
Goals	1	2
Shots on Target	1	4
Shots off Target	2	0
Hit Woodwork	0	1
Possession %	57	43
Corners	4	8
Offsides	4	2
Fouls	8	12
Disciplinary Points	8	4

Age/Height

Fulham Age	Leyton Orient Age
➤ **28 yrs, 1 mo**	➤ **25 yrs, 11 mo**

Fulham Height	Leyton Orient Height
➤ **6'**	➤ **5'11"**

Fulham got their chance in the 68th minute though when Boa Morte was bundled over in the box by Orient defender Zakuani. John stepped up but his soft penalty was easily saved by Garner.

Legwinski almost salvaged a draw for Fulham as his attempted lob from distance was touched over the bar by Garner. The resulting corner was curled in from Boa Morte and it was Legwinski who was on hand again but his header just shaved the angle of bar and post and confirmed Fulham's exit from the FA Cup.

'Monster' Player of the Match

17 Liam Rosenior

Quote

🔴 **Chris Coleman**

I put that down to offensive arrogance. I'm absolutely gutted, but good luck to Orient.

Fulham 1
Newcastle United 0

14.01.06

▶ Steed Malbranque is the goalscoring hero

Event Line

23 ⭕ ⬜	Clark
28 ⭕ ⬜	Legwinski
32 ⭕ ⬜	Carr
Half time 0-0	
46 ⭕ ⇄	Elliott > Carr
62 ⭕ ⇄	Malbranque > Radzinski
73 ⭕ ⇄	John > Legwinski
75 ⭕ ⊕	Malbranque / RF / OP / IA
	Assist: John
77 ⭕ ⇄	Chopra > N'Zogbia
80 ⭕ ⇄	O'Brien > Luque
Full time 1-0	

Fulham found the perfect repost to a disappointing Cup exit, piling on the misery for under pressure Toon manager Graeme Souness.

The Whites were full of attacking intent from the start. Tomasz Radzinski was a threat all afternoon and it was his intuitive pass that set Heidar Helguson free. The striker turned and shot but Given was equal to it with a fine stop.

Steed Malbranque was a thorn in Newcastle's side all day and it was he who broke from deep before laying a perfectly weighted ball into the path of Liam Rosenior. Rosenior's cross was met and dispatched by Helguson but his shot was denied by the woodwork.

The only goal of the game came after 73 minutes, Luis Boa Morte's hard work on the left created an opening for Collins John, his snapshot was palmed away by Shay Given but Steed Malbranque was on cue to drive in the rebound from close range.

In the closing stages of the game, Niemi pulled off a fantastic double save to deny Chopra and Bowyer. A late free kick for Newcastle brought panic for Whites' fans but Solano's set piece flew over the bar.

'Monster' Player of the Match	Quote	Premiership Milestone
35 Ian Pearce	**❝ Chris Coleman**	▶ **Debut**

We had to get rid of the poor display against Leyton Orient. We concentrated all week and psychologically it's a big win for us.

Simon Elliott made his Premiership debut, while Antti Niemi made his first Premiership appearance in the colours of Fulham.

Venue:	Craven Cottage	Referee:	A.G.Wiley - 05/06	**Fulham**
Attendance:	21,974	Matches:	26	**Newcastle United**
Capacity:	22,646	Yellow Cards:	76	
Occupancy:	97%	Red Cards:	4	

Form Coming into Fixture

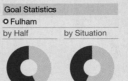

Position

- ⊙ position in league table before match

14 14 16 14 15 14 15 | 14 | 11 11 10 10 10 11 12 13

Matches

- won
- drawn
- lost
- B home match

03.12.05 vs West Brom
10.12.05 vs Birmingham City
17.12.05 vs Blackburn Rovers
26.12.05 vs Chelsea
28.12.05 vs Aston Villa
31.12.05 vs Portsmouth
02.01.06 vs Sunderland
02.01.06 vs Middlesbrough
31.12.05 vs Tottenham Hotspur
26.12.05 vs Liverpool
17.12.05 vs West Ham United
10.12.05 vs Arsenal
03.12.05 vs Aston Villa
27.11.05 vs Everton

Goals

| scored | 0 | 0 | 2 | 2 | 3 | 0 | 2 | | 2 | 0 | 0 | 4 | 1 | 1 | 0 |
| conceded | 0 | 1 | 1 | 3 | 3 | 1 | 1 | | 2 | 2 | 2 | 2 | 0 | 1 | 1 |

Goal Statistics

Fulham

by Half | by Situation

- ▶ first: 5
- second: 4
- ▶ set piece: 4
- open play: 5

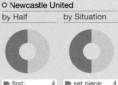

Newcastle United

by Half | by Situation

- ▶ first: 4
- second: 4
- ▶ set piece: 4
- open play: 4

Goals by Area

Fulham — Scored (Conceded)

2 (3)
7 (5)
0 (2)

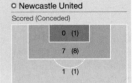

Newcastle United — Scored (Conceded)

0 (1)
7 (8)
1 (1)

Team Statistics

Starting Line-Ups

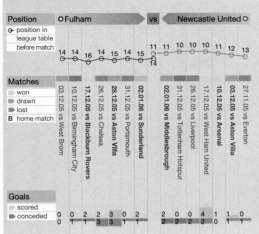

Jensen N
Boa Morte
Pearce
Helguson
Niemi
Elliott
Radzinski / Malbranqte
McBride
Knight
Legwinski / John
Rosenior

Solano
Carr / Elliott
Bowyer
Ramage
Shearer
Clark
Given
Boumsong
N'Zogbia / Chopra
Luque / O'Brien
Babayaro

▶ **4/4/2** (Diamond)   ▶ **4/5/1**

Unused Sub: Warner, Goma, Volz   Unused Sub: Harper, Brittain

Premiership Totals

	⊙Fulham	Newcastle⊙
Premiership Appearances	1,228	2,019
Team Appearances	780	1,193
Goals Scored	147	375
Assists	132	255
Clean Sheets (goalkeepers)	22	75
Yellow Cards	129	239
Red Cards	13	12
Full Internationals	9	8

Age/Height

Fulham Age	Newcastle United Age
▶ **29 yrs**	▶ **27 yrs, 7 mo**
Fulham Height	Newcastle United Height
▶ **6'**	▶ **5'10"**

Match Statistics

League Table after Fixture

		Played	Won	Drawn	Lost	For	Against	Pts
● 5	Arsenal	21	11	4	6	34	15	37
● 6	Wigan	21	11	1	9	25	26	34
● 7	Bolton	20	9	6	5	25	20	33
↑ 8	Man City	22	9	4	9	30	25	31
↓ 9	Blackburn	21	9	4	8	26	25	31
● 10	West Ham	22	8	5	9	29	31	29
↑ 11	Charlton	20	9	1	10	26	30	28
↑ 12	Fulham	22	7	5	10	26	30	26
↓ 13	Newcastle	21	7	5	9	20	24	26

Statistics

	⊙Fulham	Newcastle⊙
Goals	1	0
Shots on Target	5	4
Shots off Target	7	2
Hit Woodwork	1	0
Possession %	49	51
Corners	5	10
Offsides	4	6
Fouls	10	13
Disciplinary Points	4	8

61

West Ham United 2
Fulham 1

► Heidar Helguson is given little space in which to operate

Event Line

17 ⊙ ⊕	Ferdinand / RF / C / OA
	Assist: Harewood
28 ⊙ ⊕	Benayoun / RF / OP / IA
	Assist: Etherington
Half time 2-0	
52 ⊙ ⊕	Helguson / LF / IFK / IA
	Assist: McBride
62 ⊙ ⇄	Radzinski > Malbranque
70 ⊙ ⇄	John > McBride
77 ⊙	Boa Morte
80 ⊙	Benayoun
80 ⊙ ⇄	Dailly > Zamora
83 ⊙	Dailly
86 ⊙ ⇄	Katan > Benayoun
89 ⊙	Rosenior
90 ⊙ ⇄	Newton > Etherington
Full time 2-1	

Once again it was a tale of two wonder goals that proved to be Fulham's undoing at Upton Park as the Whites fell foul of two unstoppable first half strikes from the Hammers.

Both sides looked dangerous on the break early on, but it was Fulham who created the first real opportunity. Simon Elliott's left wing corner was met firmly by the head of Heidar Helguson whose header hit Luis Boa Morte on the line!

West Ham's first goal came completely out of the blue, following a corner on the right the ball was cleared to the edge of the area where Anton Ferdinand was waiting to thump an unstoppable volley over Niemi.

Ten minutes later and Yossi Benayoun scored one of his own to rival that of Ferdinand. The Israeli midfielder picked up the ball on the edge of the box before jinking his way into the 18-yard area and chipping a measured lob over Niemi for 2-0.

Fulham struck back early in the second half through Helguson who scored with ease when put through on goal by McBride. Although all the pressure was from the visiting side, the Whites could not find an equaliser.

'Monster' Player of the Match	Quote	Premiership Milestone
17 Liam Rosenior	❝ **Chris Coleman**	▶ **200**

In the second half we showed what a good team we can be, but in the first half we deserved to be 2-0 down.

Wayne Bridge made both his 200th Premiership appearance and his first for Fulham.

Venue:	Upton Park	Referee:	U.D.Rennie - 05/06	West Ham United
Attendance:	29,812	Matches:	25	Fulham
Capacity:	35,647	Yellow Cards:	45	
Occupancy:	84%	Red Cards:	3	

Form Coming into Fixture

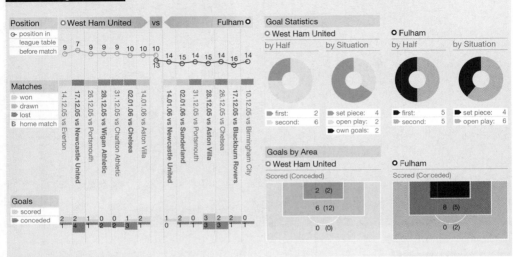

Position

- position in league table before match

O West Ham United vs Fulham O

9 7 9 9 9 10 10 10 / 13 / 14 15 14 15 14 16 14

Matches
- won
- drawn
- lost
- B home match

14.12.05 vs Everton
17.12.05 vs Newcastle United
26.12.05 vs Portsmouth
28.12.05 vs Wigan Athletic
31.12.05 vs Charlton Athletic
02.01.06 vs Chelsea
14.01.06 vs Aston Villa

14.01.06 vs Newcastle United
02.01.06 vs Sunderland
31.12.05 vs Portsmouth
28.12.05 vs Aston Villa
26.12.05 vs Chelsea
17.12.05 vs Blackburn Rovers
10.12.05 vs Birmingham City

Goals
- scored
- conceded

| 2 | 2 | 1 | 0 | 0 | 1 | 2 | | 1 | 2 | 0 | 3 | 2 | 2 | 0 |
| 1 | 4 | 1 | 2 | 2 | 3 | 1 | | 0 | 1 | 1 | 3 | 3 | 1 | 1 |

Goal Statistics

O West Ham United

by Half by Situation

- first: 2
- second: 6
- own goals: 2
- set piece: 4
- open play: 2

O Fulham

by Half by Situation

- first: 5
- second: 5
- set piece: 4
- open play: 6

Goals by Area

O West Ham United — Scored (Conceded)

| 2 (2) |
| 6 (12) |
| 0 (0) |

O Fulham — Scored (Conceded)

| 8 (5) |
| 0 (2) |

Team Statistics

Starting Line-Ups

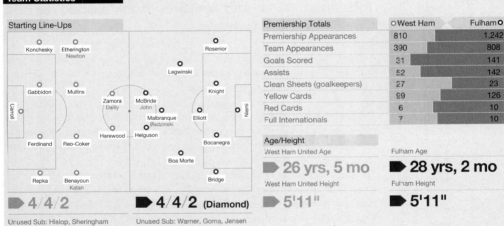

West Ham United: Konchesky, Etherington, Newton, Gabbidon, Mullins, Carroll, Ferdinand, Reo-Coker, Harewood, Repka, Benayoun/Katan, Zamora, Dailly, McBride, John, Malbranque, Radzinski, Helguson, Boa Morte

Fulham: Rosenior, Legwinski, Knight, Elliott, Niemi, Bocanegra, Bridge

West Ham: 4/4/2
Fulham: 4/4/2 (Diamond)

Unused Sub: Hislop, Sheringham
Unused Sub: Warner, Goma, Jensen N

Premiership Totals	O West Ham	Fulham O
Premiership Appearances	810	1,242
Team Appearances	390	808
Goals Scored	31	141
Assists	52	142
Clean Sheets (goalkeepers)	27	23
Yellow Cards	99	126
Red Cards	6	10
Full Internationals	7	10

Age/Height

West Ham United Age	Fulham Age
26 yrs, 5 mo	28 yrs, 2 mo
West Ham United Height	Fulham Height
5'11"	5'11"

Match Statistics

League Table after Fixture

		Played	Won	Drawn	Lost	For	Against	Pts
↑ 9	West Ham	23	9	5	9	31	32	32
↓ 10	Man City	23	9	4	10	30	27	31
● 11	Charlton	21	9	2	10	27	31	29
● 12	Everton	23	9	2	12	16	31	29
● 13	Fulham	23	7	5	11	27	32	26
● 14	Newcastle	22	7	5	10	20	25	26
● 15	Aston Villa	23	6	8	9	26	32	26
● 16	West Brom	23	6	4	13	21	32	22
● 17	Middlesbrough	22	5	7	10	27	40	22

Statistics	O West Ham	Fulham O
Goals	2	1
Shots on Target	5	6
Shots off Target	4	6
Hit Woodwork	0	0
Possession %	56	44
Corners	4	7
Offsides	4	0
Fouls	16	12
Disciplinary Points	8	8

Fulham 1
Tottenham Hotspur 0

31.01.06

➥ Carlos Bocanegra reels away after netting a late winner

Event Line

12 ○ ▣	Rasiak
23 ○ ⇄	Radzinski > Legwinski
26 ○ ⇄	Huddlestone > Reid
Half time 0-0	
57 ○ ▣	Helguson
67 ○ ▣	Jenas
70 ○ ⇄	Defoe > Rasiak
72 ○ ◢	Dawson
	2nd Bookable Offence
73 ○ ⇄	John > McBride
74 ○ ⇄	Gardner > Lennon
90 ○ ⊕	Bocanegra / H / IFK / IA
	Assist: Elliott
Full time 1-0	

A fantastic result against an ever improving Tottenham side and another brick added to the Craven Cottage fortress.

A pretty tentative opening half saw neither side giving too much ground away to the other. Chances were at a premium and neither keeper was forced to work too hard or save any truly threatening attacks.

The second half certainly brought more action and a lot more debate between the players on the pitch and the fans in the stands. Spurs' fans howled for a penalty as Jenas went down under a Boa Morte tackle, but the referee awarded a corner.

The game really heated up after 72 minutes when Spurs centre back Michael Dawson received his marching orders for a second bookable offence, a clumsy challenge on Heidar Helguson. From the resulting free kick, McBride's shot was beaten away by an alert Robinson.

With the game seemingly heading for a goalless draw, a foul by Tom Huddlestone to the left of centre saw Fulham win a free kick. Simon Elliott took it and an unmarked Carlos Bocanegra raced in to head wide of Robinson and secure another three points at home.

'Monster' Player of the Match

3 Carlos Bocanegra

Quote

🔟 Chris Coleman

It was a typical London derby that we deserved to win as Paul Robinson was by far the busier goalkeeper.

Venue:	Craven Cottage	Referee:	H.M.Webb - 05/06
Attendance:	21,081	Matches:	26
Capacity:	22,646	Yellow Cards:	62
Occupancy:	93%	Red Cards:	1

Fulham
Tottenham Hotspur

Form Coming into Fixture

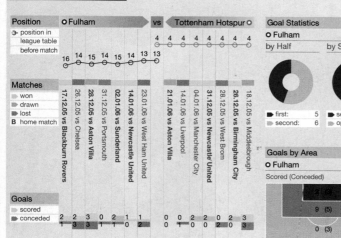

Position	Fulham	vs	Tottenham Hotspur

position in league table before match

Fulham: 16, 14, 15, 14, 15, 14, 13, 13
Tottenham Hotspur: 4, 4, 4, 4, 4, 4, 4, 4

Matches
- won
- drawn
- lost
- B home match

Fulham matches:
17.12.05 vs Blackburn Rovers
26.12.05 vs Chelsea
28.12.05 vs Aston Villa
31.12.05 vs Portsmouth
02.01.06 vs Sunderland
14.01.06 vs Newcastle United
23.01.06 vs West Ham United

Tottenham matches:
21.01.06 vs Aston Villa
14.01.06 vs Liverpool
04.01.06 vs Manchester City
31.12.05 vs Newcastle United
28.12.05 vs West Brom
26.12.05 vs Birmingham City
18.12.05 vs Middlesbrough

Goals
- scored
- conceded

Fulham scored: 2 2 3 0 2 1 1
Fulham conceded: 1 3 3 1 1 0 2

Tottenham scored: 0 0 2 2 0 2 3
Tottenham conceded: 0 1 0 0 2 0 3

Goal Statistics

Fulham
by Half / by Situation

| first: | 5 | set piece: | 5 |
| second: | 6 | open play: | 6 |

Tottenham Hotspur
by Half / by Situation

| first: | 3 | set piece: | 3 |
| second: | 6 | open play: | 6 |

Goals by Area

Fulham
Scored (Conceded)
2 (0)
9 (5)
0 (3)

Tottenham Hotspur
Scored (Conceded)
0 (1)
7 (5)
2 (0)

Team Statistics

Starting Line-Ups

Fulham:
Niemi
Rosenior
Knight
Bocanegra
Legwinski (Radzinski)
Elliott
Malbranque
Helguson
McBride (John)
Boa Morte
Bridge

Tottenham Hotspur:
Robinson
Kelly
King
Carrick
Dawson
Reid (Huddlestone)
Jenas
Keane
Rasiak (Defoe)
Stalteri
Lennon (Gardner)

4/4/2 (Diamond)   **4/4/2**

Unused Sub: Warner, Goma, Jensen N
Unused Sub: Cerny, Jackson

Premiership Totals	Fulham	Tottenham
Premiership Appearances	1,255	1,162
Team Appearances	821	694
Goals Scored	142	143
Assists	143	99
Clean Sheets (goalkeepers)	23	40
Yellow Cards	128	79
Red Cards	10	3
Full Internationals	10	10

Age/Height

	Fulham	Tottenham Hotspur
Age	28 yrs, 2 mo	23 yrs, 11 mo
Height	5'11"	6'

Match Statistics

League Table after Fixture

		Played	Won	Drawn	Lost	For	Against	Pts
● 4	Tottenham	24	11	8	5	31	20	41
...		...	...	...	...	...	...	...
● 13	Fulham	24	8	5	11	28	32	29
● 14	Newcastle	22	7	5	10	20	25	26
● 15	Aston Villa	23	6	8	9	28	32	26
↑ 16	Middlesbrough	23	6	7	10	30	40	25
↓ 17	West Brom	24	6	5	13	21	32	23
● 18	Birmingham	22	5	4	13	20	31	19
● 19	Portsmouth	23	4	5	14	16	39	17

Statistics	Fulham	Tottenham
Goals	1	0
Shots on Target	8	3
Shots off Target	4	4
Hit Woodwork	0	0
Possession %	51	49
Corners	4	9
Offsides	2	5
Fouls	9	11
Disciplinary Points	4	18

▶ Brian McBride demonstrates his aerial prowess

Event Line

6 ⊙ ⊕ Bocanegra / RF / OG / IA	
Assist: Park	
14 ⊙ ⊕ Ronaldo / RF / DFK / OA	
Assist: Saha	
17 ⊙ ■ Rosenior	
22 ⊙ ⊕ McBride / H / OP / IA	
Assist: Rosenior	
23 ⊙ ⊕ Saha / LF / OP / IA	
Assist: van Nistelrooy	
35 ⊙ ■ Smith	
37 ⊙ ⊕ Helguson / H / OP / 6Y	
Assist: Bridge	
38 ⊙ ■ Brown	
44 ⊙ ■ Neville	
Half time 3-2	
46 ⊙ ⇄ Radzinski > Brown	
62 ⊙ ■ Boa Morte	
69 ⊙ ⇄ Vidic > Neville	
69 ⊙ ⇄ Rooney > Park	
76 ⊙ ⇄ John > Helguson	
79 ⊙ ■ Evra	
81 ⊙ ⇄ Bardsley > Evra	
86 ⊙ ⊕ Ronaldo / RF / OP / IA	
Assist: van Nistelrooy	
Full time 4-2	

Fulham matched and at times outplayed the Red Devils, but in the end were undone to give United a scoreline that did not accurately reflect the game.

It took United just six minutes to find the back of the net, Park's deflected shot hitting Bocanegra and looping over Niemi. United doubled their lead when a deviating Ronaldo free kick completely flummoxed Niemi.

Fulham struck back after 22 minutes, Liam Rosenior was released down the right by Malbranque and his perfectly floated delivery was powerfully headed home by McBride from 10 yards out.

United took just a minute to increase their lead, ex-Fulham striker Louis Saha on hand to make it 3-1 after van Nistelrooy's shot was parried.

Fulham brought themselves right back into the game once more, making it five goals in the first half. Wayne Bridge outpaced Park to place a pinpoint centre to the far post where Helguson slammed home a perfect header beyond van der Sar.

United put the game beyond doubt in the 86th minute when Ronaldo netted his brace having fired a low shot past Niemi.

'Monster' Player of the Match	Quote	Premiership Milestone
10 Heidar Helguson	⁶⁶ Chris Coleman	▶ **150**
	I thought my guys were fantastic, dug their heels in and were always in the game.	Tomasz Radzinski made his 150th Premiership appearance.

Venue:	Old Trafford	Referee:	M.Atkinson - 05/06		Manchester United
Attendance:	67,844	Matches:	25		Fulham
Capacity:	73,006	Yellow Cards:	52		
Occupancy:	93%	Red Cards:	2		

Form Coming into Fixture

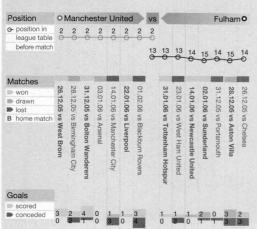

Position
- position in league table before match

O Manchester United: 2 2 2 2 2 2 2 2
vs Fulham O: 13 13 13 14 15 14 15 14

Matches
- won
- drawn
- lost
- B home match

26.12.05 vs West Brom / 28.12.05 vs Birmingham City / 31.12.05 vs Bolton Wanderers / 03.01.06 vs Arsenal / 14.01.06 vs Manchester City / 22.01.06 vs Liverpool / 01.02.06 vs Blackburn Rovers

31.01.06 vs Tottenham Hotspur / 23.01.06 vs West Ham United / 14.01.06 vs Newcastle United / 02.01.06 vs Sunderland / 31.12.05 vs Portsmouth / 28.12.05 vs Aston Villa / 26.12.05 vs Chelsea

Goals
- scored
- conceded

| scored | 3 | 2 | 4 | 0 | 1 | 1 | 3 | | 1 | 1 | 1 | 2 | 0 | 3 | 2 |
| conceded | 0 | 2 | 1 | 0 | 3 | 0 | 4 | | 0 | 2 | 0 | 1 | 1 | 3 | 3 |

Goal Statistics

O Manchester United

by Half | by Situation
- first: 6 | set piece: 4
- second: 8 | open play: 9
| own goals: 1

O Fulham

by Half | by Situation
- first: 4 | set piece: 5
- second: 6 | open play: 5

Goals by Area

O Manchester United
Scored (Conceded)

5 (4)
9 (6)
0 (0)

O Fulham
Scored (Conceded)

9 (4)
0 (3)

Team Statistics

Starting Line-Ups

Evra / Ronaldo / Bardsley
Silvestre / Richardson / Saha / Helguson John / Elliott / Knight
van der Sar / Brown / Smith / van Nistelrooy McBride / Brown Radzinski / Bocanegra / Niemi
Neville Vidic / Park Rooney / Boa Morte / Bridge

Malbranque / Rosenior

4/4/2 | **4/4/2**

Unused Sub: Steele, Fletcher | Unused Sub: Warner, Goma, Jensen N

Premiership Totals

	O Man Utd	Fulham O
Premiership Appearances	1,572	1,211
Team Appearances	1,110	706
Goals Scored	236	137
Assists	196	142
Clean Sheets (goalkeepers)	53	24
Yellow Cards	184	119
Red Cards	13	10
Full Internationals	13	10

Age/Height

Manchester United Age
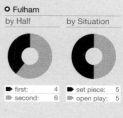 **25 yrs, 9 mo**

Fulham Age
27 yrs, 11 mo

Manchester United Height
5'11"

Fulham Height
5'11"

Match Statistics

League Table after Fixture

		Played	Won	Drawn	Lost	For	Against	Pts
● 2	Man Utd	25	15	6	4	49	26	51
...	...	...	...	...	...	...	...	...
↓ 14	Fulham	25	8	5	12	30	36	29
● 15	Newcastle	24	8	5	11	22	28	29
↑ 16	West Brom	25	7	5	13	23	32	26
↓ 17	Middlesbrough	24	6	7	11	30	44	25
● 18	Birmingham	24	5	5	14	21	34	20
● 19	Portsmouth	25	4	6	15	17	42	18
● 20	Sunderland	24	2	3	19	17	45	9

Statistics

	O Man Utd	Fulham O
Goals	4	2
Shots on Target	14	7
Shots off Target	7	3
Hit Woodwork	0	0
Possession %	59	41
Corners	8	5
Offsides	3	1
Fouls	10	14
Disciplinary Points	16	8

Fulham 6
West Brom 1

▶ Heidar Helguson gets the party started at Craven Cottage

Event Line

4 O ⊕ Helguson / RF / OP / IA	
Assist: McBride	
29 O ▨ Wallwork	
40 O ⊕ Helguson / H / IFK / 6Y	
Assist: Elliott	
Half time 2-0	
46 O ⇄ Martinez > Gaardsoe	
46 O ⇄ Ellington > Horsfield	
46 O ▨ Helguson	
48 O ⊕ Radzinski / RF / OP / IA	
Assist: Malbranque	
49 O ▨ Radzinski	
58 O ⊕ Davies C / H / CG / IA	
Assist: Helguson	
61 O ▨ Martinez	
61 O ⇄ Hoult > Kuszczak	
64 O ⇄ John > Helguson	
83 O ⊕ John / RF / OP / 6Y	
Assist: Radzinski	
85 O ⊕ Campbell / RF / OP / IA	
Assist: Inamoto	
86 O ▨ Boa Morte	
90 O ⊕ John / LF / OP / IA	
Assist: Radzinski	
Full time 6-1	

Fans would happily take a six goal scoreline once every season and this one saw the Whites hammer a poor West Brom side at the Cottage.

Fulham got off to a brilliant start. A long clearance from Antti Niemi was met by McBride and his flick on fell into the path of Helguson who scored with a low, crashing volley. The Whites doubled their lead with 40 minutes gone, as Helguson grabbed a second with a header from six yards out.

It was 3-0 within two minutes of the second half as Malbranque released Radzinski to open his account for the season, an understandable but perhaps slightly over-exuberant celebration also saw the Canadian pick up a booking.

The dubious goals panel were called in for Fulham's fourth, Helguson denied a hat-trick after a heavy deflection off Curtis Davies. With under 10 minutes to go Fulham made it five as substitute Collins John scored.

There was a late consolation for West Brom, Kevin Campbell scored from close range after Inamoto released him. If the game wasn't beyond doubt before it soon was as Fulham made it 6-1, John bagging himself a late brace in the process.

'Monster' Player of the Match

10 Heidar Helguson

Quote

❝ Chris Coleman

If we put the ball in the box, Brian McBride and Heidar Helguson will get goals. They caused havoc at Manchester United last week and did the same today.

Form Coming into Fixture

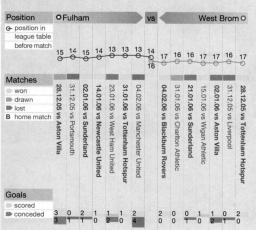

Position

- ○ position in league table before match

| | 15 | 14 | 15 | 14 | 13 | 13 | 13 | 14 16 | 17 | 16 | 16 | 17 | 17 | 16 | 17 |

Matches
- won
- drawn
- lost
- B home match

28.12.05 vs Aston Villa · 31.12.05 vs Portsmouth · 02.01.06 vs Sunderland · 14.01.06 vs Newcastle United · 23.01.06 vs West Ham United · 31.01.06 vs Tottenham Hotspur · 04.02.06 vs Manchester United · 04.02.06 vs Blackburn Rovers · 31.01.06 vs Charlton Athletic · 21.01.06 vs Sunderland · 15.01.06 vs Wigan Athletic · 02.01.06 vs Aston Villa · 31.12.05 vs Liverpool · 28.12.05 vs Tottenham Hotspur

Goals
- scored
- conceded

| scored | 3 | 0 | 2 | 1 | 1 | 1 | 2 | | 2 | 0 | 0 | 1 | 1 | 0 | 2 |
| conceded | 3 | 1 | 1 | 0 | 2 | 0 | 4 | | 0 | 0 | 1 | 0 | 2 | 1 | 0 |

Goal Statistics

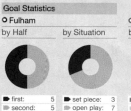

○ Fulham

by Half	by Situation
first: 5	set piece: 3
second: 5	open play: 7

○ West Bromwich Albion

by Half	by Situation
first: 3	set piece: 1
second: 3	open play: 5

Goals by Area

○ Fulham
Scored (Conceded)

9 (6)

0 (3)

○ West Bromwich Albion
Scored (Conceded)

1 (1)

4 (3)

1 (0)

Team Statistics

Starting Line-Ups

Bridge, Boa Morte, Bocanegra, Helguson, John, Campbell, Niemi, Elliott, Malbranque, Knight, McBride / Ellington, Horsfield / Ellington, Radzinski, Volz, Inamoto, Albrechtsen, Wallwork, Davies C, Hoult, Kuszczak, Quashie, Baardsen / Martinez, Greening, Clement

▶ **4/4/2** (Diamond)   ▶ **4/4/2**

Unused Sub: Warner, Goma, Jensen N, Legwinski

Unused Sub: Carter, Kozak

Premiership Totals

	○ Fulham	West Brom ○
Premiership Appearances	1,200	1,165
Team Appearances	766	528
Goals Scored	137	119
Assists	138	98
Clean Sheets (goalkeepers)	24	8
Yellow Cards	111	93
Red Cards	8	6
Full Internationals	10	5

Age/Height

Fulham Age	West Bromwich Albion Age
▶ **28 yrs**	▶ **27 yrs, 4 mo**
Fulham Height	West Bromwich Albion Height
▶ **5'11"**	▶ **6'**

Match Statistics

League Table after Fixture

		Played	Won	Drawn	Lost	For	Against	Pts
●	9 Blackburn	25	11	4	10	31	31	37
↑	10 Everton	26	11	3	12	19	32	36
↓	11 Man City	25	10	4	11	33	28	34
↓	12 Charlton	24	10	3	11	30	34	33
↑	13 Fulham	26	9	5	12	36	37	32
↑	14 Newcastle	25	9	5	11	24	29	32
↓	15 Aston Villa	26	7	9	10	32	35	30
↑	16 Middlesbrough	25	7	7	11	33	44	28
↓	17 West Brom	26	7	5	14	24	38	26

Statistics

	○ Fulham	West Brom ○
Goals	6	1
Shots on Target	7	6
Shots off Target	4	5
Hit Woodwork	0	0
Possession %	52	48
Corners	4	7
Offsides	3	3
Fouls	19	14
Disciplinary Points	12	8

Bolton Wanderers 2
Fulham 1

➤ Tomasz Radzinski pressurises Kevin Davies

Event Line

22 ⚪ ⊕	Helguson / H / IFK / IA	
	Assist: Elliott	
36 ⚪ ■	Boa Morte	
42 ⚪ ■	Nolan	
45 ⚪ ⊕	Helguson / RF / OG / 6Y	
	Assist: N'Gotty	
Half time 1-1		
60 ⚪ ⇄	Speed > Diagne-Faye	
68 ⚪ ⊕	Nolan / RF / OP / IA	
	Assist: Davies	
75 ⚪ ⇄	John > McBride	
75 ⚪ ⇄	Diop > Radzinski	
82 ⚪ ⇄	Vaz Te > Nakata	
90 ⚪ ⇄	Ben Haim > Okocha	
Full time 2-1		

The Reebok Stadium's reputation as a tough place to visit held fast for Fulham's last game in February as a Kevin Nolan goal claimed all the spoils for the Trotters.

Man of the moment, Heidar Helguson, struck once again for Fulham in the 22nd minute as he rose highest to nod home a beautifully flighted Simon Elliott free kick.

Bolton looked to reply straight away and thought they had made a breakthrough when Kevin Nolan put the ball into the net, but much to the dismay of the home crowd the goal was ruled out for offside.

With the whistle pursed on the referee's lips Bolton won a corner, Stelios attempted to deliver but it was cleared straight back to him, his second cross was dangerous and caused confusion in the box and, in an attempt to clear, Helguson could only smash it into his own net.

Bolton took a lot of heart from this lucky goal and they managed to make it 2-1 following some good work by Kevin Davies. Davies played the ball into Nolan who jinked his way through two weak Fulham tackles before sliding the ball past Warner for what would prove to be the winning goal.

'Monster' Player of the Match

10 Heidar Helguson

Quote

❝ Chris Coleman

For the first 45 minutes we were the better side, but we didn't capitalise on the chances we created.

Venue:	Reebok Staduim	Referee:	P.Dowd - 05/06	Bolton Wanderers
Attendance:	23,104	Matches:	34	Fulham
Capacity:	28,723	Yellow Cards:	133	
Occupancy:	80%	Red Cards:	5	

Form Coming into Fixture

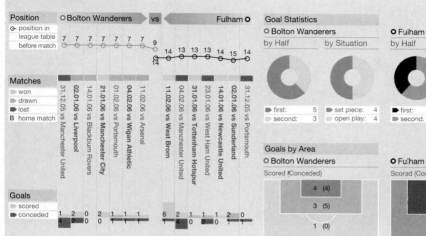

Position

- ○ Bolton Wanderers vs Fulham ○
- ○ position in league table before match

Matches
- won
- drawn
- lost
- B home match

Matches (Bolton):
- 31.12.05 vs Manchester United
- 02.01.06 vs Liverpool
- 14.01.06 vs Blackburn Rovers
- 21.01.06 vs Manchester City
- 01.02.06 vs Portsmouth
- 04.02.06 vs Wigan Athletic
- 11.02.06 vs Arsenal

Matches (Fulham):
- 11.02.06 vs West Brom
- 04.02.06 vs Manchester United
- 31.01.06 vs Tottenham Hotspur
- 23.01.06 vs West Ham United
- 14.01.06 vs Newcastle United
- 02.01.06 vs Sunderland
- 31.12.05 vs Portsmouth

Goals
- scored
- conceded

Bolton: scored 1 2 0 2 1 1 1 1 / conceded 4 2 0 0 1 1 1 1
Fulham: scored 6 2 1 1 1 2 0 / conceded 1 4 0 2 0 1

Goal Statistics

○ Bolton Wanderers — by Half | by Situation
- first: 5
- second: 3
- set piece: 4
- open play: 4

○ Fulham — by Half | by Situation
- first: 5
- second: 8
- set piece: 3
- open play: 9
- own goals: 1

Goals by Area

○ Bolton Wanderers — Scored (Conceded)
- 4 (4)
- 3 (5)
- 1 (0)

○ Fulham — Scored (Conceded)
- 10 (6)
- 0 (3)

Team Statistics

Starting Line-Ups

Bolton Wanderers:
- Gardner
- Giannakopoulos
- Nakata / Vaz Te
- N'Gotty
- Jaaskelainen
- Okocha / Ben Haim
- Davies
- Jaidi
- Diagne-Faye / Speed
- O'Brien
- Nolan

Fulham:
- Volz
- Radzinski / Diop
- Knight
- McBride / John
- Malbranque
- Elliott
- Warner
- Helguson
- Bocanegra
- Boa Morte
- Bridge

▶ 4/5/1

▶ 4/4/2 (Diamond)

Unused Sub: Walker, Borgetti

Unused Sub: Goma, Jensen N, Rosenior

Premiership Totals

	○ Bolton	Fulham ○
Premiership Appearances	1,646	1,185
Team Appearances	1,104	832
Goals Scored	187	150
Assists	153	143
Clean Sheets (goalkeepers)	47	2
Yellow Cards	217	124
Red Cards	11	10
Full Internationals	10	10

Age/Height

Bolton Wanderers Age ▶ 28 yrs, 4 mo
Fulham Age ▶ 27 yrs, 10 mo
Bolton Wanderers Height ▶ 5'11"
Fulham Height ▶ 6'

Match Statistics

League Table after Fixture

		Played	Won	Drawn	Lost	For	Against	Pts
↑ 6	Bolton	25	11	9	5	32	24	42
↓ 7	Arsenal	27	12	5	10	39	22	41
↓ 8	West Ham	26	12	5	9	39	34	41
↓ 9	Wigan	27	12	4	11	32	34	40
• 10	Man City	27	11	4	12	36	31	37
• 11	Newcastle	27	10	6	11	26	29	36
• 12	Everton	27	11	3	13	19	34	36
• 13	Charlton	27	10	5	12	32	37	35
• 14	Fulham	27	9	5	13	37	39	32

Statistics

	○ Bolton	Fulham ○
Goals	2	1
Shots on Target	5	6
Shots off Target	8	4
Hit Woodwork	0	1
Possession %	50	50
Corners	8	5
Offsides	10	1
Fouls	13	13
Disciplinary Points	4	4

Fulham 0
Arsenal 4

04.03.06

➤ Luis Boa Morte attempts to outsprint Emmanuel Eboue

Event Line

31 ⚽ Henry / LF / OP / IA	
Assist: Diaby	
35 ⚽ Adebayor / LF / OP / IA	
Assist: Ljungberg	
Half time 0-2	
61 ⇄ John > Helguson	
68 ▢ Diaby	
72 ⇄ Bergkamp > Adebayor	
77 ⚽ Henry / RF / OP / IA	
Assist: Ljungberg	
79 ⇄ Fabregas > Hleb	
84 ⇄ Reyes > Henry	
86 ⚽ Fabregas / RF / OP / IA	
Assist: Flamini	
Full time 0-4	

Arsenal had been having a weak season by their high standards but on this occasion everything clicked for the men from N5 as Fulham chased shadows for much of the afternoon.

Arsenal started off in menacing fashion and it was only the fine form of Tony Warner that kept the Gunners at bay. The visiting team eventually breached Fulham's defence just after the half hour mark when Diaby got the ball to Henry. The Frenchman accelerated past Volz and cracked a left footed shot past Warner.

Four minutes later and it was 2-0, this time thanks to Adebayor who ran on to a Ljungberg pass to score from 10 yards.

After the break, and with quarter of an hour to go, Fulham tried to pull one back through Malbranque but his low drive was well held by Lehmann.

Eventually, however, it was Arsenal who added the gloss to the scoreline getting two late goals to leave Fulham with their worst defeat of the season. Henry got his second of the game as he bore down on goal before curling the ball effortlessly past Warner. With time running out substitute Cesc Fabregas made it four, as he side footed a simple goal from a Flamini cross.

'Monster' Player of the Match

30 Tony Warner

Quote

🔓 Chris Coleman

It was the worst performance we have had at home this season, but that was the best display from an Arsenal team against us.

Venue:	Craven Cottage	Referee:	R.Styles - 05/06		Fulham
Attendance:	22,397	Matches:	32		Arsenal
Capacity:	22,646	Yellow Cards:	107		
Occupancy:	99%	Red Cards:	4		

Form Coming into Fixture

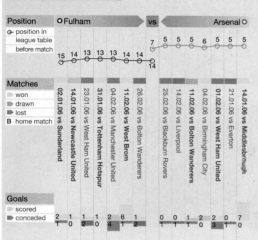

Position — O Fulham vs Arsenal O
- position in league table before match

Fulham: 15 14 13 13 13 14 14 / 14
Arsenal: 7 5 5 5 6 5 5 5

Matches
- won
- drawn
- lost
- B home match

Fulham matches:
- 02.01.06 vs Sunderland
- 14.01.06 vs Newcastle United
- 23.01.06 vs West Ham United
- 31.01.06 vs Tottenham Hotspur
- 04.02.06 vs Manchester United
- 11.02.06 vs West Brom
- 26.02.06 vs Bolton Wanderers

Arsenal matches:
- 25.02.06 vs Blackburn Rovers
- 14.02.06 vs Liverpool
- 11.02.06 vs Bolton Wanderers
- 04.02.06 vs Birmingham City
- 01.02.06 vs West Ham United
- 21.01.06 vs Everton
- 14.01.06 vs Middlesbrough

Goals
- scored
- conceded

Fulham: scored 2 1 1 1 2 6 1 / conceded 1 0 2 0 4 1 2
Arsenal: scored 0 0 1 2 2 0 7 / conceded 1 1 1 0 3 1 0

Goal Statistics

O Fulham — by Half / by Situation
- first: 6
- second: 8
- set piece: 4
- open play: 9
- own goals: 1

O Arsenal — by Half / by Situation
- first: 6
- second: 6
- set piece: 2
- open play: 10

Goals by Area

O Fulham — Scored (Conceded)
3 (1)
11 (6)
0 (3)

O Arsenal — Scored (Conceded)
2 (2)
9 (5)
1 (0)

Team Statistics

Starting Line-Ups

Fulham: Rosenior, Boa Morte, Goma, Helguson, John, Elliott, Malbranque, McBride, Knight, Radzinski, Volz, Warner

Arsenal: Hleb, Eboue, Fabregas, Gilberto Silva, Toure, Adebayor, Bergkamp, Henry, Reyes, Diaby, Senderos, Lehmann, Ljungberg, Flamini

4/4/2 (Diamond) | **4/4/2**

Unused Sub: Crossley, Bocanegra, Jensen N, Elrich | Unused Sub: Poom, Djourou

Premiership Totals

	O Fulham	Arsenal O
Premiership Appearances	1,063	1,269
Team Appearances	876	1,269
Goals Scored	139	314
Assists	133	275
Clean Sheets (goalkeepers)	2	38
Yellow Cards	128	125
Red Cards	9	4
Full Internationals	9	12

Age/Height

Fulham Age	Arsenal Age
28 yrs, 1 mo	**25 yrs, 8 mo**
Fulham Height	Arsenal Height
6'	**6'**

Match Statistics

League Table after Fixture

		Played	Won	Drawn	Lost	For	Against	Pts
↑ 5	Arsenal	28	13	5	10	43	22	44
...	...	...	...	...	...	...	...	...
↑ 14	Aston Villa	28	8	10	10	33	35	34
↑ 15	Middlesbrough	27	9	7	11	36	44	34
↓ 16	Fulham	28	9	5	14	37	43	32
• 17	West Brom	28	7	5	16	25	42	26
• 18	Birmingham	27	6	5	16	22	38	23
• 19	Portsmouth	28	4	6	18	18	48	18
• 20	Sunderland	27	2	4	21	18	49	10

Statistics

	O Fulham	Arsenal O
Goals	0	4
Shots on Target	4	11
Shots off Target	3	7
Hit Woodwork	0	0
Possession %	54	46
Corners	0	7
Offsides	4	4
Fouls	10	11
Disciplinary Points	0	4

Everton 3
Fulham 1

Everton

► Heidar Helguson bears down on goal

Event Line

14 ⊙ ⊕ Beattie / RF / P / IA	
	Assist: Beattie
36 ⊙ ⊕ Beattie / RF / IFK / OA	
	Assist: Cahill
36 ⊙ ■ Rosenior	
43 ⊙ ⇄ Christanval > Elliott	
Half time 2-0	
55 ⊙ ⊕ McFadden / LF / OP / OA	
	Assist: Beattie
57 ⊙ ■ Neville	
74 ⊙ ⇄ John > Helguson	
77 ⊙ ⇄ Kilbane > McFadden	
77 ⊙ ⇄ Davies > Valente	
81 ⊙ ■ Bocanegra	
83 ⊙ ⇄ van der Meyde > Cahill	
86 ⊙ ⊕ John / RF / P / IA	
	Assist: John
88 ⊙ ■ Stubbs	
Full time 3-1	

Everton secured Fulham's third successive League defeat and, in so doing, pushed the Whites further towards the wrong end of the table.

Fulham got off to the worst possible start as referee Uriah Rennie awarded a penalty for a Zat Knight foul on Beattie as the Everton striker chased a long ball into the box. Beattie picked himself up to dispatch the penalty past Tony Warner.

There was no chance with Everton's second goal, however, as James Beattie scored with an inch perfect chip over Tony Warner into the far corner of the net after the ball was knocked back to him by Tim Cahill.

James McFadden later netted the goal of the game as he smashed a 30-yard volley past Warner following a neat flick down by Beattie.

Fulham, however, almost got back into the game, Phillippe Christanval's shot on the turn, from a deflected Boa Morte free kick, flying narrowly over the bar.

It was too little too late for Fulham. With five minutes remaining the Whites were awarded their own spot kick after Collins John was fouled by Hibbert. John coolly slotted the penalty past Wright but it was of little consolation.

'Monster' Player of the Match

7 Mark Pembridge

Quote

❝ Chris Coleman

I can't describe it really. I am as disappointed as I have been in my short managerial career. It was a poor, unacceptable performance.

Venue:	Goodison Park	Referee:	U.D.Rennie - 05/06	Everton
Attendance:	36,515	Matches:	34	Fulham
Capacity:	40,569	Yellow Cards:	66	
Occupancy:	90%	Red Cards:	4	

Form Coming into Fixture

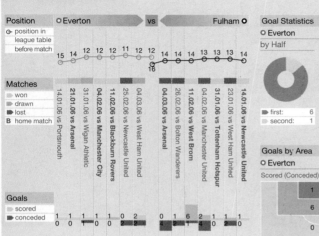

Position
- position in league table before match

O Everton vs Fulham O

15 14 12 12 12 11 12 12 | 14 14 14 13 13 13 14
16

Matches
- won
- drawn
- lost
- B home match

14.01.06 vs Portsmouth
21.01.06 vs Arsenal
31.01.06 vs Wigan Athletic
04.02.06 vs Manchester City
11.02.06 vs Blackburn Rovers
25.02.06 vs Newcastle United
04.03.06 vs West Ham United
04.03.06 vs Arsenal
26.02.06 vs Bolton Wanderers
11.02.06 vs West Brom
04.02.06 vs Manchester United
31.01.06 vs Tottenham Hotspur
23.01.06 vs West Ham United
14.01.06 vs Newcastle United

Goals
	scored	conceded
	1 1 1 1 1 0 2	0 1 6 2 1 1 1
	0 0 1 0 0 2 2	4 2 1 4 0 2 0

Goal Statistics

O Everton

by Half

| first: | 6 |
| second: | 1 |

by Situation

set piece:	3
open play:	2
own goals:	2

O Fulham

by Half

| first: | 5 |
| second: | 7 |

by Situation

set piece:	4
open play:	7
own goals:	1

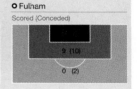

Goals by Area

O Everton

Scored (Conceded)

| 1 (2) |
| 6 (2) |
| 0 (1) |

O Fulham

Scored (Conceded)

| 9 (10) |
| 0 (2) |

Team Statistics

Starting Line-Ups

Wright
Valente — Davies — Arteta
Stubbs — Neville
McFadden — Kilbane
Weir — Cahill — van der Meyde
Hibbert — Osman
Beattie

Helguson — John
Elliott — Christanval
Knight
McBride — Pembridge
Bocanegra
Boa Morte
Malbranque — Rosenior
Volz
Warner

▶ 4/4/2   ▶ 4/5/1

Unused Sub: Westerveld, Yobo

Unused Sub: Crossley, Goma, Jensen N

Premiership Totals

	O Everton	Fulham O
Premiership Appearances	1,727	1,067
Team Appearances	942	820
Goals Scored	152	125
Assists	127	134
Clean Sheets (goalkeepers)	28	2
Yellow Cards	198	131
Red Cards	12	9
Full Internationals	10	10

Age/Height

Everton Age	Fulham Age
▶ 28 yrs	▶ 27 yrs, 10 mo
Everton Height	Fulham Height
▶ 5'11"	▶ 6'

Match Statistics

League Table after Fixture

	Played	Won	Drawn	Lost	For	Against	Pts
↑ 11 Everton	29	12	4	13	24	37	40
↓ 12 Newcastle	28	11	6	11	29	30	39
● 13 Charlton	28	10	6	12	32	37	36
● 14 Aston Villa	29	8	10	11	33	37	34
● 15 Middlesbrough	27	9	7	11	36	44	34
● 16 Fulham	29	9	5	15	38	46	32
● 17 West Brom	29	7	6	16	26	43	27
● 18 Birmingham	28	6	6	16	23	39	24
● 19 Portsmouth	29	5	6	18	20	49	21

Statistics

	O Everton	Fulham O
Goals	3	1
Shots on Target	8	4
Shots off Target	8	5
Hit Woodwork	0	0
Possession %	61	39
Corners	8	4
Offsides	1	1
Fouls	15	12
Disciplinary Points	8	8

Liverpool 5
Fulham 1

➡ Michael Brown is tracked by Fernando Morientes

Event Line

16 ⊙ ⊕ Fowler / H / C / 6Y	
	Assist: Garcia
25 ⊙ ⊕ John / RF / OP / IA	
	Assist: Boa Morte
31 ⊙ ▪ Brown	
34 ⊙ ⊕ Brown / LF / OG / 6Y	
	Assist: Kewell
Half time 2-1	
68 ⊙ ⇄ Cisse > Fowler	
69 ⊙ ⇄ Christanval > Knight	
71 ⊙ ⊕ Morientes / LF / C / 6Y	
	Assist: Agger
71 ⊙ ▪ Bridge	
78 ⊙ ⇄ McBride > Radzinski	
81 ⊙ ⇄ Crouch > Morientes	
88 ⊙ ⇄ Warnock > Kewell	
89 ⊙ ⊕ Crouch / RF / OP / 6Y	
	Assist: Gerrard
90 ⊙ ⊕ Warnock / RF / OP / IA	
	Assist: Finnan
90 ⊙ ▪ John	
Full time 5-1	

Liverpool put five away at Anfield as Fulham slumped to an embarrassing 5-1 loss to further compound a run of four defeats for Chris Coleman's men.

It was always going to be a tough test for a side yet to win away from home and after 16 minutes it looked an even taller order, Robbie Fowler darting in at the far post to power in a header from a corner – his first goal since returning to Merseyside.

Fulham did not seem deterred though and netted an equaliser nine minutes later through Collins John. A perfectly weighted ball from Luis Boa Morte released John and the Dutchman coolly slotted the ball past Jose Reina in the Liverpool goal.

Liverpool restored their lead just after half an hour as Michael Brown turned the ball into his own net following a Kewell cross.

Into the second half and it was 3-1 to Liverpool as Morientes capitalised on some hesitant defending following a Gerrard corner. Liverpool poured salt on the wound with two late goals, Crouch struck first to make it 4-1 as he was first to react to a driven Gerrard effort. Warnock then made it five in stoppage time.

'Monster' Player of the Match	Quote
9 Michael Brown	⓰ **Chris Coleman**

It looks as if we have been battered after those last few minutes, but I cannot criticise the players for their performance.

Venue:	Anfield	Referee:	A.G.Wiley - 05/06	Liverpool
Attendance:	42,293	Matches:	35	Fulham
Capacity:	45,362	Yellow Cards:	106	
Occupancy:	93%	Red Cards:	7	

Form Coming into Fixture

Position

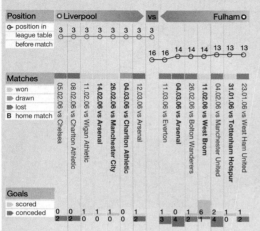

	O Liverpool	vs	Fulham O

position in league table before match: Liverpool 3 3 3 3 3 3 3 3 — Fulham 16 16 14 14 14 13 13 13

Matches:
- won
- drawn
- lost
- B home match

Liverpool matches: 05.02.06 vs Chelsea, 08.02.06 vs Charlton Athletic, 11.02.06 vs Wigan Athletic, 14.02.06 vs Arsenal, 26.02.06 vs Manchester City, 04.03.06 vs Charlton Athletic, 12.03.06 vs Arsenal

Fulham matches: 11.03.06 vs Everton, 04.03.06 vs Arsenal, 26.02.06 vs Bolton Wanderers, 11.02.06 vs West Brom, 04.02.06 vs Manchester United, 31.01.06 vs Tottenham Hotspur, 23.01.06 vs West Ham United

Goals:
- scored: Liverpool 0 0 1 1 1 0 1 — Fulham 1 0 1 6 2 1 1
- conceded: Liverpool 2 2 0 0 0 0 2 — Fulham 3 4 2 1 4 0 2

Goal Statistics

O Liverpool
by Half	by Situation

- first: 2
- second: 2
- set piece: 1
- open play: 3

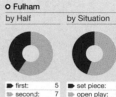

O Fulham
by Half	by Situation

- first: 5
- second: 7
- set piece: 5
- open play: 6
- own goals: 1

Goals by Area

O Liverpool
Scored (Conceded)

1 (1)
3 (5)
0 (0)

O Fulham
Scored (Conceded)

3 (0)
9 (11)
0 (4)

Team Statistics

Starting Line-Ups

Liverpool: Reina; Traore, Kewell (Warnock), Agger, Hamann, Morientes (Crouch), John, Carragher, Gerrard, Fowler (Cisse), Finnan, Garcia

Fulham: Malbranque, Rosenior, Brown, Knight (Christanval), Warner, Radzinski (McBride), Pembridge, Pearce, Boa Morte, Bridge

Liverpool: ▶ 4/4/2
Fulham: ▶ 4/4/1/1

Unused Sub: Dudek, Hyypia

Unused Sub: Crossley, Jensen N, Helguson

Premiership Totals	O Liverpool	Fulham O
Premiership Appearances	1,834	1,525
Team Appearances	1,386	753
Goals Scored	310	158
Assists	209	175
Clean Sheets (goalkeepers)	17	2
Yellow Cards	203	144
Red Cards	13	12
Full Internationals	13	9

Age/Height

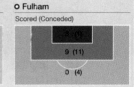

Liverpool Age	Fulham Age
▶ 27 yrs	▶ 28 yrs, 6 mo
Liverpool Height	Fulham Height
▶ 6'	▶ 6'

Match Statistics

League Table after Fixture

		Played	Won	Drawn	Lost	For	Against	Pts
● 3	Liverpool	30	17	7	6	39	20	58
...		...	...	...	...	...	...	...
● 14	Aston Villa	29	8	10	11	33	37	34
● 15	Middlesbrough	28	9	7	12	37	46	34
● 16	Fulham	30	9	5	16	39	51	32
● 17	West Brom	29	7	6	16	26	43	27
● 18	Birmingham	28	6	6	16	23	39	24
● 19	Portsmouth	29	5	6	18	20	49	21
● 20	Sunderland	29	2	4	23	19	52	10

Statistics	O Liverpool	Fulham O
Goals	5	1
Shots on Target	10	4
Shots off Target	8	3
Hit Woodwork	1	1
Possession %	53	47
Corners	8	2
Offsides	5	10
Fouls	8	12
Disciplinary Points	0	12

► Luis Boa Morte skips away from Didier Drogba

Event Line

17 ○ ⊕ Boa Morte / LF / OP / IA	
Assist: Malbranque	
26 ○ ⇄ Drogba > Cole J	
26 ○ ⇄ Duff > Wright-Phillips	
29 ○ ■ Huth	
Half time 1-0	
46 ○ ⇄ Carvalho > Huth	
53 ○ ■ Brown	
57 ○ ■ Carvalho	
60 ○ ■ Drogba	
71 ○ ⇄ Helguson > John	
89 ○ ⇄ Christanval > Malbranque	
90 ○ ■ Gallas	
Foul	
90 ○ ■ Makelele	
Full time 1-0	

A day that will forever live in the memories of the largest crowd at Craven Cottage in recent times. This was a victory 27 years in the waiting, the second part of the season's SW6 derby battle.

Unfazed by the lofty position of their opponents the Whites set out to attack from the first kick of this pulsating encounter. Malbranque, on the right, slipped the ball inside Gallas and into the path of Moritz Volz, the German youth international was brought down by John Terry but the referee waved away the penalty protests.

The vital goal for Fulham came on 17 minutes. Steed Malbranque's shot hit Robert Huth and the ball dropped to Luis Boa Morte, who hit it past Petr Cech.

Fulham continued to look solid going into half-time as Chelsea made changes to try and find the breakthrough. The Blues came out in the second half intent on attack and thought they had equalized in the 57th minute. The Drogba goal, however, was ruled out for an obvious handball.

Late drama, with Chelsea down to 10 men following Gallas' sending off and with two minutes remaining, John Terry sent in a thumping header which Crossley dealt with superbly to tip over the bar and ensure Fulham's historic victory.

'Monster' Player of the Match	Quote	Premiership Milestone
4 Steed Malbranque	🆔 **Chris Coleman**	► **22,486**
	Three points against anyone would have been sweet, but against Chelsea in a local derby was even sweeter.	The attendance of 22,486 was a Premiership record at Craven Cottage.

Venue:	Craven Cottage	Referee:	M.L.Dean - 05/06		Fulham
Attendance:	22,486	Matches:	29		Chelsea
Capacity:	22,646	Yellow Cards:	82		
Occupancy:	99%	Red Cards:	7		

Form Coming into Fixture

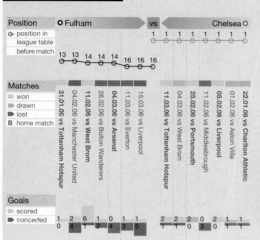

Position
- position in league table before match

O Fulham vs **Chelsea O**

Fulham: 13 13 14 14 14 16 16 16
Chelsea: 1 1 1 1 1 1 1 1

Matches
- won
- drawn
- lost
- B home match

Fulham matches:
- 31.01.06 vs Tottenham Hotspur
- 04.02.06 vs Manchester United
- 11.02.06 vs West Brom
- 26.02.06 vs Bolton Wanderers
- 04.03.06 vs Arsenal
- 11.03.06 vs Everton
- 15.03.06 vs Liverpool

Chelsea matches:
- 11.03.06 vs Tottenham Hotspur
- 04.03.06 vs West Brom
- 25.02.06 vs Portsmouth
- 11.02.06 vs Middlesbrough
- 05.02.06 vs Liverpool
- 01.02.06 vs Aston Villa
- 22.01.06 vs Charlton Athletic

Goals
- scored
- conceded

Fulham goals: scored 1 2 6 1 0 1 1 / conceded 0 4 2 4 3 5
Chelsea goals: scored 2 2 2 0 2 1 1 / conceded 0 3 0

Goal Statistics

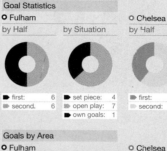

O Fulham

by Half:
- first: 6
- second: 6

by Situation:
- set piece: 4
- open play: 7
- own goals: 1

O Chelsea

by Half:
- first: 4
- second: 6

by Situation:
- set piece: 2
- open play: 8

Goals by Area

O Fulham
Scored (Conceded)
9 (11)
0 (3)

O Chelsea
Scored (Conceded)
2 (2)
7 (5)
1 (0)

Team Statistics

Starting Line-Ups

Fulham: Crossley, Rosenior, Pearce, Knight, Volz, Boa Morte, Pembridge, Brown, McBride, Malbranque / Christanval, John / Helguson

Unused Sub: Warner, Jensen N, Radzinski

4/4/2 (Diamond)

Chelsea: Cech, Ferreira, Huth / Carvalho, Terry, Gallas, Essien, Makelele, Lampard, Wright-Phillips / Duff, Crespo, Cole J / Drogba

Unused Sub: Cudicini, Maniche

4/3/3

Premiership Totals

	O Fulham	Chelsea O
Premiership Appearances	1,480	1,584
Team Appearances	797	1,083
Goals Scored	137	211
Assists	144	194
Clean Sheets (goalkeepers)	50	37
Yellow Cards	156	164
Red Cards	13	6
Full Internationals	8	14

Age/Height

Fulham Age: **28 yrs, 5 mo**
Chelsea Age: **26 yrs, 8 mo**

Fulham Height: **5'11"**
Chelsea Height: **6'**

Match Statistics

League Table after Fixture

		Played	Won	Drawn	Lost	For	Against	Pts
●	1 Chelsea	30	24	3	3	58	19	75
...		...	...	...	...	...	...	...
↑	14 Fulham	31	10	5	16	40	51	35
↓	15 Aston Villa	30	8	10	12	34	41	34
↓	16 Middlesbrough	29	9	7	13	39	49	34
●	17 West Brom	30	7	6	17	27	45	27
●	18 Birmingham	29	6	6	17	23	41	24
●	19 Portsmouth	30	6	6	18	24	51	24
●	20 Sunderland	30	2	4	24	19	54	10

Statistics

	O Fulham	Chelsea O
Goals	1	0
Shots on Target	4	4
Shots off Target	3	6
Hit Woodwork	1	1
Possession %	40	60
Corners	0	16
Offsides	2	6
Fouls	12	13
Disciplinary Points	4	28

Aston Villa 0
Fulham 0

25.03.06

➡ Ian Pearce proves too strong for Luke Moore

Half time 0-0

58 ⟳ ⇄ Agbonlahor > Hendrie

62 ⟳ ⇄ Radzinski > John

73 ⟳ ⇄ Angel > Moore

Full time 0-0

The Whites followed up their historic derby day success with a hard fought draw against Villa. The scoreline didn't tell the whole tale, however, as Steed Malbranque had three decent chances that might have given Fulham that elusive first away victory.

Collins John had the first chance for Fulham but dragged his shot from the right side of the box wide. John got a second chance moments later as he was first to react to a Brian McBride cross from the right but his side footed volley flew over.

Fulham had to rely on some desperate defending on the half hour mark as first Crossley and then a double block by Moritz Volz kept things level.

Steed Malbranque had three attempts on goal in the second half, with the latter two forcing Thomas Sorensen in the Villa goal to produce some agile keeping.

It was always going to be a game that needed something special to break the deadlock but, irrespective of the hard work and intuitive play by Malbranque and Brown in the Fulham midfield, the goal wouldn't come.

'Monster' Player of the Match

4 Steed Malbranque

Quote

🔊 **Chris Coleman**

We showed the commitment and desire required. It was not always pretty, but we competed as a team.

Venue:	Villa Park	Referee:	L.Mason - 05/06	**Aston Villa**
Attendance:	32,605	Matches:	27	**Fulham**
Capacity:	42,573	Yellow Cards:	65	
Occupancy:	77%	Red Cards:	2	

Form Coming into Fixture

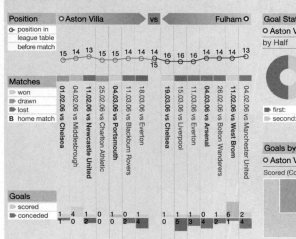

Position
- position in league table before match

Matches
- won
- drawn
- lost
- B home match

15 14 13 15 15 14 14 14 15 16 16 16 14 14 14 13

01.02.06 vs Chelsea
04.02.06 vs Middlesbrough
11.02.06 vs Newcastle United
25.02.06 vs Charlton Athletic
04.03.06 vs Portsmouth
11.03.06 vs Blackburn Rovers
18.03.06 vs Everton
19.03.06 vs Chelsea
15.03.06 vs Liverpool
11.03.06 vs Everton
04.03.06 vs Arsenal
26.02.06 vs Bolton Wanderers
11.02.06 vs West Brom
04.02.06 vs Manchester United

Goals
- scored
- conceded

| scored | 1 | 4 | 1 | 0 | 1 | 0 | 1 | | 1 | 1 | 1 | 0 | 1 | 6 | 2 |
| conceded | 1 | 0 | 2 | 0 | 0 | 2 | 4 | | 0 | 5 | 3 | 4 | 2 | 1 | 4 |

Goal Statistics

○ Aston Villa

by Half	by Situation

- first: 4
- second: 4
- set piece: 2
- open play: 6

○ Fulham

by Half	by Situation

- first: 7
- second: 5
- set piece: 3
- open play: 8
- own goals: 1

Goals by Area

○ Aston Villa
Scored (Conceded)

2 (4)
6 (4)
0 (1)

○ Fulham
Scored (Conceded)

9 (5)
9 (11)
0 (3)

Team Statistics

Starting Line-Ups

Sorensen — Bouma, Barry, Ridgewell, Davis, Phillips, John, Malbranque, Moore Angel, McCann, Hughes, De la Cruz, Hendrie Agbonlahor

Volz, Brown, Knight, Radzinski, Pembridge, McBride, Boa Morte, Pearce, Resenior, Crossley

▶ 4/4/2
Unused Sub: Taylor, Cahill, Gardner

▶ 4/4/2 (Diamond)
Unused Sub: Warner, Christanval, Goma, Jensen N

Premiership Totals	○ Aston Villa	Fulham ○
Premiership Appearances	1,772	1,601
Team Appearances	1,122	843
Goals Scored	203	157
Assists	154	165
Clean Sheets (goalkeepers)	68	51
Yellow Cards	198	152
Red Cards	9	13
Full Internationals	10	7

Age/Height

Aston Villa Age	Fulham Age
▶ **26 yrs, 5 mo**	▶ **28 yrs, 9 mo**
Aston Villa Height	Fulham Height
▶ **5'11"**	▶ **5'11"**

Match Statistics

League Table after Fixture

		Played	Won	Drawn	Lost	For	Against	Pts
●	7 Bolton	28	13	9	6	39	28	48
●	8 Wigan	31	14	4	13	36	38	46
↑	9 West Ham	30	13	6	11	46	45	45
↓	10 Everton	31	13	4	14	29	41	43
●	11 Man City	31	12	4	15	39	37	40
●	12 Newcastle	30	11	6	13	30	35	39
●	13 Charlton	30	11	6	13	34	41	39
●	14 Fulham	32	10	6	16	40	51	36
●	15 Aston Villa	31	8	11	12	34	41	35

Statistics	○ Aston Villa	Fulham ○
Goals	0	0
Shots on Target	6	3
Shots off Target	4	6
Hit Woodwork	0	0
Possession %	51	49
Corners	8	4
Offsides	9	1
Fouls	11	8
Disciplinary Points	0	0

Fulham 1
Portsmouth 3

► Steed Malbranque dances away from Pedro Mendes

Event Line

1 ○ ⊕	O'Neil / RF / OF / IA
	Assist: Mwaruwari
10 ○ ⊕	Malbranque / RF / OP / OA
24 ○ ⊕	Lua Lua / RF / OP / IA
	Assist: Mwaruwari
34 ○ ⇄	Christanval > Pearce
Half time 1-2	
55 ○ ▢	O'Neil
62 ○ ⊕	O'Neil / RF / IFK / OA
	Assist: Lua Lua
66 ○ ⇄	Stefanovic > D'Alessandro
66 ○ ⇄	Helguson > John
69 ○ ⇄	Todorov > Mwaruwari
69 ○ ▢	Malbranque
70 ○ ▢	Mendes
72 ○ ⇄	Radzinski > Pembridge
74 ○ ■	Brown
	Foul
89 ○ ⇄	Karadas > Lua Lua
90 ○ ▢	Helguson
Full time 1-3	

A disappointing afternoon for the Whites as relegation threatened Pompey took all the spoils in a must win game for the South Coast side.

With the game just 30 seconds old, Gary O'Neil made the most of a defensive lapse from Wayne Bridge to open the scoring and give the large travelling Portsmouth support hope of a vital win.

With 10 minutes gone a piece of magic from Steed Malbranque rightly got Fulham back into the game. Having received a throw from the left the Frenchman spun off Mendes before curling a delightful 18-yard shot past Kiely in the Portsmouth goal.

Portsmouth regained their lead in the 23rd minute as LuaLua chased a throughball to nudge home the visitors' second of the game. With an hour gone Harry Redknapp's side then made it three, with another fortuitous moment as Gary O'Neil's attempted strike took a massive deflection off Phillippe Christanval, leaving Crossley with no chance.

Fulham's woes were further compounded with a little over 15 minutes remaining as Michael Brown got his marching orders for a mis-timed tackle on ex-Whites midfielder Sean Davis.

'Monster' Player of the Match	Quote
20 Brian McBride	⑥ **Chris Coleman**

I could see this display coming. We need to be at it straight away or else we're climbing mountains.

Venue:	Craven Cottage	Referee:	C.J.Foy - 05/06		Fulham
Attendance:	22,322	Matches:	34		Portsmouth
Capacity:	22,646	Yellow Cards:	78		
Occupancy:	99%	Red Cards:	8		

Form Coming into Fixture

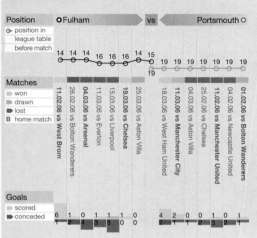

Position
- position in league table before match

Fulham vs Portsmouth

14 14 14 16 16 16 14 15
19 19 19 19 19 19 19 19

Matches
- won
- drawn
- lost
- B home match

11.02.06 vs West Brom
26.02.06 vs Bolton Wanderers
04.03.06 vs Arsenal
11.03.06 vs Everton
15.03.06 vs Liverpool
19.03.06 vs Chelsea
25.03.06 vs Aston Villa
18.03.06 vs West Ham United
11.03.06 vs Manchester City
04.03.06 vs Aston Villa
25.02.06 vs Chelsea
11.02.06 vs Manchester United
04.02.06 vs Newcastle United
01.02.06 vs Bolton Wanderers

Goals
| scored | 6 1 0 1 1 1 0 | 4 2 0 0 1 0 1 |
| conceded | 1 2 4 3 5 0 0 | 2 1 1 2 3 2 1 |

Goal Statistics

Fulham

by Half  by Situation

first:	5	set piece:	3
second:	5	open play:	6
		own goals:	1

Portsmouth

by Half 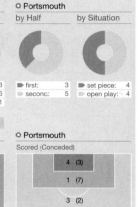 by Situation

| first: | 3 | set piece: | 4 |
| second: | 5 | open play: | 4 |

Goals by Area

Fulham
Scored (Conceded)

8 (8)
0 (2)

Portsmouth
Scored (Conceded)

4 (3)
1 (7)
3 (2)

Team Statistics

Starting Line-Ups

Bridge, Boa Morte, Pearce Christanval, Crossley, Pembridge Radzinski, John Helguson, Malbranque, Lua Lua Karadas, McBride, Mwaruwari Todorov, Knight, Brown, Volz, Davis, Mendes, O'Neil, Priske, Primus, Kiely, O'Brien, D'Alessandro Stefanovic, Taylor

▶ 4/4/2 (Diamond)   ▶ 4/4/2

Unused Sub: Warner, Rosenior   Unused Sub: Ashdown, Routledge

Premiership Totals

	Fulham	Portsmouth
Premiership Appearances	1,823	1,094
Team Appearances	855	477
Goals Scored	173	63
Assists	184	52
Clean Sheets (goalkeepers)	52	52
Yellow Cards	163	96
Red Cards	12	7
Full Internationals	10	10

Age/Height

Fulham Age	Portsmouth Age
▶ 29 yrs	▶ 27 yrs, 7 mo
Fulham Height	Portsmouth Height
▶ 5'11"	▶ 5'11"

Match Statistics

League Table after Fixture

		Played	Won	Drawn	Lost	For	Against	Pts
●	10 Everton	32	13	5	14	31	43	44
●	11 Charlton	31	12	6	13	37	42	42
↑	12 Newcastle	32	12	6	14	34	39	42
↓	13 Man City	31	12	4	15	39	37	40
●	14 Middlesbrough	30	10	7	13	43	52	37
●	15 Fulham	33	10	6	17	41	54	36
●	16 Aston Villa	32	8	11	13	34	46	35
●	17 West Brom	32	7	6	19	28	49	27
↑	18 Portsmouth	31	7	6	18	27	52	27

Statistics

	Fulham	Portsmouth
Goals	1	3
Shots on Target	4	7
Shots off Target	6	3
Hit Woodwork	1	0
Possession %	51	49
Corners	7	8
Offsides	4	5
Fouls	9	16
Disciplinary Points	20	8

Fulham 2
Charlton Athletic 1

15.04.06

▶ Luis Boa Morte is the two-goal hero at Craven Cottage

Event Line	
15 ○ ⊕ Boa Morte / LF / DFK / OA	
Assist: Helguson	
26 ○ ⊕ Euell / H / C / 6Y	
Assist: Hreidarsson	
30 ○ ⊕ Boa Morte / RF / OP / IA	
Assist: McBride	
Half time 2-1	
60 ○ ⇄ Thomas > Kishishev	
63 ○ ⇄ Christanval > Elliott	
80 ○ ⇄ Bothroyd > Holland	
Full time 2-1	

Following Fulham's abandoned visit to the Stadium of Light on April 8 the Whites were back in more familiar surroundings for the visit of South London rivals Charlton Athletic and, on the day, an inspired Luis Boa Morte performance was the difference between the sides.

An early free kick was awarded to Fulham after 14 minutes on the far right hand side of the pitch, Boa Morte showed a real piece of opportunism by curling the ball around the Charlton wall and in at Myhre's near post.

Fulham's lead lasted just 10 minutes, Herman Hreidarsson knocking back a half-clearance for an oblivious Jason Euell to divert past Niemi.

There was nothing fortuitous about Fulham's winner five minutes later. Boa Morte picked up possession from Brian McBride, before sprinting past Charlton defenders' despairing tackles and scoring low past Myhre to make it 2-1.

The second half saw Fulham almost increase their lead but, with the pressure mounting, Charlton defended well and the score stayed at 2-1.

'Monster' Player of the Match	Quote	Premiership Milestone
11 Luis Boa Morte	❝ **Steve Kean**	▶ **25**

We hope that is enough for us. This win puts more daylight between us and the teams at the bottom.

Luis Boa Morte's first goal was his 25th in the Premiership for Fulham.

Venue:	Craven Cottage	Referee:	M.Atkinson - 05/06		Fulham
Attendance:	19,146	Matches:	34		Charlton Athletic
Capacity:	22,646	Yellow Cards:	72		
Occupancy:	85%	Red Cards:	2		

Form Coming into Fixture

Position

- O position in league table before match

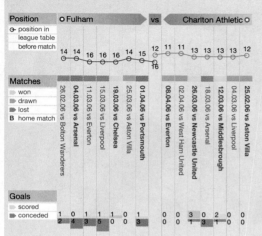

Fulham vs Charlton Athletic

14 14 16 16 16 14 15 16 12 11 11 13 13 13 13 12

Matches

- won
- drawn
- lost
- B home match

26.02.06 vs Bolton Wanderers
04.03.06 vs Arsenal
11.03.06 vs Everton
15.03.06 vs Liverpool
19.03.06 vs Chelsea
25.03.06 vs Aston Villa
01.04.06 vs Portsmouth
08.04.06 vs Everton
02.04.06 vs West Ham United
26.03.06 vs Newcastle United
18.03.06 vs Arsenal
12.03.06 vs Middlesbrough
04.03.06 vs Liverpool
25.02.06 vs Aston Villa

Goals

- scored
- conceded

| scored | 1 | 0 | 1 | 1 | 1 | 0 | 1 | | 0 | 0 | 3 | 0 | 2 | 0 | 0 |
| conceded | 2 | 4 | 3 | 5 | 0 | 0 | 3 | | 0 | 0 | 1 | 3 | 1 | 0 | 0 |

Goal Statistics

O Fulham

by Half | by Situation

- first: 4
- second: 1
- set piece: 2
- open play: 3

O Charlton Athletic

by Half | by Situation

- first: 2
- second: 3
- set piece: 1
- open play: 3
- own goals: 1

Goals by Area

O Fulham
Scored (Conceded)

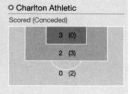

0	(6)
4	(9)
1	(3)

O Charlton Athletic
Scored (Conceded)

3	(0)
2	(3)
0	(2)

Team Statistics

Starting Line-Ups

Bridge, Boa Morte, Pearce, Elliott Christanval, McBride, Bent D, Niemi, Knight, Diop, Helguson, Bent M, Rosenior, Malbranque

Kishishev Thomas, Spector, Holland Bothroyd, Perry, Euell, Sorondo, Myhre, Ambrose, Hreidarsson

▶ 4/4/2   **▶ 4/4/2**

Unused Sub: Crossley, Volz, John, Radzinski

Unused Sub: Andersen, Powell, Sankofa

Premiership Totals

	O Fulham	Charlton O
Premiership Appearances	1,201	1,607
Team Appearances	678	720
Goals Scored	113	153
Assists	122	83
Clean Sheets (goalkeepers)	24	32
Yellow Cards	120	167
Red Cards	13	8
Full Internationals	9	8

Age/Height

Fulham Age	Charlton Athletic Age
▶ 28 yrs, 8 mo	**▶ 27 yrs, 6 mo**
Fulham Height	Charlton Athletic Height
▶ 6'	**▶ 6'**

Match Statistics

League Table after Fixture

		Played	Won	Drawn	Lost	For	Against	Pts
●	12 Charlton	34	12	8	14	38	44	44
●	13 Man City	34	12	4	18	40	41	40
●	14 Middlesbrough	33	11	7	15	45	55	40
↑	15 Fulham	34	11	6	17	43	55	39
↓	16 Aston Villa	33	8	12	13	34	46	36
↑	17 Portsmouth	34	8	8	18	31	55	32
↓	18 Birmingham	33	7	8	18	25	45	29
●	19 West Brom	34	7	7	20	29	52	28
●	20 Sunderland	33	2	6	25	21	57	12

Statistics

	O Fulham	Charlton O
Goals	2	1
Shots on Target	4	7
Shots off Target	2	3
Hit Woodwork	0	1
Possession %	46	54
Corners	2	12
Offsides	1	3
Fouls	12	16
Disciplinary Points	0	0

▶ Future Fulham signing Jimmy Bullard gets to grips with Heidar Helguson

Event Line

45 O ⊕ Malbranque / LF / OP / IA	
Assist: Boa Morte	
Half time 1-0	
57 O ▪ McCulloch	
63 O ▪ Diop	
72 O ⇄ Radzinski > Helguson	
76 O ▪ Boa Morte	
84 O ▪ Radzinski	
85 O ▪ McBride	
85 O ⇄ Christanval > Elliott	
87 O ⇄ Connolly > Teale	
90 O ▪ Chimbonda	
Full time 1-0	

In a complete reverse of the corresponding fixture at the JJB in October, it was Wigan who controlled large parts of the game but Fulham who got the all important goal to steal victory, this time at Craven Cottage.

The game almost started perfectly for Fulham as Steed Malbranque unleashed a shot that had Wigan keeper Mike Pollitt at full stretch to deny the Frenchman. Wigan recovered from the early scare and proceeded to stamp their authority on the game. Bullard and Teale were at the centre of everything creative for Wigan, the best chance falling to Jason Roberts who only managed to head tamely wide.

An unlikely breakthrough came for Fulham with half time fast approaching, a perfectly weighted pass from Boa Morte split the defence and Steed Malbranque was on hand to rifle the ball past Pollitt and into the roof of the net for the lead.

The second half continued in much the same way as the first, Wigan controlled a lot of the possession and looked the more likely to score. With the game coming to an end and Wigan applying increased pressure, Fulham had Niemi to thank for some late heroics which earned the Whites all three points.

'Monster' Player of the Match	Quote
4 Steed Malbranque	⓰ **Chris Coleman**

We're at a stage in the season when we need points. Many times this season we have played well and come away with nothing.

Venue:	Craven Cottage	Referee:	R.Styles - 05/06		Fulham
Attendance:	17,149	Matches:	42		Wigan Athletic
Capacity:	22,646	Yellow Cards:	129		
Occupancy:	76%	Red Cards:	6		

Form Coming into Fixture

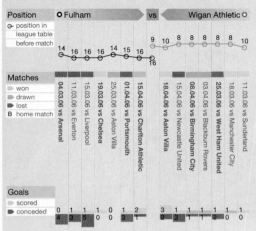

Position
- position in league table before match

O Fulham   vs   Wigan Athletic O

Matches
- won
- drawn
- lost
- B home match

Goals
- scored
- conceded

Goal Statistics

O Fulham

by Half · by Situation

- first: 5
- second: 1
- set piece: 2
- open play: 4

O Wigan Athletic

by Half · by Situation

- first: 4
- second: 5
- set piece: 5
- open play: 4

Goals by Area

O Fulham
Scored (Conceded)

2 (3)
4 (8)
2 (3)

O Wigan Athletic
Scored (Conceded)

2 (3)
4 (6)
3 (0)

Team Statistics

Starting Line-Ups

Niemi
Bridge · Boa Morte
Pearce · Elliott (Christanval)
Helguson (Radzinski) · Camara
McBride · Roberts
Knight · Diop
Rosenior · Malbranque

Teale (Connolly) · Chimbonda
Bullard · Henchoz
Kavanagh · Jackson
McCulloch · Baines
Pollitt

▶ 4/4/2   ▶ 4/4/2

Unused Sub: Crossley, Volz, John

Unused Sub: Wright, Ziegler, Johansson, Thompson

Premiership Totals

	O Fulham	Wigan O
Premiership Appearances	1,368	728
Team Appearances	755	313
Goals Scored	147	50
Assists	150	47
Clean Sheets (goalkeepers)	24	3
Yellow Cards	125	82
Red Cards	13	3
Full Internationals	10	7

Age/Height

Fulham Age	Wigan Athletic Age
▶ 29 yrs	▶ 29 yrs, 2 mo
Fulham Height	Wigan Athletic Height
▶ 6'	▶ 5'11"

Match Statistics

League Table after Fixture

		Played	Won	Drawn	Lost	For	Against	Pts
●	9 Wigan	36	15	6	15	42	46	51
●	10 West Ham	35	14	7	14	48	52	49
●	11 Charlton	36	13	8	15	41	49	47
●	12 Everton	36	13	7	16	31	47	46
●	13 Middlesbrough	34	12	7	15	47	55	43
↑	14 Fulham	35	12	6	17	44	55	42
↓	15 Man City	34	12	4	18	40	41	40
↓	16 Aston Villa	35	9	12	14	39	50	39
●	17 Portsmouth	36	9	8	19	34	58	35

Statistics

	O Fulham	Wigan O
Goals	1	0
Shots on Target	6	10
Shots off Target	6	13
Hit Woodwork	0	0
Possession %	45	55
Corners	4	8
Offsides	5	2
Fouls	11	9
Disciplinary Points	16	8

➡ Collins John celebrates his equaliser with Luis Boa Morte

Event Line

26 ○ ⇄	Christanval > Knight
45 ○ ▪	Earton
Half time 0-0	
66 ○ ⇄	Samaras > Vassell
66 ○ ⇄	John > Helguson
68 ○ ▪	Diop
69 ○ ⊕	Dunne / RF / IFK / IA
	Assist: Richards
77 ○ ▪	Christanval
79 ○ ▪	Malbranque
80 ○ ⇄	Flood > Sibierski
84 ○ ⊕	John / LF / OP / IA
	Assist: Boa Morte
90 ○ ⊕	Malbranque / RF / OP / IA
	Assist: Boa Morte
Full time 1-2	

At last, the first away win of the season! It was the moment Fulham's devoted travelling fans had been waiting for and it was a feat achieved against a very good Manchester City side.

Fulham looked bright from the outset and could have been ahead through Rosenior after only 45 seconds, but his shot from a Helguson cut back went agonisingly wide. The first half saw chances for both sides but both David James and Antti Niemi were in fine form to keep the scores level.

It was Manchester City who opened the scoring through a Richard Dunne shot from close range after Fulham had failed to clear their lines following a City free-kick. With only six minutes remaining and Fulham seemingly condemned to another away defeat, Boa Morte surged into the box and provided Collins John with a chance that he tucked away with ease.

With only stoppage time left to decide the outcome, Fulham fans were readying themselves for a decent away point. However, Steed Malbranque had other ideas; he was released by Boa Morte and ran across the face of the 18 yard box before unleashing an unstoppable drive to send the travelling fans into delirium.

'Monster' Player of the Match	Quote	Premiership Milestone
17 Liam Rosenior	**❝ Chris Coleman**	➡ **150**

	Our first away win of the season was a long time in coming, but the way we did it made it extra special.	Luis Boa Morte made his 150th Premiership appearance in the colours of Fulham.

Venue:	City of Manchester	Referee:	P.Walton - 05/06	**Manchester City**
Attendance:	41,128	Matches:	41	**Fulham**
Capacity:	48,000	Yellow Cards:	123	
Occupancy:	86%	Red Cards:	6	

Form Coming into Fixture

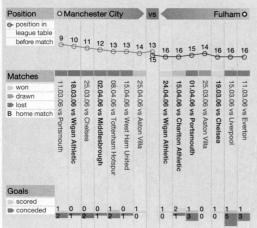

Position
- position in league table before match

Matches
- won
- drawn
- lost
- B home match

Goals
- scored
- conceded

Goal Statistics

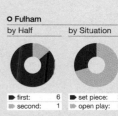

o Manchester City

by Half | by Situation

| first: | 0 | set piece: | 1 |
| second: | 3 | open play: | 2 |

o Fulham

by Half | by Situation

| first: | 6 | set piece: | 2 |
| second: | 1 | open play: | 5 |

Goals by Area

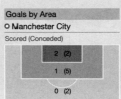

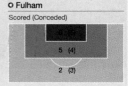

o Manchester City
Scored (Conceded)

2 (2)
1 (5)
0 (2)

o Fulham
Scored (Conceded)

5 (4)
2 (3)

Team Statistics

Starting Line-Ups

Manchester City: James; Distin, Riera, Richards, Barton, Vassell (Samaras), Helguson (John), Dunne, Reyna, Sibierski (Flood), Sommeil, Sinclair

Fulham: Niemi; Malbranque, Rosenior, Diop, Knight (Christanval), McBride, Elliott, Pearce, Boa Morte, Bridge

4/4/1/1   **4/4/2**

Unused Sub: Weaver, Jihai, Musampa   Unused Sub: Crossley, Volz, Radzinski

Premiership Totals

	o Man City	Fulham o
Premiership Appearances	1,703	1,292
Team Appearances	801	769
Goals Scored	136	134
Assists	121	129
Clean Sheets (goalkeepers)	131	25
Yellow Cards	159	130
Red Cards	10	13
Full Internationals	6	10

Age/Height

Manchester City Age	Fulham Age
27 yrs, 3 mo	**28 yrs, 1 mo**

Manchester City Height	Fulham Height
6'	**6'**

Match Statistics

League Table after Fixture

		Played	Won	Drawn	Lost	For	Against	Pts
•	6 Blackburn	36	17	6	13	48	42	57
•	7 Newcastle	37	16	7	14	46	42	55
•	8 Bolton	35	14	10	11	47	39	52
•	9 Wigan	37	15	6	16	43	48	51
•	10 West Ham	36	14	7	15	49	54	49
↑	11 Everton	37	14	7	16	32	47	49
↓	12 Charlton	37	13	8	16	41	51	47
↑	13 Fulham	36	13	6	17	46	56	45
↓	14 Man City	36	13	4	19	42	43	43

Statistics

	o Man City	Fulham o
Goals	1	2
Shots on Target	10	7
Shots off Target	9	5
Hit Woodwork	0	0
Possession %	48	52
Corners	9	6
Offsides	3	0
Fouls	11	12
Disciplinary Points	4	12

Sunderland 2
Fulham 1

▶ Collins John gets the better of Gary Breen

Event Line

18 ⚽ ⇄ Radzinski > Boa Morte	
29 ◻ Caldwell	
32 ⚽ ⊕ Le Tallec / H / OP / 6Y	
Assist: Welsh	
42 ◻ McCartney	
Half time 1-0	
50 ⚽ ◻ Elliott	
52 ⚽ ◻ Christanval	
56 ◻ Pearce	
57 ⚽ ⊕ Brown / RF / OP / 6Y	
Assist: Nosworthy	
60 ⚽ ⇄ John > McBride	
63 ◻ Brown	
69 ⚽ ⇄ Brown > Pearce	
74 ⚽ ⇄ Kyle > Hoyte	
76 ⚽ ⊕ Radzinski / LF / OP / IA	
Assist: John	
81 ⚽ ⇄ Murphy D > Le Tallec	
87 ◻ Whitehead	
90 ⚽ ◻ Bridge	
Full time 2-1	

This was a game that Fulham fans, in hindsight, would have liked to have seen finished at the first time of asking, albeit in the Arctic conditions of April 8. In the rearranged fixture, however, Sunderland managed to get their only home win of the campaign.

In a scrappy start Fulham's chances took an early blow, with Luis Boa Morte hobbling off the field with a thigh injury.

The Mackems took the lead just after the half hour mark when Anthony Le Tallec got the faintest of touches on an Andy Welsh cross to guide the ball past Mark Crossley.

Boa Morte's replacement, Tomasz Radzinski, almost scored a swift equaliser but a resolute Sunderland defence snuffed out the danger. The relegated side then doubled their lead when Mark Crossley could only parry a Nyron Nosworthy shot and Chris Brown was on hand to slot the ball home.

Radzinski gave Fulham hope late on as he rifled home a sweet left foot shot.

'Monster' Player of the Match	Quote	Premiership Milestone
13 Tomasz Radzinski	❝ **Chris Coleman**	**50**
	I'm disappointed at the fashion in which we lost the game, but I can't be too hard on the guys.	Papa Bouba Diop made his 50th Premiership appearance.

Venue: Stadium of Light
Attendance: 28,226
Capacity: 48,300
Occupancy: 58%

Referee: M.A.Riley - 05/06
Matches: 38
Yellow Cards: 126
Red Cards: 10

Sunderland
Fulham

Form Coming into Fixture

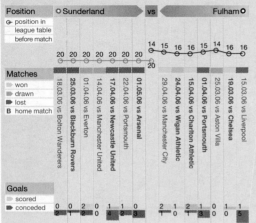

Position
- position in league table before match

Sunderland vs Fulham

20	20	20	20	20	20	20	20	14	15	16	16	15	14	16	16

Matches
- won
- drawn
- lost
- B home match

18.03.06 vs Bolton Wanderers
25.03.06 vs Blackburn Rovers
01.04.06 vs Everton
14.04.06 vs Manchester United
17.04.06 vs Newcastle United
22.04.06 vs Portsmouth
01.05.06 vs Arsenal
29.04.06 vs Manchester City
24.04.06 vs Wigan Athletic
15.04.06 vs Charlton Athletic
01.04.06 vs Portsmouth
25.03.06 vs Aston Villa
19.03.06 vs Chelsea
15.03.06 vs Liverpool

Goals
- scored
- conceded

0	0	2	0	1	1	0		2	1	2	1	0	1	1
2	1	2	0	4	2	3		1	0	3	0	0	5

Goal Statistics

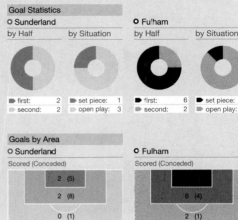

Sunderland

by Half | by Situation

- first: 2
- second: 2
- set piece: 1
- open play: 3

Fulham

by Half | by Situation

- first: 6
- second: 2
- set piece: 1
- open play: 7

Goals by Area

Sunderland — Scored (Conceded)

- 2 (5)
- 2 (8)
- 0 (1)

Fulham — Scored (Conceded)

- 6 (4)
- 2 (1)

Team Statistics

Starting Line-Ups

McCartney, Welsh, Caldwell, Miller, Le Tallec (Murphy D), McBride (John), Brown, Helguson, Breen, Whitehead, Nosworthy, Hoyte (Kyle), Davis

Malbranque, Rosenior, Diop, Christanval, Elliott, Pearce (Brown), Boa Morte (Radzinski), Bridge, Crossley

4/4/2   **4/4/2**

Unused Sub: Alnwick, Collins D, Leadbitter

Unused Sub: Warner, Volz

Premiership Totals

	Sunderland	Fulham
Premiership Appearances	560	1,529
Team Appearances	358	740
Goals Scored	16	169
Assists	17	160
Clean Sheets (goalkeepers)	4	52
Yellow Cards	77	149
Red Cards	4	14
Full Internationals	4	10

Age/Height

Sunderland Age **25 yrs**   Fulham Age **28 yrs, 10 mo**

Sunderland Height **6'**   Fulham Height **5'11"**

Match Statistics

League Table after Fixture

	Played	Won	Drawn	Lost	For	Against	Pts
12 Charlton	37	13	8	16	41	51	47
13 Middlesbrough	37	12	9	16	48	57	45
14 Fulham	37	13	6	18	47	58	45
15 Man City	37	13	4	20	43	46	43
16 Aston Villa	37	9	12	16	40	54	39
17 Portsmouth	37	10	8	19	36	59	38
18 Birmingham	37	8	10	19	28	49	34
19 West Brom	37	7	8	22	29	56	29
20 Sunderland	37	3	6	28	25	67	15

Statistics

	Sunderland	Fulham
Goals	2	1
Shots on Target	3	2
Shots off Target	0	8
Hit Woodwork	0	0
Possession %	54	46
Corners	10	6
Offsides	3	2
Fouls	18	6
Disciplinary Points	16	16

► Michael Brown bursts forward from midfield

Event Line

Half time 0-0

51	○ ■	Graham
56	○ ⇄	Helguson > John
62	○ ⇄	Walker > Christie
70	○ ⇄	Padzinski > McBride
81	○ ⇄	Craddock > Graham
84	○ ⊕	Helguson / RF / P / IA
		Assist: Helguson
85	○ ⇄	Cooper > Kennedy

Full time 1-0

Whilst Fulham looked to make one final push up the table, Middlesbrough had their eyes firmly set on their UEFA Cup Final appearance in Eindhoven three days later, and their squad selection showed this. A virtual youth team turned out for Boro with the average age of the squad just over 21.

Although Fulham struggled to settle and put together coherent passing moves, the forward duo of Collins John and McBride were a constant threat. It was John who had the best chances, heading wide after a deep Bridge cross and poking the ball agonisingly wide when played through by Diop.

The youthful tenacity of the Boro side was causing problems and the worst almost happened soon after the restart. Danny Graham appeared to score, but the goal was chalked off for handball and Graham was booked.

Fulham's breakthrough finally arrived courtesy of second half substitute Heidar Helguson. Having superbly controlled a Christanval pass he was unceremoniously bundled over in the area by Wheater and it was Helguson who dusted himself off to score from 12 yards, rounding off Fulham's season with their 13th home win.

'Monster' Player of the Match

19 Phillippe Christanval

Quote

❝ **Chris Coleman**

I have been pleased with my players this season. Thirteen home wins is terrific and is top-five form.

Venue:	Craven Cottage	Referee:	M.R.Halsey - 05/06		**Fulham**
Attendance:	22,434	Matches:	36		**Middlesbrough**
Capacity:	22,646	Yellow Cards:	54		
Occupancy:	99%	Red Cards:	6		

Form Coming into Fixture

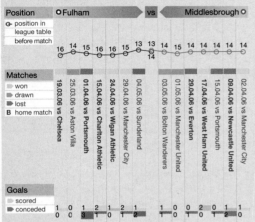

Position

O Fulham vs Middlesbrough O

- position in league table before match

16 14 15 16 16 15 13 13 14 15 14 14 14 14 14
14

Matches
- won
- drawn
- lost
- B home match

19.03.06 vs Chelsea
25.03.06 vs Aston Villa
01.04.06 vs Portsmouth
15.04.06 vs Charlton Athletic
24.04.06 vs Wigan Athletic
29.04.06 vs Manchester City
04.05.06 vs Sunderland
03.05.06 vs Bolton Wanderers
01.05.06 vs Manchester United
29.04.06 vs Everton
17.04.06 vs West Ham United
15.04.06 vs Portsmouth
09.04.06 vs Newcastle United
02.04.06 vs Manchester City

Goals
- scored: 1 0 1 2 1 2 1 | 1 0 0 2 0 1 1
- conceded: 0 0 3 1 0 1 2 | 1 0 1 0 1 2 0

Goal Statistics

O Fulham

by Half | by Situation

- first: 5 | set piece: 1
- second: 3 | open play: 7

O Middlesbrough

by Half | by Situation

- first: 2 | set piece: 2
- second: 3 | open play: 3

Goals by Area

O Fulham
Scored (Conceded)

6 (3)

2 (1)

O Middlesbrough
Scored (Conceded)

0 (1)

4 (3)

1 (1)

Team Statistics

Starting Line-Ups

Rosenior | Bridge | Morrison | Davies
Bocanegra | Diop | Kennedy Cooper | Bates
Niemi | McBride Radzinski | Christie Walker | Turnbull
Christanval | Brown | John Helguson | Graham Craddock | Cattermole | Wheater
Volz | Malbranque | Johnson | Taylor

▶ 4/4/2 ▶ 4/4/2

Unused Sub: Crossley, Goma, Elliott   Unused Sub: Knight, McMahon

Premiership Totals	O Fulham	Boro O
Premiership Appearances	1,161	525
Team Appearances	695	325
Goals Scored	135	45
Assists	118	30
Clean Sheets (goalkeepers)	25	0
Yellow Cards	115	64
Red Cards	6	0
Full Internationals	9	1

Age/Height

Fulham Age	Middlesbrough Age
▶ **27 yrs, 7 mo**	▶ **21 yrs, 6 mo**
Fulham Height	Middlesbrough Height
▶ **5'11"**	▶ **6'**

Match Statistics

League Table after Fixture

		Played	Won	Drawn	Lost	For	Against	Pts
●	6 Blackburn	38	19	6	13	51	42	63
●	7 Newcastle	38	17	7	14	47	42	58
●	8 Bolton	38	15	11	12	49	41	56
●	9 West Ham	38	16	7	15	52	55	55
●	10 Wigan	38	15	6	17	45	52	51
●	11 Everton	38	14	8	16	34	49	50
↑	12 Fulham	38	14	6	18	48	58	48
↓	13 Charlton	38	13	8	17	41	55	47
↓	14 Middlesbrough	38	12	9	17	48	58	45

Statistics	O Fulham	Boro O
Goals	1	0
Shots on Target	4	3
Shots off Target	5	3
Hit Woodwork	0	0
Possession %	51	49
Corners	8	4
Offsides	2	3
Fouls	8	12
Disciplinary Points	0	4

Season Review 2005/06

The history books may not look back on 2005/06 as Fulham Football Club's most illustrious campaign to date but, nevertheless, it will be remembered as an emotional rollercoaster ride in which the Whites' top flight security was ultimately achieved at Fortress Craven Cottage.

Just as the Club's magnificent home form was contrasted by its disappointing results on the road, 2005/06 will be remembered for joy and despair in seemingly equal measure. The tragic death of Fulham legend Johnny Haynes, in October 2005, cast a heavy shadow over the season's proceedings but, in front of the newly renamed Johnny Haynes Stand, the Maestro's memory was honoured with historic victories over Premiership Champions, Chelsea, and European Champions, Liverpool.

Luis Boa Morte scores against Chelsea

Indeed, Craven Cottage – boasting record breaking gates throughout the campaign – bore witness to a home season in which Premiership safety was secured with a string of memorable victories and a bank of points. West Brom crumbled to a 6-1 thumping and other highlights included Man City, Bolton, Blackburn, Sunderland and Charlton all losing 2-1 and Everton, Newcastle and Tottenham going home on the end of a 1-0 beating. Visiting teams, on the whole, did not enjoy their trip to the Thames in 2005/06.

Away from SW6, however, the Whites' story was a very different one. Defeat followed defeat on the road as Chris Coleman's men were ignored by Lady Luck and repeatedly punished for failing to take their chances. Points were few and far between away from the familiar surrounds of the Cottage and low points of the season included a 4-1 defeat at Arsenal, a 5-1 humiliation at Anfield, a heart wrenching last minute 1-0 loss at Wigan and an equally disappointing 1-0 defeat at Portsmouth. The contrast in form was staggering.

The 2005/06 campaign, however, started back in August 2005 as the Whites faced somewhat of a goalkeeping crisis. With the departure of Dutchman Edwin van der Sar to Manchester United in the Summer, Mark Crossley looked set to haul himself comfortably in to the number one shirt. However, injuries to Crossley and newly recruited Jaroslav Drobny in pre-season meant that another shot stopper had to be found before the season got underway.

Having already started the season with Cardiff City, Tony Warner, a former Liverpool trainee, was recruited on loan to cover the crocked 'keepers. Warner literally grabbed his chance with both hands and produced some memorable early season displays, including a string of fine saves and a penalty stop at Highbury as the Whites crashed to an unrealistic 4-1 defeat to Arsenal.

Indeed, having drawn 0-0 at home to Birmingham on the opening day of the season and losing 2-1 at Ewood Park it took until the end of the month for Chris Coleman's men to pick up their first three points of 05/06. Everton were the visitors to Craven Cottage on that occasion and hero of the hour, Brian McBride, duly obliged by side footing home the winner in the second half.

September saw the Whites claim just one Premiership point, away at St James' Park, as West Ham became one of the few teams to take the spoils at Craven Cottage and Tottenham comfortably saw out a 1-0 win at White Hart Lane. In the Second Round of the Carling Cup, however, the Whites entertained Lincoln City under the floodlights at the Cottage. What followed was one of the most dramatic League Cup games in recent history as the League Two side refused to lie down. With the score precariously balanced at 4-4 at the end of extra time it took until the 120th minute for Brian McBride to nod home the winner from a free kick. The 5365 fans present that evening had witnessed a large dollop of Carling Cup magic.

Manchester United were the first visitors to the Cottage in October 2005 as an action packed first half saw Collins John put one past the returning van der Sar from Fulham's first attack, after just one minute. The Reds, however, came straight back after quarter of an hour with two in two minutes as Ruud van Nistelrooy slotted away a penalty and Wayne Rooney put United 2-1 up. Not to be outdone though, Claus Jensen levelled the scores in the 27th minute with a curling free kick that bent inside the far post. At the end of a pulsating first half, however, van Nistelrooy broke clear of the Whites' offside trap to net United's winner in another classic match between the two sides.

A fortnight later, on October 18, 2005 – the day after Fulham drew 1-1 with Charlton at The Valley – the tragic news of Johnny Haynes' death rocked the Club. A true Fulham and England legend Haynes made a staggering 658 appearances for the Whites, scoring 158 goals and becoming Fulham's most capped England player (56 in total, 22 as Captain) in the process. His death, at the age of 71, came as a huge blow to all those who knew him and who knew of him. Tributes poured in to the Club over the following week, led by his best friend and former

Fulham team-mate Tosh Chamberlain who said of his old pal; "I was totally in awe of him. He was a genius on the pitch and a perfectionist and as much as it was a delight to play with Johnny it was more the fact that he was my friend and it was great to be out there with him. I'll miss him always."

A subdued crowd paid their respects to The Maestro the following weekend as European Champions, Liverpool, were the visitors to the Cottage. An immaculately observed period of silence preceded the game and, once underway, the Whites set about honouring their greatest ever player with an emphatic display and a 2-0 victory, goals coming from Collins John in the first half and Luis Boa Morte in injury time at the end of the second.

The remainder of October ended in disappointing fashion as West Brom saw off Chris Coleman's Carling Cup hopes when they visited the Cottage for the Third Round clash. Fulham's former InterToto Cup hero, Junichi Inamoto, scored a spectacular injury time winner to take the Baggies through as 3-2 winners. The following weekend's trip to Wigan also ended in last minute defeat as Pascal Chimbonda headed the Latics' 91st minute winner at the JJB.

November was a microcosm of Fulham's entire 2005/06 season. Home wins against Manchester City – in which Andy Cole's return to his former club was overshadowed by a Steed Malbranque brace – and Bolton, who fell victim to a Brian McBride double, were contrasted by defeat at Middlesbrough, despite a Collins John contender for goal of the season. Nevertheless, three wins on the bounce at Craven Cottage had kept Fulham's points haul healthy going in to the busy December calendar.

Six games in December, either side of Christmas, provided their usual added pressures at the midway point of the season. The month started with a double trip to the Midlands, first up were West Brom where the Whites valiantly saw out a 0-0 draw to secure a point, despite losing Luis Boa Morte to a double booking and subsequent red card at the end of the first half. The trip to Birmingham a week later proved to be another frustrating affair as, despite having defended well for most of the game, Nicky Butt headed home the winner for Steve Bruce's men with six minutes left to play.

The emotional tribute to Johnny Haynes

With no points from the last two games, the pressure was on once again as the Whites entertained Blackburn back at the Cottage on the Saturday before Christmas. Goals from Papa Bouba Diop at the end of the first half and Boa Morte – returning from suspension – in the second 45 were enough to secure the points, despite a nervy end to the game following a Zat Knight own goal in the 89th minute.

Stamford Bridge beckoned on Boxing Day 2005 and, as always, the Whites gave their neighbours a real run for their money on their own turf. In a five goal thriller Fulham came from 2-0 down to equalise through Brian McBride and a Heidar Helguson penalty in the second half, eventually being undone by a Crespo goal 15 minutes from the end.

The remainder of the festive calendar saw a battling 3-3 draw at home against Villa and a 1-0 New Year's Eve defeat at Fratton Park. However, whereas December had wielded just five points from six games, January saw an altogether healthier points haul. Sunderland, Newcastle and Tottenham all made the journey to SW6, leaving with nothing for their troubles. Indeed, in a reversal of their away fortunes it was Fulham's turn to grab the latest of late winners against Spurs as Carlos Bocanegra headed home from six yards in the 90th minute to break the deadlock and secure the points.

January also saw the Whites fall at the first hurdle in the FA Cup as League Two Leyton Orient deservedly earned their place in the Fourth Round with a 2-1 victory at Craven Cottage. The second defeat of the month, by the same scoreline, came at Upton Park in the League.

Nine goals in three games is a decent return by anyone's reckoning but when only one of those games ends in victory, as happened back in February, questions are inevitably asked. The shortest month's biggest victory, however, came unsurprisingly at Craven Cottage when West Brom – who had last been to the ground to knock the Whites out of the Carling Cup – crumbled as Chris Coleman's men smashed six past Bryan Robson's side. Once again though there were no points to show on the road as Manchester United ran out 4-2 winners at Old Trafford and Bolton took the spoils in a 2-1 win at the Reebok.

March 2006 will ultimately be remembered for one game and one game alone, Fulham versus Chelsea on Sunday 19th. The Whites had lost the three preceding games, at home to Arsenal and away to Everton and Liverpool, leaking 12 goals in the process. The signs were not good for the visit of Jose Mourinho's Champions elect. However, during an afternoon that will forever be remembered as one of Fulham's finest and bravest performances, a 17th minute Luis Boa Morte goal proved enough to take the points and the plaudits in the SW6 derby. Fulham fans had waited 27 years for this win and victory tasted sweet.

With the end of the season now in sight Chris Coleman's focus was firmly on securing the Club's Premiership status for the sixth successive season and a point at Villa towards the end of March was still not enough. Defeat at home to Portsmouth on April Fool's Day and the snow induced abandonment of the away game at Sunderland – when Brian McBride had scored an early goal to put Fulham 1-0 up – meant that wins against Charlton and Wigan at home would be enough to ensure safety.

The Addicks succumbed to two memorable goals from Luis Boa Morte at the Cottage in April – the first a cheeky free kick that found its way inside the near post and the second following a mazy solo run after the South East London side had equalised through Jason Euell. The last evening game at the Cottage later that month saw a strong Wigan side dominate large portions of the game in front of the Sky cameras. However, the Whites could not be broken down and a goal from Steed Malbranque towards the end of the first half was enough to secure the three points that guaranteed another season of Premiership football on the banks of the Thames in 2006/07.

With three games to go – Man City and Sunderland away and Middlesbrough at home – Chris Coleman had accomplished his primary objective and secured Fulham's place amongst the elite for the new season. 'Job done' may well be the phrase by which most people sum up 2005/06 but, on reflection, it has shown that this team is capable of beating the very best in the land and that Craven Cottage is indeed the most formidable of fortresses. In short, there's no place quite like home.

Premiership Results Table

Legend:
- ■ Won
- ■ Drawn
- ■ Lost
- Yellow Card
- Red Card
- Goal
- 45 Time of 1st Sub
- 45 Time of 2nd Sub
- 45 Time of 3rd Sub
- 45 Time of Goal
- 45 Time of Assist

Match: | Players: | Substitutes:

Date	H/A	Opponent	H/T	F/T	Pos	First Team											Subs 1st	2nd	3rd
13-08	H	Birmingham	0-0	0-0	08	Warner	Volz	Knight	Rehman	Jensen N	Legwinski 36	Jensen C	Malbranque	Legwinski 36	Boa Morte	McBride	Elrich 46	Elrich 90	–
20-08	A	Blackburn	0-1	1-2	14	Warner	Volz	Knight	Rehman	Jensen N 49	Malbranque	Diop	Radzinski	McBride	Helguson	John 89	Helguson 81	John 89	–
24-08	A	Arsenal	1-1	1-4	16	Warner	Volz	Knight	Rehman 45	Jensen N	Malbranque	Jensen C 22	Boa Morte 24	Radzinski	McBride	John	John 64	–	–
27-08	A	Everton	0-1	1-0	14	Warner	Volz 57	Knight	Rehman	Jensen N	Malbranque 90	Diop	Boa Morte	Radzinski 22	McBride 57	–	–	–	–
10-09	H	Newcastle	1-0	1-1	12	Warner	Volz	Knight	Bocanegra 20	Jensen N	Jensen C	Diop	Boa Morte 13	Radzinski	McBride 13	John	Helguson 81	–	–
17-09	A	West Ham	0-1	0-1	16	Warner	Volz	Knight	Bocanegra 45	Jensen N	Malbranque 66	Diop	Boa Morte 21	John	Radzinski	McBride	Christanval 80	–	–
26-09	A	Tottenham	0-1	0-1	17	Warner	Volz	Knight 16	Bocanegra	Jensen N	Diop	Diop 62	Jensen C	Boa Morte	John 87	McBride	Radzinski 77	–	–
01-10	H	Man Utd	2-3	2-3	17	Warner	Knight 16	Bocanegra	Jensen N	Diop 60	Christanval 29	Boa Morte 28 87	Helguson 72	Radzinski 35	McBride	Rosenior 69	Rosenior 78	–	–
17-10	A	Charlton	1-0	1-0	17	Crossley	Volz	Knight	Bocanegra	Jensen N	Malbranque 28 87	Christanval 29	Jensen C 30	Diop	Boa Morte 90	McBride	Warner 63	Rosenior 82	–
22-10	H	Liverpool	1-0	2-0	15	Crossley	Volz 42	Knight	Bocanegra	Jensen N	Malbranque	Jensen C 30	Diop	B.Morte 06 39 45	Radzinski	McBride	John 30	McBride	–
29-10	A	Wigan	0-0	0-1	15	Warner	Volz	Goma	Bocanegra	Jensen N	Legwinski 06	Christanval	Diop 70	Boa Morte	Radzinski	Helguson	Helguson 77	–	–
05-11	H	Man City	2-1	2-1	14	Warner	Volz	Goma	Bocanegra	Jensen N	Legwinski 09 70	John 09 70	Malbranque	Boa Morte	Radzinski	McBride	Helguson 78	–	–
20-11	A	Middlesbrough	1-0	2-3	14	Crossley 18	Volz	Knight	Goma	Jensen N 31	Rosenior 51	John	Malbranque	B.Morte 45	Radzinski	McBride	Knight 70	Legwinski 71	–
27-11	H	Bolton	2-0	2-1	14	Crossley	Volz	Knight	Rosenior	Bocanegra 88	John	Malbranque	Boa Morte 45	Boa Morte	McBride 51	Legwinski 61	Helguson 78	–	–
03-12	A	West Brom	0-0	0-0	14	Crossley	Volz	Goma	Rosenior	John	Malbranque	Diop 82	John 45	McBride	Radzinski 04	Helguson 32	McBride 04 18	Legwinski 70	–
10-12	H	Birmingham	0-0	1-0	14	Crossley	Knight 67	Goma	Bocanegra	Jensen N	Christanval	Christanval 52	Malbranque	B.Morte 45 52	Radzinski 71	McBride	Knight 49	Warner 71	–
17-12	A	Blackburn	1-0	2-1	15	Crossley	Knight 29	Goma	Rosenior	Jensen N	Legwinski 65	Diop 45	Boa Morte 61	Radzinski	Helguson 55	McBride 29 56	Legwinski 69	Elrich 71	–
26-12	A	Chelsea	1-2	2-3	15	Crossley	Leacock	Goma	Bocanegra	Rosenior 41	Christanval 62	Christanval	Boa Morte	Radzinski 13 32	Helguson 32	McBride 13 61	Jensen N 57	John	–
28-12	H	Aston Villa	2-1	3-3	15	Crossley	Leacock	Goma	Bocanegra	Elrich	Legwinski	Boa Morte 61	Radzinski	Helguson 56	John 89	Warner 71	Ehrich	–	–
31-12	A	Portsmouth	1-1	1-0	15	Warner	Leacock 45	Goma	Bocanegra	Diop	Legwinski 59	Boa Morte	Radzinski	Helguson 22	John 89	John	Bocanegra 85 59	–	–
02-01	H	Sunderland	1-1	2-1	14	Warner	Leacock	Goma	Pearce	Rosenior	Elrich 43 61	Boa Morte	Radzinski	Helguson 61 40	John	Helguson 61 40	John 75	Bocanegra 85 59	–
14-01	A	Newcastle	0-0	1-0	12	Warner	Volz	Knight	Rosenior 36	Diop	Malbranque	Boa Morte	Radzinski	McBride 43	Helguson 52	John	M'branque 66	Jensen N	–
23-01	H	West Ham	0-2	1-2	13	Niemi	Volz	Knight	Pearce	Bridge	Elliott 28	Legwinski 28	Boa Morte 77	Radzinski	McBride	John 75	John 73	–	–
31-01	A	Tottenham	0-1	0-1	13	Niemi	Rosenior 89	Knight	Bridge	Elliott 90	Legwinski	Boa Morte	Radzinski	McBride 52	Diop	McBride 70	–	–	–
04-02	A	West Brom	2-3	2-4	13	Niemi	Rosenior	Knight	Bridge 37	Bocanegra 90	John	Malbranque	Boa Morte 62	B.Morte 45 52	McBride 22	John 37	Radzinski 23	John 73	–
11-02	H	Bolton	1-2	1-2	14	Niemi	Knight	Bocanegra	Bridge	R'zmski 49 93 90	Christanval	Malbranque	B.Morte 45 52	McBride 48	Helguson 37	John 83 90	Radzinski	Christanval 89	–
11-02	A	West Brom	2-0	6-1	13	Niemi	Rosenior 17 22	Knight	Bridge 90	Christanval 62	John 40	Boa Morte 17	Malbranque 17	John 17	McBride 04	John 76	Warner 78	–	–
26-02	H	Bolton	2-0	6-1	14	Volz	Knight	Bocanegra	Bridge	Christanval	Boa Morte 36	Boa Morte	Radzinski	McBride 13 61	John 28	Jensen N 57	Ehrich 78	–	–
04-03	A	Arsenal	0-2	0-4	15	Volz	Knight	Bocanegra	Bridge 71	Rosenior	Elliott	Malbranque	Radzinski	McBride	Helguson 22	Christanval 69	McBride 73	–	–
11-03	H	Everton	0-2	1-3	16	Volz	Knight	Goma	Rosenior	Bocanegra 81	Pembridge	Malbranque	Radzinski	McBride	John	Christanval 63	–	–	–
15-03	H	Charlton	2-1	2-1	15	Volz	Knight	Goma	Bocanegra	Pembridge	Elliott 22	Malbranque	Boa Morte	Radzinski	McBride	John	Christanval 34	Helguson 90 66	–
19-03	A	Chelsea	1-0	1-0	16	Volz	Knight	Goma	Rosenior	Bocanegra	Pembridge	Brown 53	Boa Morte 17	Radzinski	McBride	Helguson 71	Christanval 89	–	–
25-03	H	Aston Villa	0-0	0-0	14	Volz	Knight	Goma	Rosenior	Bocanegra	Pembridge	Brown	Boa Morte	McBride	John	Radzinski 62	–	–	–
01-04	A	Portsmouth	1-1	1-2	14	Crossley	Knight	Goma	Pearce	Rosenior	Brown 74	Malbranque 107	Boa Morte	Radzinski	McBride 30	John	Helguson 90 66	–	–
04-04	A	Charlton	0-2	0-4	14	Crossley	Knight	Goma	Pearce	Bridge	Brown	Boa Morte	Radzinski	Elliott	McBride 15	John 109	Christanval 43	John 86 86	–
15-03	H	Wigan	2-1	2-1	15	Knight	Pearce	Bridge	Malbranque 45	Diop 63	Radzinski	Elliott	Helguson 15	McBride 30	John	John	Radzinski 84 72	Christanval	–
15-03	H	Liverpool	0-2	1-5	16	Knight	Pearce	Bridge	Malbranque 9 10	Diop 68	Boa Morte 45 76	Radzinski	McBride 85	Helguson	John	C'stanval 77 26	McBride	–	–
24-04	A	Wigan	1-0	1-0	14	Niemi	Knight	Pearce	Bridge 71	Malbranque 45	Boa Morte 84 90	Radzinski	Helguson 85	John 84	John 84	John 84	Christanval 69	Christanval 84	–
29-04	A	Man City	0-0	0-0	13	Niemi	Rosenior	Knight	Pearce	Bridge	Diop	Malbranque	Radzinski	Helguson	John	C'stanval 52	Helguson 23	–	–
04-05	H	Sunderland	0-1	1-2	14	Sunderland	Niemi	Rosenior	Christanval 52	Pearce 56	Bridge 90	Malbranque	Diop	Boa Morte 50	Radzinski	McBride	H'gson 64 84 56	John 76	–
07-05	A	Middlesbrough	0-0	1-0	12	Niemi	Volz	Knight	Bocanegra	Rosenior	Malbranque	Brown	Bridge	John	McBride	Radzinski	Brown 60	–	–

1

Mark Crossley
Goalkeeper

Season Review 05/06

It was an injury plagued season for Fulham's number one but this didn't stop the Barnsley-born shot stopper from playing his part in some of the biggest games of the campaign.

Cruelly sidelined a week before the first game of the season, Crossley battled back to make his first appearance against Manchester United at the Cottage in early October. Even with the signing of Niemi and Warner, Crossley maintained his challenge for the number one shirt. Donning the gloves for Fulham's derby day clash with Chelsea in March, Crossley made a number of crucial saves to ensure a historic three points and a clean sheet against the Champions.

Player Details:

Date of Birth:	16.06.1969
Place of Birth:	Barnsley
Nationality:	Welsh
Height:	6'3"
Weight:	16st 1lb
Foot:	Left

Player Performance 05/06

League Performance

Percentage of total possible time player was on pitch   ⊖ position in league table at end of month

Month:	Aug	Sep	Oct	Nov	Dec	Jan	Feb	Mar	Apr	May	Total
	0%	0%	68%	33%	80%	0%	0%	40%	25%	50%	33%
Position	14	17	15	14	15	13	14	15	13	12	
Team Pts:	4/12	1/9	4/12	6/9	5/18	9/12	3/9	4/15	9/12	3/6	48/114
Team Gls F:	3	2	5	6	7	5	9	3	6	2	48
Team Gls A:	6	4	5	5	9	3	7	12	5	2	58
Total mins:	0	0	243	90	431	0	0	180	90	90	1,124
Starts (sub):	0	0	3	1	5	0	0	2	1	1	13
Goals:	0	0	0	0	0	0	0	0	0	0	0
Assists:	0	0	0	1	0	0	0	0	0	0	1
Clean sheets:	0	0	0	0	1	0	0	2	0	0	3
Cards (Y/R):	0	0	0	0	0	0	0	0	0	0	0

League Performance Totals

Clean Sheets
- ▶ Crossley: 3
- ▬ Team-mates: 7
- **Total: 10**

Assists
- ▶ Crossley: 1
- ▬ Team-mates: 46
- **Total: 47**

Cards
- ▶ Crossley: 0
- ▬ Team-mates: 66
- **Total: 66**

Cup Games

	Apps	CS	Cards
European	0	0	0
FA Cup	0	0	0
Carling Cup	0	0	0
Total	**0**	**0**	**0**

Career History

Career Milestones

Club Debut:
vs Wigan (A), L 1-0, League Cup
▶ **23.09.03**

First Goal Scored for the Club:
▶ **—**

Time Spent at the Club:
▶ **3 Seasons**

Full International:
▶ **Wales**

Premiership Totals

92-06
Appearances	204
Clean Sheets	52
Assists	1
Yellow Cards	2
Red Cards	1

Clubs

Year	Club	Apps	CS
03-06	Fulham	23	5
02-03	Stoke City	12	7
00-03	Middlesbrough	31	11
98-98	Millwall	14	3
90-90	Man Utd	0	0
87-00	Nottm Forest	393	

Off the Pitch

Age:

- ▶ Crossley: 36 years, 11 months
- ▬ Team: 28 years, 11 months
- ∣ League: 26 years, 11 months

Height:
- ▶ Crossley: 6'3"
- ▬ Team: 5'11"
- ∣ League: 5'11"

Weight:
- ▶ Crossley: 16st 1lb
- ▬ Team: 13st 2lb
- ∣ League: 12st

16 Ricardo Batista
Goalkeeper

Season Review 05/06

Although the young Portuguese goalkeeper only made one full First Team appearance for the Whites last season it was in Fulham's largest scoring game, a 5-4 Carling Cup win over Lincoln City.

An exciting prospect who has benefited greatly from being involved with the First Team set-up, Ricardo was loaned out to MK Dons for a month in January and following a successful initial spell his loan deal was extended to the end of the season.

Player Detail:

Date of Birth:	19.11.1986
Place of Birth:	Setubal
Nationality:	Portuguese
Height:	6'1"
Weight:	12st 6lb
Foot:	Right

Player Performance 05/06

League Performance

Percentage of total possible time player was on pitch   ⊖ position in league table at end of month

Month:	Aug	Sep	Oct	Nov	Dec	Jan	Feb	Mar	Apr	May	Total
	14	17	15	14	15	13	14	15	13	12	
	0%	0%	0%	0%	0%	0%	0%	0%	0%	0%	0%
Team Pts:	4/12	1/9	4/12	6/9	5/18	9/12	3/9	4/15	9/12	3/6	48/114
Team Gls F:	3	2	5	6	7	5	9	3	6	2	48
Team Gls A:	6	4	5	5	9	3	7	12	5	2	58
Total mins:	0	0	0	0	0	0	0	0	0	0	
Starts (sub):	0	0	0	0	0	0	0	0	0	0	0
Goals:	0	0	0	0	0	0	0	0	0	0	0
Assists:	0	0	0	0	0	0	0	0	0	0	0
Clean sheets:	0	0	0	0	0	0	0	0	0	0	0
Cards (Y/R):	0	0	0	0	0	0	0	0	0	0	0

League Performance Totals

Clean Sheets
- Batista: 0
- Team-mates: 10
- **Total:** 10

Assists
- Batista: 0
- Team-mates: 47
- **Total:** 47

Cards
- Batista: 0
- Team-mates: 66
- **Total:** 66

Cup Games

	Apps	CS	Cards
European	0	0	0
FA Cup	0	0	0
Carling Cup	1	0	0
Total	**1**	**0**	**0**

Career History

Career Milestones

Club Debut:
vs Lincoln City (H), W 5-4, League Cup
 **21.09.05**

Time Spent at the Club:
 **2 Seasons**

First Goal Scored for the Club:
—
 **—**

Full International:
▶ —

Premiership Totals

92-06

Appearances	0
Clean Sheets	0
Assists	0
Yellow Cards	0
Red Cards	0

Clubs

Year	Club	Apps	CS
06-06	MK Dons	9	2
04-06	Fulham	1	0
	Vitoria Setubal		

Off the Pitch

Age:
- ▶ Batista: 19 years, 6 months
- Team: 28 years, 11 months
- | League: 26 years, 11 months

Height:
- ▶ Batista: 6'1"
- Team: 5'11"
- | League: 5'11"

Weight:
- ▶ Batista: 12st 6lb
- Team: 13st 2lb
- | League: 12st

30 Tony Warner
Goalkeeper

Player Details:

Date of Birth:	11.05.1974
Place of Birth:	Liverpool
Nationality:	Trinidad & Tobagan
Height:	6'3"
Weight:	15st 6lb
Foot:	Right

Season Review 05/06

With the season fast approaching Fulham were having to face up to the fact that they were without their two first choice keepers, as both Drobny and Crossley had picked up knee injuries.

Tony Warner was initially drafted in on loan from Cardiff City as a stop gap replacement while the injury situation improved, but such were his performances that he was offered a permanent contract in January. Tony was excellent at St. James' Park, keeping new signing Michael Owen at bay and at Highbury where he saved a Lauren penalty. He was on hand to replace Niemi and Crossley throughout the campaign.

Player Performance 05/06

League Performance

Percentage of total possible time player was on pitch   ⊙ position in league table at end of month

Month:	Aug	Sep	Oct	Nov	Dec	Jan	Feb	Mar	Apr	May	Total
	100%	100%	33%	67%	20%	25%	30%	60%	0%	0%	43%
Team Pts:	4/12	1/9	4/12	6/9	5/18	9/12	3/9	4/15	9/12	3/6	48/114
Team Gls F:	3	2	5	6	7	5	9	3	6	2	48
Team Gls A:	6	4	5	5	9	3	7	12	5	2	58
Total mins:	360	270	117	180	109	90	90	270	0	0	1,486
Starts (sub):	4	3	1 (1)	2	1 (1)	1	1	3	0	0	16 (2)
Goals:	0	0	0	0	0	0	0	0	0	0	0
Assists:	0	0	0	0	0	0	0	0	0	0	0
Clean sheets:	2	0	0	0	0	0	0	0	0	0	2
Cards (Y/R):	0	0	0	0	0	0	0	0	0	0	0

League Performance Totals

Clean Sheets

▶ Warner: 2
▶ Team-mates: 8
Total: 10

Assists

▶ Warner: 0
▶ Team-mates: 47
Total: 47

Cards

▶ Warner: 0
▶ Team-mates: 66
Total: 66

Cup Games

	Apps	CS	Cards
European	0	0	0
FA Cup	1	0	0
Carling Cup	1	0	0
Total	**2**	**0**	**0**

Career History

Career Milestones

Club Debut:
vs Birmingham (H), D 0-0, Prem.
 **13.08.05**

First Goal Scored for the Club:
—
 **—**

Time Spent at the Club:
▶ **1 Season**

Full International:
▶ **Trinidad & Tobago**

Premiership Totals
92-06

Appearances	18
Clean Sheets	2
Assists	0
Yellow Cards	0
Red Cards	0

Clubs

Year	Club	Apps	CS
05-06	Fulham	20	2
04-06	Cardiff City	30	6
99-04	Millwall	225	75
99-99	Aberdeen		
98-99	Celtic		
97-97	Swindon Town	3	1
90-99	Liverpool	0	0

Off the Pitch

Age:
▶ Warner: 32 years
▶ Team: 28 years, 11 months
| League: 26 years, 11 months

Height:
▶ Warner: 6'3"
▶ Team: 5'11"
| League: 5'11"

Weight:
▶ Warner: 15st 6lb
▶ Team: 13st 2lb
| League: 12st

29 Antti Niemi
Goalkeeper

Player Details:

Date of Birth:	31.05.1972
Place of Birth:	Oulu
Nationality:	Finnish
Height:	6'1"
Weight:	12st 12lb
Foot:	Right

Season Review 05/06

The Icelandic stopper was brought in from Southampton in January to further bolster the strong contingent of goalkeeping ability at the Club.

Antti slotted in straight away and made a good impression from the outset with a commanding display against Newcastle which saw him at his agile best to deny Chopra and Bowyer. It seemed that Niemi had cemented his place between the sticks only for an injury in the warm-up for the Bolton game to sideline him. Back in goal towards the end of season, however, the 34-year-old once again showed his obvious talent with a string of fine saves.

Player Performance 05/06

League Performance

Percentage of total possible time player was on pitch   ⊙ position in league table at end of month

Month:	Aug	Sep	Oct	Nov	Dec	Jan	Feb	Mar	Apr	May	Total
	0%	0%	0%	0%	0%	75%	67%	0%	75%	50%	24%
Position	14	17	15	14	15	13	14	15	13	12	
Team Pts:	4/12	1/9	4/12	6/9	5/18	9/12	3/9	4/15	9/12	3/6	48/114
Team Gls F:	3	2	5	6	7	5	9	3	6	2	48
Team Gls A:	6	4	5	5	9	3	7	12	5	2	58
Total mins:	0	0	0	0	0	270	180	0	270	90	810
Starts (sub):	0	0	0	0	0	3	2	0	3	1	9
Goals:	0	0	0	0	0	0	0	0	0	0	0
Assists:	0	0	0	0	0	0	0	0	0	0	0
Clean sheets:	0	0	0	0	0	2	0	0	1	1	4
Cards (Y/R):	0	0	0	0	0	0	0	0	0	0	0

League Performance Totals

Clean Sheets
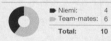
- Niemi: 4
- Team-mates: 6
- **Total: 10**

Assists
- Niemi: 0
- Team-mates: 47
- **Total: 47**

Cards

- Niemi: 0
- Team-mates: 66
- **Total: 66**

Cup Games

	Apps	CS	Cards
European	0	0	0
FA Cup	0	0	0
Carling Cup	0	0	0
Total	**0**	**0**	**0**

Career History

Career Milestones

Club Debut:
vs Newcastle (H), W 1-0, Premiership
▶ **14.01.06**

Time Spent at the Club:
▶ **0.5 Seasons**

First Goal Scored for the Club:
—
▶ **—**

Full International:
▶ **Finland**

Premiership Totals

92-06

Appearances	90
Clean Sheets	26
Assists	1
Yellow Cards	1
Red Cards	0

Clubs

Year	Club	Apps	CS
06-06	Fulham	9	4
02-06	Southampton	123	38
99-02	Hearts		
99-99	Charlton Ath	0	0
97-99	Rangers		
	FC Copenhagen		
	HJK Helsinki		

Off the Pitch

Age:

- Niemi: 34 years
- Team: 28 years, 11 months
- League: 26 years, 11 months

Height:
- Niemi: 6'1"
- Team: 5'11"
- League: 5'11"

Weight:
- Niemi: 12st 12lb
- Team: 13st 2lb
- League: 12st

25

Jaroslav Drobny
Goalkeeper

Player Details:

Date of Birth:	18.10.1979
Place of Birth:	Pocatky, Czech Rep.
Nationality:	Czech
Height:	6'3"
Weight:	13st 5lb
Foot:	Right

Season Review 05/06

The former Czech Under 21 International was brought in to challenge for the number one jersey in June 2005, having signed a pre-contract agreement to join Fulham back in January 2005.

Drobny played a major part in the Whites' pre-season campaign but suffered a knee cartilage injury which meant he missed the beginning of the campaign. Further injury to Mark Crossley, meanwhile, saw Tony Warner joining the Club on loan to cover goalkeeping duties. The permanent signing of Warner and the arrival of Antti Niemi meant that Drobny fell down the pecking order and, to ensure he benefited from regular First Team action, he signed for Dutch side ADO den Haag for the rest of the season in late January.

www.fulhamfc.com
Follow the action all the way to the net!

3
Carlos Bocanegra
Defence

Season Review 05/06

Having spent much of the 04/05 season confined to a left back role, Boca returned to his preferred central defensive position for the start of the 05/06 season and the change benefited his performances from the off.

Carlos replaced Rehman in the heart of the Whites defence early in the season to form a solid partnership with Zat Knight. It was only some niggling injuries that denied Boca a more consistent run in the team. The highlight of the former Chicago Fire defender's campaign was his last gasp header against Tottenham Hotspur that stole all three points for the Whites in January.

Player Details:

Date of Birth:	25.05.1979
Place of Birth:	Alta Loma
Nationality:	American
Height:	5'9"
Weight:	12st 11lb
Foot:	Left/Right

Player Performance 05/06

League Performance

Percentage of total possible time player was on pitch

⊕ position in league table at end of month

Month:	Aug	Sep	Oct	Nov	Dec	Jan	Feb	Mar	Apr	May	Total
	25%	100%	100%	67%	56%	50%	100%		13	50%	54%
	14	17	15	14	15	13	14	15	0%	12	
								20%			
Team Pts:	4/12	1/9	4/12	6/9	5/18	9/12	3/9	4/15	9/12	3/6	48/114
Team Gls F:	3	2	5	6	7	5	9	3	6	2	48
Team Gls A:	6	4	5	5	9	3	7	12	5	2	58
Total mins:	90	270	360	180	301	180	270	90	0	90	1,831
Starts (sub):	1	3	4	2	3 (1)	2	3	1	0	1	20 (1)
Goals:	0	0	0	0	0	1	0	0	0	0	1
Assists:	0	0	0	0	0	0	0	0	0	0	0
Clean sheets:	1	0	1	0	1	1	0	0	0	1	5
Cards (Y/R):	0	2	0	1	1	0	0	1	0	0	5

League Performance Totals

Goals

- ▶ Bocanegra: 1
- ▷ Team-mates: 46
- **Total: 47**
- ▶ own goals: 1

Assists

- ▶ Bocanegra: 0
- ▷ Team-mates: 47
- **Total: 47**

Cards

- ▶ Bocanegra: 5
- ▷ Team-mates: 61
- **Total: 66**

Cup Games

	Apps	Goals	Cards
European	0	0	0
FA Cup	0	0	0
Carling Cup	1	0	0
Total	**1**	**0**	**0**

Career History

Career Milestones

Club Debut:

vs Newcastle (A), L 3-1, Premiership

▶ **19.01.04**

First Goal Scored for the Club:

vs Portsmouth (A), L 4-3, Premiership

▶ **30.08.04**

Time Spent at the Club:

▶ **2.5 Seasons**

Full International:

▶ **USA**

Premiership Totals

92-06

Appearances	64
Goals	2
Assists	0
Yellow Cards	11
Red Cards	1

Clubs

Year	Club	Apps	Gls
04-06	Fulham	76	2
	Chicago Fire		

Off the Pitch

Age:

- ▶ Bocanegra: 27 years
- ▷ Team: 28 years, 11 months
- | League: 26 years, 11 months

Height:

- ▶ Bocanegra: 5'9"
- ▷ Team: 5'11"
- | League: 5'11"

Weight:

- ▶ Bocanegra: 12st 11lb
- ▷ Team: 13st 2lb
- | League: 12st

31

Wayne Bridge
Defence

Season Review 05/06

January saw a real coup for Fulham as the Whites snapped up left back Wayne Bridge on loan from Chelsea for the second half of the 05/06 campaign.

Having moved down the Kings Road Bridge's first appearance came in the narrow defeat to West Ham but it was clear from his first game that his undeniable quality would be a huge asset for the remainder of the season. His impressive performances against Tottenham at home and Manchester United away typified the sort of player Bridge is. A solid defensive display nullified the threat of Spurs' Aaron Lennon and, against United, he displayed the sort of cavalier attacking approach which persuaded Chelsea to originally part with £7 million for his services.

Player Details:

Date of Birth:	05.08.1980
Place of Birth:	Southampton
Nationality:	English
Height:	5'9"
Weight:	12st 8lb
Foot:	Left

Player Performance 05/06

League Performance

Percentage of total possible time player was on pitch ↻ position in league table at end of month

Month:	Aug	Sep	Oct	Nov	Dec	Jan	Feb	Mar	Apr	May	Total
	0%	0%	0%	0%	0%	50%	100%	20%	100%	100%	32%
	14	17	15	14	15	13	14	15	13	12	
Team Pts:	4/12	1/9	4/12	6/9	5/18	9/12	3/9	4/15	9/12	3/6	48/114
Team Gls F:	3	2	5	6	7	5	9	3	6	2	48
Team Gls A:	6	4	5	5	9	3	7	12	5	2	58
Total mins:	0	0	0	0	0	180	270	90	360	180	1,080
Starts (sub):	0	0	0	0	0	2	3	1	4	2	12
Goals:	0	0	0	0	0	0	0	0	0	0	0
Assists:	0	0	0	0	0	0	1	0	0	0	1
Clean sheets:	0	0	0	0	0	1	0	0	1	1	3
Cards (Y/R):	0	0	0	0	0	0	0	1	0	1	2

League Performance Totals

Goals
- Bridge: 0
- Team-mates: 47
- **Total: 47**
- own goals: 1

Assists
- Bridge: 1
- Team-mates: 46
- **Total: 47**

Cards
- Bridge: 2
- Team-mates: 64
- **Total: 66**

Cup Games

	Apps	Goals	Cards
European	0	0	0
FA Cup	0	0	0
Carling Cup	0	0	0
Total	**0**	**0**	**0**

Career History

Career Milestones

Club Debut:
vs West Ham (A), L 2-1, Premiership
▶ **23.01.06**

Time Spent at the Club:
▶ **0.5 Seasons**

First Goal Scored for the Club:
—
▶ **—**

Full International:
▶ **England**

Premiership Totals
92-06

Appearances	211
Goals	3
Assists	15
Yellow Cards	9
Red Cards	0

Clubs

Year	Club	Apps	Gls
06-06	Fulham	12	0
03-06	Chelsea	75	3
97-03	Southampton	173	2

Off the Pitch

Age:
- Bridge: 25 years, 9 months
- Team: 28 years, 11 months
- League: 26 years, 11 months

Height:
- Bridge: 5'9"
- Team: 5'11"
- League: 5'11"

Weight:
- Bridge: 12st 8lb
- Team: 13st 2lb
- League: 12st

19 Phillippe Christanval
Defence

Season Review 05/06

Former French international Christanval was a transfer coup for Fulham as, not being attached to a club, Chris Coleman snapped him up on a free.

Having looked comfortable at either centre half or in the middle of the park on his debut against Lincoln City, Christanval appeared to be a shrewd acquisition. He further cemented his credentials with a solid first half performance against Charlton Athletic, but an injury sidelined the Frenchman until December. A run of games over the festive period then saw Christanval make a commanding central midfield pairing with Sylvain Legwinski. In and out of the side all season he proved himself a valuable addition to the squad.

Player Details:

Date of Birth:	31.08.1979
Place of Birth:	Paris
Nationality:	French
Height:	6'2"
Weight:	13st 3lb
Foot:	Right

Player Performance 05/06

League Performance

Percentage of total possible time player was on pitch — position in league table at end of month

Month:	Aug	Sep	Oct	Nov	Dec	Jan	Feb	Mar	Apr	May	Total
	0%	4%	10%	0%	67%	0%	0%	15%	42%	100%	24%
Team Pts:	4/12	1/9	4/12	6/9	5/18	9/12	3/9	4/15	9/2	3/6	48/114
Team Gls F:	3	2	5	6	7	5	9	3	6	2	48
Team Gls A:	6	4	5	5	9	3	7	12	5	2	58
Total mins:	0	10	35	0	360	0	0	69	152	180	806
Starts (sub):	0	0 (1)	1	0	4	0	0	0 (3)	0 (4)	2	7 (8)
Goals:	0	0	0	0	0	0	0	0	0	0	0
Assists:	0	0	0	0	0	0	0	0	0	0	0
Clean sheets:	0	0	0	0	0	0	0	0	0	1	1
Cards (Y/R):	0	0	1	0	1	0	0	0	1	1	4

League Performance Totals

Goals

- Christanval: 0
- Team-mates: 47

Total: 47

- own goals: 1

Assists

- Christanval: 0
- Team-mates: 47

Total: 47

Cards

- Christanval: 4
- Team-mates: 62

Total: 66

Cup Games

	Apps	Goals	Cards
European	0	0	0
FA Cup	0	0	0
Carling Cup	1	0	1
Total	**1**	**0**	**1**

Career History

Career Milestones

Club Debut:

vs West Ham (H), L 1-2, Premiership

▶ **17.09.05**

First Goal Scored for the Club:

—

▶ **—**

Time Spent at the Club:

▶ **1 Season**

Full International:

▶ **France**

Premiership Totals

92-06

Appearances	15
Goals	0
Assists	0
Yellow Cards	4
Red Cards	0

Clubs

Year	Club	Apps	Gls
05-06	Fulham	16	0
	Marseille		
	Barcelona		
	AS Monaco		

Off the Pitch

Age:

- Christanval: 27 years, 9 months
- Team: 28 years, 11 months
- League: 26 years, 11 months

Height:

- Christanval: 6'2"
- Team: 5'11"
- League: 5'11"

Weight:

- Christanval: 13st 3lb
- Team: 13st 2lb
- League: 12st

109

Alain Goma
Defence

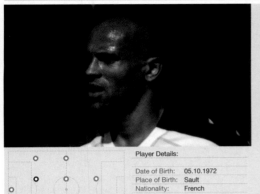

The 2005/06 season proved to be somewhat of a frustrating year for Fulham's 'Rock' as he was in and out of the side throughout.

Partnering both Zat Knight and Carlos Bocanegra in the centre of defence Goma had a good spell in the side towards the end of 2005 but failed to secure a more regular spot in the starting XI. His contributions were nevertheless typically solid.

Player Details:

Date of Birth:	05.10.1972
Place of Birth:	Sault
Nationality:	French
Height:	6'
Weight:	13st 10lb
Foot:	Right/Left

Player Performance 05/06

League Performance

Percentage of total possible time player was on pitch   ⟳ position in league table at end of month

Month:	Aug	Sep	Oct	Nov	Dec	Jan	Feb	Mar	Apr	May	Total
	0%	0%	100%	100%	83%	0%	0%	20%	0%	0%	34%
(position)	14	17	15	14	15	13	14	15	13	12	
Team Pts:	4/12	1/9	4/12	6/9	5/18	9/12	3/9	4/15	9/12	3/6	48/114
Team Gls F:	3	2	5	6	7	5	9	3	6	2	48
Team Gls A:	6	4	5	5	9	3	7	12	5	2	58
Total mins:	0	0	360	270	450	0	0	90	0	0	1,170
Starts (sub):	0	0	4	3	5	0	0	1	0	0	13
Goals:	0	0	0	0	0	0	0	0	0	0	0
Assists:	0	0	0	0	0	0	0	0	0	0	0
Clean sheets:	0	0	1	0	1	0	0	0	0	0	2
Cards (Y/R):	0	0	0	0	0	0	0	0	0	0	0

League Performance Totals

Goals
- Goma: 0
- Team-mates: 47
- **Total: 47**
- own goals: 1

Assists
- Goma: 0
- Team-mates: 47
- **Total: 47**

Cards
- Goma: 0
- Team-mates: 66
- **Total: 66**

Cup Games

	Apps	Goals	Cards
European	0	0	0
FA Cup	1	0	0
Carling Cup	1	0	0
Total	**2**	**0**	**0**

Career History

Career Milestones

Club Debut:
vs Portsmouth (A), D 1-1, Champ.
➡ 21.04.01
Time Spent at the Club:
➡ 5 Seasons

First Goal Scored for the Club:
—
➡ —
Full International:
➡ France

Premiership Totals
92-06

Appearances	147
Goals	1
Assists	2
Yellow Cards	24
Red Cards	1

Clubs

Year	Club	Apps	Gls
01-06	Fulham	152	0
99-01	Newcastle Utd	41	1
	Paris-SG		
	AJ Auxerre		

Off the Pitch

Age:
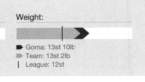
- Goma: 33 years, 7 months
- Team: 28 years, 11 months
- League: 26 years, 11 months

Height:
- Goma: 6'
- Team: 5'11"
- League: 5'11"

Weight:
- Goma: 13st 10lb
- Team: 13st 2lb
- League: 12st

33 Niclas Jensen
Defence

Player Details:
Date of Birth:	17.08.1974
Place of Birth:	Copenhagen
Nationality:	Danish
Height:	5'9"
Weight:	12st 4lb
Foot:	Left

Season Review 05/06

A summer signing from Borussia Dortmund, Niclas Jensen slotted straight into the left back berth and made it his own during the early stages of the season.

Jensen amassed a total of 15 appearances up to mid-January, marking some of the toughest opponents in the game, Ronaldo and Robben to name but two. The January transfer window saw the acquisition of highly rated left back Wayne Bridge from West London rivals Chelsea, however, and this – allied with the tremendous form of Fulham youngster Liam Rosenior – saw increased competition for the Danish international's place in the team.

Player Performance 05/06

League Performance
Percentage of total possible time player was on pitch — position in league table at end of month

Month:	Aug	Sep	Oct	Nov	Dec	Jan	Feb	Mar	Apr	May	Total
	100%	100%	94%	67%	6%	29%	0%	0%	0%	0%	38%
Team Pts:	4/12	1/9	4/12	6/9	5/18	9/12	3/9	4/15	9/12	3/6	48/114
Team Gls F:	3	2	5	6	7	5	9	3	6	2	48
Team Gls A:	6	4	5	9	3	7	12	5	2		58
Total mins:	360	270	339	180	33	105	0	0	0	0	1,287
Starts (sub):	4	3	4	2	0 (1)	1 (1)	0	0	0	0	14 (2)
Goals:	0	0	0	0	0	0	0	0	0	0	0
Assists:	1	0	0	0	0	0	0	0	0	0	1
Clean sheets:	2	0	0	0	0	1	0	0	0	0	3
Cards (Y/R):	0	0	0	1	0	0	0	0	0	0	1

Position in league table at end of month: 14, 17, 15, 14, 15, 13, 14, 15, 13, 12

League Performance Totals

Goals
- Jensen N: 0
- Team-mates: 47
- **Total: 47**
- own goals: 1

Assists
- Jensen N: 1
- Team-mates: 46
- **Total: 47**

Cards
- Jensen N: 1
- Team-mates: 65
- **Total: 66**

Cup Games
	Apps	Goals	Cards
European	0	0	0
FA Cup	1	0	0
Carling Cup	0	0	0
Total	**1**	**0**	**0**

Career History

Career Milestones

Club Debut:
vs Birmingham (H), D 0-0, Prem.

 **13.08.05**

Time Spent at the Club:

 1 Season

First Goal Scored for the Club:
—

 **—**

Full International:

 Denmark

Premiership Totals
92-06
Appearances	49
Goals	1
Assists	1
Yellow Cards	6
Red Cards	1

Clubs
Year	Club	Apps	Gls
05-06	Fulham	17	0
03-05	Borussia Dortmund		
02-03	Man City	56	2
	PSV Eindhoven		
	FC Copenhagen		

Off the Pitch

Age:

- Jensen N: 31 years, 9 months
- Team: 28 years, 11 months
- League: 26 years, 11 months

Height:
- Jensen N: 5'9"
- Team: 5'11"
- League: 5'11"

Weight:
- Jensen N: 12st 4lb
- Team: 13st 2lb
- League: 12st

6

Zat Knight
Defence

Season Review 05/06

Almost ever present throughout the season – bar a short spell in October and November – Zat displayed a solid level of consistency in the heart of the Whites' back line, partnering Carlos Bocanegra, Alain Goma and Ian Pearce.

Picked by England Manager Sven Goran Erickson for England's tour of the USA early in the season.

Player Details:

Date of Birth:	02.05.1980
Place of Birth:	Solihull
Nationality:	English
Height:	6'5"
Weight:	15st 9lb
Foot:	Right

Player Performance 05/06

League Performance

Percentage of total possible time player was on pitch   ⟲ position in league table at end of month

Month:	Aug	Sep	Oct	Nov	Dec	Jan	Feb	Mar	Apr	May	Total
	100%	96%	0%	33%	87%	100%	100%	95%	82%	0%	74%
	14	17	15	14	15	13	14	15	13	12	
Team Pts:	4/12	1/9	4/12	6/9	5/18	9/12	3/9	4/15	9/12	3/6	48/114
Team Gls F:	3	2	5	6	7	5	9	3	6	2	48
Team Gls A:	6	4	5	5	9	3	7	12	5	2	58
Total mins:	360	260	0	90	470	360	270	429	296	0	2,535
Starts (sub):	4	3	0	1	5 (1)	4	3	5	4	0	29 (1)
Goals:	0	0	0	0	0	0	0	0	0	0	0
Assists:	0	0	0	0	1	0	0	0	0	0	1
Clean sheets:	2	0	0	0	0	2	0	2	1	0	7
Cards (Y/R):	0	1	0	0	1	0	0	0	0	0	2

League Performance Totals

Goals
- ▶ Knight: 0
- ▶ Team-mates: 47
- **Total: 47**
- ● own goals: 1

Assists
- ▶ Knight: 1
- ▶ Team-mates: 46
- **Total: 47**

Cards
- ▶ Knight: 2
- ▶ Team-mates: 64
- **Total: 66**

Cup Games

	Apps	Goals	Cards
European	0	0	0
FA Cup	1	0	0
Carling Cup	1	0	1
Total	**2**	**0**	**1**

Career History

Career Milestones

Club Debut:
vs Northampton (H), W 4-1, Lge Cup

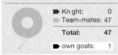 **05.09.00**

Time Spent at the Club:

▶ **7.5 Seasons**

First Goal Scored for the Club:
vs Watford (A), D 1-1, FA Cup

▶ **08.01.05**

Full International:

▶ **England**

Premiership Totals
92-06

Appearances	123
Goals	1
Assists	3
Yellow Cards	9
Red Cards	2

Clubs

Year	Club	Apps	Gls
00-00	Peterborough	8	0
99-06	Fulham	153	2

Off the Pitch

Age:

- ▶ Knight: 26 years
- ▶ Team: 28 years, 11 months
- | League: 26 years, 11 months

Height:

- ▶ Knight: 6'5"
- ▶ Team: 5'11"
- | League: 5'11"

Weight:

- ▶ Knight: 15st 9lb
- ▶ Team: 13st 2lb
- | League: 12st

22

Dean Leacock
Defence

Season Review 05/06

Another product of the successful Fulham Academy, Dean Leacock was looking to add the odd First Team appearance in 05/06 to his already impressive displays in the Reserve side.

A swath of injuries, however, saw Dean called upon to fill the right back berth for a run of five games in December and early January. He performed admirably and highlighted to the management the potential that he undoubtedly has.

Player Details:

Date of Birth:	10.06.1984
Place of Birth:	Croydon
Nationality:	English
Height:	6'2"
Weight:	12st 10lb
Foot:	Right

Player Performance 05/06

League Performance

Percentage of total possible time player was on pitch   ⊙ position in league table at end of month

Month:	Aug	Sep	Oct	Nov	Dec	Jan	Feb	Mar	Apr	May	Total
					61%						
	-14	17	15	14	15	13	14	15	13	12	
	0%	0%	0%	0%	25%		0%	0%	0%	0%	12%
Team Pts:	4/12	1/9	4/12	6/9	5/18	9/12	3/9	4/15	9/12	3/6	48/114
Team Gls F:	3	2	5	6	7	5	9	3	6	2	48
Team Gls A:	6	4	5	5	9	3	7	12	5	2	58
Total mins:	0	0	0	0	327	90	0	0	0	0	417
Starts (sub):	0	0	0	0	4	1	0	0	0	0	5
Goals:	0	0	0	0	0	0	0	0	0	0	0
Assists:	0	0	0	0	0	0	0	0	0	0	0
Clean sheets:	0	0	0	0	0	0	0	0	0	0	0
Cards (Y/R):	0	0	0	0	0	1	0	0	0	0	1

League Performance Totals

Goals

▶ Leacock:	0
▶ Team-mates:	47
Total:	**47**
▶ own goals:	1

Assists

▶ Leacock:	0
▶ Team-mates:	47
Total:	**47**

Cards

▶ Leacock:	1
▶ Team-mates:	65
Total:	**66**

Cup Games

	Apps	Goals	Cards
European	0	0	0
FA Cup	0	0	0
Carling Cup	2	0	0
Total	**2**	**0**	**0**

Career History

Career Milestones

Club Debut:

vs Wigan (A), L 2-1, League Cup

 **04.12.02**

Time Spent at the Club:

 **5 Seasons**

First Goal Scored for the Club:

—

▶ —

Full International:

▶ —

Premiership Totals

92-06

Appearances	9
Goals	0
Assists	0
Yellow Cards	3
Red Cards	0

Clubs

Year	Club	Apps	Gls
04-05	Coventry City	16	0
01-06	Fulham	13	0

Off the Pitch

Age:

- ▶ Leacock: 21 years, 11 months
- ▶ Team: 28 years, 11 months
- | League: 26 years, 11 months

Height:

- ▶ Leacock: 6'2"
- ▶ Team: 5'11"
- | League: 5'11"

Weight:

- ▶ Leacock: 12st 10lb
- ▶ Team: 13st 2lb
- | League: 12st

35 Ian Pearce
Defence

Season Review 05/06

Ever dependable defender Ian Pearce made a valuable contribution to the side in the second half of the campaign as injuries saw him get a run in the starting line-up from January.

Most notably he proved a rock in the centre of defence when Champions Chelsea visited the Cottage in March, repeatedly denying Drogba and Crespo a sniff at goal.

Player Details:

Date of Birth:	07.05.1974
Place of Birth:	Bury St Edmunds
Nationality:	English
Height:	6'3"
Weight:	16st 7lb
Foot:	Right/Left

Player Performance 05/06

League Performance

Percentage of total possible time player was on pitch   ⊙ position in league table at end of month

Month:	Aug	Sep	Oct	Nov	Dec	Jan	Feb	Mar	Apr	May	Total
	0%	0%	0%	0%	0%	50%	0%	60%	84%	12%	24%
	14	17	15	14	15	13	14	15	13		
Team Pts:	4/12	1/9	4/12	6/9	5/18	9/12	3/9	4/15	9/12	3/6	48/114
Team Gls F:	3	2	5	6	7	5	9	3	6	2	48
Team Gls A:	6	4	5	5	9	3	7	12	5	2	58
Total mins:	0	0	0	0	0	180	0	270	304	69	823
Starts (sub):	0	0	0	0	0	2	0	3	4	1	10
Goals:	0	0	0	0	0	0	0	0	0	0	0
Assists:	0	0	0	0	0	0	0	0	0	0	0
Clean sheets:	0	0	0	0	0	1	0	2	1	0	4
Cards (Y/R):	0	0	0	0	0	0	0	0	0	1	1

League Performance Totals

Goals
- ▶ Pearce: 0
- ▶ Team-mates: 47
- **Total: 47**
- ▶ own goals: 1

Assists
- ▶ Pearce: 0
- ▶ Team-mates: 47
- **Total: 47**

Cards
- ▶ Pearce: 1
- ▶ Team-mates: 65
- **Total: 66**

Cup Games

	Apps	Goals	Cards
European	0	0	0
FA Cup	1	0	1
Carling Cup	1	0	1
Total	**2**	**0**	**2**

Career History

Career Milestones

Club Debut:
vs Tottenham (H), W 2-1, Premiership

▶ **31.01.04**

First Goal Scored for the Club:
—

▶ **—**

Time Spent at the Club:

▶ **2.5 Seasons**

Full International:

▶ **—**

Premiership Totals
92-06

Appearances	214
Goals	10
Assists	4
Yellow Cards	16
Red Cards	3

Clubs

Year	Club	Apps	Gls
04-06	Fulham	37	0
97-04	West Ham	163	10
93-97	Blackburn	81	3
91-93	Chelsea	5	0

Off the Pitch

Age:

- ▶ Pearce: 32 years
- ▶ Team: 28 years, 11 months
- | League: 26 years, 11 months

Height:
- ▶ Pearce: 6'3"
- ▶ Team: 5'11"
- | League: 5'11"

Weight:
- ▶ Pearce: 16st 7lb
- ▶ Team: 13st 2lb
- | League: 12st

17 Liam Rosenior
Defence

Player Details:

Date of Birth:	09.07.1984
Place of Birth:	London
Nationality:	English
Height:	5'8"
Weight:	11st 11lb
Foot:	Right/Left

Player Performance 05/06

League Performance

Percentage of total possible time player was on pitch   position in league table at end of month

Month:	Aug	Sep	Oct	Nov	Dec	Jan	Feb	Mar	Apr	May	Total
	0%	0%	6%	33%	100%	96%	86%	100%	75%	100%	58%
	14	17	15	14	15	13	14	15	13	12	
Team Pts:	4/12	1/9	4/12	6/9	5/18	9/12	3/9	4/15	9/12	3/6	48/114
Team Gls F:	3	2	5	6	7	5	9	3	6	2	48
Team Gls A:	6	4	5	5	9	3	7	12	5	2	58
Total mins:	0	0	21	90	540	345	90	450	270	180	1,986
Starts (sub):	0	0	0 (2)	1	6	4	1	5	3	2	22 (2)
Goals:	0	0	0	0	0	0	0	0	0	0	0
Assists:	0	0	0	0	0	0	1	0	0	0	1
Clean sheets:	0	0	0	0	1	2	0	2	1	1	7
Cards (Y/R):	0	0	0	1	1	1	1	1	0	0	5

League Performance Totals

Goals

- Rosenior: 0
- Team-mates: 47
- **Total: 47**
- own goals: 1

Assists
- Rosenior: 1
- Team-mates: 46
- **Total: 47**

Cards
- Rosenior: 5
- Team-mates: 61
- **Total: 66**

Cup Games

	Apps	Goals	Cards
European	0	0	0
FA Cup	1	0	1
Carling Cup	2	1	0
Total	**3**	**1**	**1**

Career History

Career Milestones

Club Debut:
vs Boston Utd (A), W 1-4, Lge Cup
 **22.09.04**

Time Spent at the Club:
 2.5 Seasons

First Goal Scored for the Club:
vs Lincoln City (H), W 5-4, Lge Cup
 **21.09.05**

Full International:
▶ —

Premiership Totals
92-06

Appearances	41
Goals	0
Assists	2
Yellow Cards	8
Red Cards	1

Clubs

Year	Club	Apps	Gls
04-04	Torquay Utd	10	0
03-06	Fulham	50	1
02-03	Bristol City	28	3

Off the Pitch

Age:
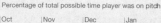
- Rosenior: 21 years, 10 months
- Team: 28 years, 11 months
- League: 26 years, 11 months

Height:
- Rosenior: 5'8"
- Team: 5'11"
- League: 5'11"

Weight:
- Rosenior: 11st 11lb
- Team: 13st 2lb
- League: 12st

2

Moritz Volz
Defence

Moritz Volz was an ever present for Fulham in all Premiership encounters until a broken rib sidelined the young German international in early December, ruling him out until February.

His adventurous attacking play was highlighted as he proved to be a thorn in the side of opposing defences with his intelligent forward runs and ability to deliver menacing crosses. Competition for the right back berth was fierce this season, however, as Moritz battled with team-mate Liam Rosenior throughout.

Player Details:

Date of Birth:	21.01.1983
Place of Birth:	Siegen
Nationality:	German
Height:	5'9"
Weight:	12st 8lb
Foot:	Right

Player Performance 05/06

League Performance

Percentage of total possible time player was on pitch   ⊕ position in league table at end of month

Month:	Aug	Sep	Oct	Nov	Dec	Jan	Feb	Mar	Apr	May	Total
	100%	100%	100%	100%	13%	0%	67%	80%	25%	50%	60%
	14	17	15	14	15	13	14	15	13	12	
Team Pts:	4/12	1/9	4/12	6/9	5/18	9/12	3/9	4/15	9/12	3/6	48/114
Team Gls F:	3	2	5	6	7	5	9	3	6	2	48
Team Gls A:	6	4	5	5	9	3	7	12	5	2	58
Total mins:	360	270	360	270	70	0	180	360	90	90	2,050
Starts (sub):	4	3	4	3	1	0	2	4	1	1	23
Goals:	0	0	0	0	0	0	0	0	0	0	0
Assists:	1	0	0	0	0	0	0	0	0	0	1
Clean sheets:	2	0	1	0	0	0	0	2	0	1	6
Cards (Y/R):	0	0	2	0	0	0	0	0	0	0	2

League Performance Totals

Goals
- Volz: 0
- Team-mates: 47
- **Total: 47**
- own goals: 1

Assists
- Volz: 1
- Team-mates: 46
- **Total: 47**

Cards
- Volz: 2
- Team-mates: 64
- **Total: 66**

Cup Games

	Apps	Goals	Cards
European	0	0	0
FA Cup	0	0	0
Carling Cup	1	0	0
Total	**1**	**0**	**0**

Career History

Career Milestones

Club Debut:
vs Middlesbrough (H), W 3-2, Prem.
➧ **16.08.03**

Time Spent at the Club:
➧ **3 Seasons**

First Goal Scored for the Club:
vs Watford (H), W 2-0, FA Cup
➧ **19.01.05**

Full International:
➧ **—**

Premiership Totals

92-06

Appearances	87
Goals	0
Assists	2
Yellow Cards	12
Red Cards	0

Clubs

Year	Club	Apps	Gls
03-06	Fulham	98	1
03-03	Wimbledon	10	1
00-04	Arsenal	2	0
	Schalke 04		

Off the Pitch

Age:
- ➧ Volz: 23 years, 4 months
- Team: 28 years, 11 months
- | League: 26 years, 11 months

Height:
- ➧ Volz: 5'9"
- Team: 5'11"
- | League: 5'11"

Weight:
- ➧ Volz: 12st 8lb
- Team: 13st 2lb
- | League: 12st

11 Luis Boa Morte
Midfield

Season Review 05/06

A massive season for the Portuguese international as he assumed the mantle of Club Captain following the departure of Lee Clark last summer.

Boa grasped his new found responsibility with both hands, offering guidance and support to his team-mates both on and off the pitch. Playing in a variety of roles, in the middle of the park as well as his more familiar left flank role, Boa chipped in with seven goals, including the unforgettable winner against Chelsea at the Cottage in March.

Player Details:

Date of Birth:	04.08.1977
Place of Birth:	Lisbon
Nationality:	Portuguese
Height:	5'8"
Weight:	12st 8lb
Foot:	Left

Player Performance 05/06

League Performance

Percentage of total possible time player was on pitch   ⊖ position in league table at end of month

Month:	Aug	Sep	Oct	Nov	Dec	Jan	Feb	Mar	Apr	May	Total
	100%	100%	100%	56%	83%	100%	100%	100%	100%	10%	89%
	14	17	15	14	15	13	14	15	13	12	
Team Pts:	4/12	1/9	4/12	6/9	5/18	9/12	3/9	4/15	9/12	3/6	48/114
Team Gls F:	3	2	5	6	7	5	9	3	6	2	48
Team Gls A:	6	4	5	5	9	3	7	12	5	2	58
Total mins:	360	270	360	151	450	360	270	450	360	18	3,049
Starts (sub):	4	3	4	2	5	4	3	5	4	1	35
Goals:	0	1	1	0	1	0	0	1	2	0	6
Assists:	0	1	1	2	2	0	0	1	3	0	10
Clean sheets:	2	0	1	0	1	2	0	2	1	0	9
Cards (Y/R):	1	1	1	1	0/1	1	3	0	1	0	9/1

League Performance Totals

Goals

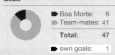

▶ Boa Morte:	6
▶ Team-mates:	41
Total:	**47**
▶ own goals:	1

Assists

▶ Boa Morte:	10
▶ Team-mates:	37
Total:	**47**

Cards

▶ Boa Morte:	10
▶ Team-mates:	56
Total:	**66**

Cup Games

	Apps	Goals	Cards
European	0	0	0
FA Cup	1	0	0
Carling Cup	1	1	1
Total	**2**	**1**	**1**

Career History

Career Milestones

Club Debut:
vs Crewe (H), W 2-0, Championship

 **12.08.00**

First Goal Scored for the Club:
vs Stockport (H), W 4-1, Champ.

▶ **26.08.00**

Time Spent at the Club:

▶ **6 Seasons**

Full International:

▶ **Portugal**

Premiership Totals
92-06

Appearances	190
Goals	27
Assists	38
Yellow Cards	43
Red Cards	5

Clubs

Year	Club	Apps	Gls
00-06	Fulham	235	54
99-01	Southampton	17	1
97-99	Arsenal	40	4
	Sporting Lisbon		

Off the Pitch

Age:

▶ Boa Morte: 28 years, 9 months
▶ Team: 28 years, 1 months
| League: 26 years, 11 months

Height:

▶ Boa Morte: 5'8"
▶ Team: 5'11"
| League: 5'11"

Weight:

▶ Boa Morte: 12st 8lb
▶ Team: 13st 2lb
| League: 12st

9
Michael Brown
Midfield

Season Review 05/06

Fulham's last January signing, Brown was brought from London rivals Tottenham Hotspur to bolster the Whites' midfield options.

It was a frustrating start for Brown, however, after he picked up a slight hamstring strain on his debut against Manchester United at Old Trafford. Reinstalled to the Whites' starting line-up by mid-March he immediately formed a good partnership with Mark Pembridge in the centre of midfield. Sent off against Portsmouth for a foul on Sean Davis, Brown didn't really get the sort of run in the side that he needed to show his true potential this term but, nevertheless, he has undoubtedly been a great addition to the squad.

Player Details:

Date of Birth:	25.01.1977
Place of Birth:	Hartlepool
Nationality:	English
Height:	5'8"
Weight:	11st 11lb
Foot:	Right

Player Performance 05/06

League Performance

Percentage of total possible time player was on pitch   ○- position in league table at end of month

Month:	Aug	Sep	Oct	Nov	Dec	Jan	Feb	Mar	Apr	May	Total
	0%	0%	0%	0%	0%	0%	17%	60%	25%	62%	15%
	14	17	15	14	15	13	14	15	13	12	
Team Pts:	4/12	1/9	4/12	6/9	5/18	9/12	3/3	4/15	9/12	3/6	48/114
Team Gls F:	3	2	5	6	7	5	9	3	6	2	48
Team Gls A:	6	4	5	5	9	3	7	12	5	2	58
Total mins:	0	0	0	0	0	0	46	270	90	111	517
Starts (sub):	0	0	0	0	0	0	1	3	1	1 (1)	6 (1)
Goals:	0	0	0	0	0	0	0	0	0	0	0
Assists:	0	0	0	0	0	0	0	0	0	0	0
Clean sheets:	0	0	0	0	0	0	0	2	0	1	3
Cards (Y/R):	0	0	0	0	0	0	0	2	0/1	0	2/1

League Performance Totals

Goals
- Brown: 0
- Team-mates: 47
- **Total:** 47
- own goals: 1

Assists
- Brown: 0
- Team-mates: 47
- **Total:** 47

Cards
- Brown: 3
- Team-mates: 63
- **Total:** 66

Cup Games

	Apps	Goals	Cards
European	0	0	0
FA Cup	0	0	0
Carling Cup	0	0	0
Total	**0**	**0**	**0**

Career History

Career Milestones

Club Debut:
vs Man Utd (A), L 4-2, Premiership
 04.02.06

Time Spent at the Club:
0.5 Seasons

First Goal Scored for the Club:
—

Full International:
—

Premiership Totals
92-06

Appearances	78
Goals	2
Assists	6
Yellow Cards	17
Red Cards	2

Clubs

Year	Club	Apps	Gls
06-06	Fulham	7	0
04-06	Tottenham	64	3
99-04	Sheff Utd	174	36
99-99	Portsmouth	4	0
97-97	Hartlepool Utd	6	1
94-00	Man City	111	5

Off the Pitch

Age:

- Brown: 29 years, 4 months
- Team: 28 years, 11 months
- League: 26 years, 11 months

Height:
- Brown: 5'8"
- Team: 5'11"
- League: 5'11"

Weight:
- Brown: 11st 11lb
- Team: 13st 2lb
- League: 12st

18 Ahmad Elrich
Midfield

Regarded as one of the most exciting prospects to come out of Australia in recent years, Fulham snapped up Elrich from Korean side Busan I'cons.

As with many of Fulham's summer signings Ahmad made his first full start in Fulham's Carling Cup game against Lincoln City. His pace and eye for a pass proved useful but the winger found it hard to break in to the First Team on a regular basis and in March he joined Norwegian side FC Lyn on loan for the remainder of the season.

Player Details:

Date of Birth:	30.05.1981
Place of Birth:	Sydney
Nationality:	Australian
Height:	5'9"
Weight:	12st 4lb
Foot:	Right

Player Performance 05/06

League Performance

Percentage of total possible time player was on pitch   position in league table at end of month

Month:	Aug	Sep	Oct	Nov	Dec	Jan	Feb	Mar	Apr	May	Total
Position	14	17	15	14	15	13	14	15	13	12	
%	0%	0%	23%	0%	13%	0%	0%	0%	0%	0%	5%
Team Pts:	4/12	1/9	4/12	6/9	5/18	9/12	3/9	4/15	9/12	3/6	48/114
Team Gls F:	3	2	5	6	7	5	9	3	6	2	48
Team Gls A:	6	4	5	5	9	3	7	12	5	2	58
Total mins:	0	0	84	0	71	0	0	0	0	0	155
Starts (sub):	0 (1)	0	1 (1)	0	1 (2)	0	0	0	0	0	2 (4)
Goals:	0	0	0	0	0	0	0	0	0	0	0
Assists:	0	0	0	0	0	0	0	0	0	0	0
Clean sheets:	0	0	1	0	0	0	0	0	0	0	1
Cards (Y/R):	0	0	0	0	0	0	0	0	0	0	0

League Performance Totals

Goals

Elrich:	0
Team-mates:	47
Total:	**47**
own goals:	1

Assists

Elrich:	0
Team-mates:	47
Total:	**47**

Cards

Elrich:	0
Team-mates:	66
Total:	**66**

Cup Games

	Apps	Goals	Cards
European	0	0	0
FA Cup	1	0	0
Carling Cup	2	0	0
Total	**3**	**0**	**0**

Career History

Career Milestones

Club Debut:
vs Birmingham (H) D 0-0, Prem.
13.08.05

First Goal Scored for the Club:
—
—

Time Spent at the Club:
1 Season

Full International:
Australia

Premiership Totals

92-06

Appearances	6
Goals	0
Assists	0
Yellow Cards	0
Red Cards	0

Clubs

Year	Club	Apps	Gls
06-06	Lyn Oslo		
05-06	Fulham	9	0
	Busan I'cons		
	Parramatta Power	120	19

Off the Pitch

Age:
- Elrich: 25 years
- Team: 28 years, 11 months
- League: 26 years, 11 months

Height:
- Elrich: 5'9"
- Team: 5'11"
- League: 5'11"

Weight:
- Elrich: 12st 4lb
- Team: 13st 2lb
- League: 12st

8 Claus Jensen
Midfield

Player Details:

Date of Birth:	22.04.1977
Place of Birth:	Nykobing
Nationality:	Danish
Height:	5'9"
Weight:	13st 7lb
Foot:	Right/Left

Season Review 05/06

A frustrating and injury plagued season for the Danish international which was all the more disappointing as Jensen came into this season in great form.

In the early stages of the campaign he formed an excellent central midfield partnership with Papa Bouba Diop. It was Jensen's goal against Arsenal that gave Whites' fans early hope of an upset against the former Champions. It seemed Jensen saved his goals for past Champions of the Premier League as he notched again against Manchester United at the Cottage with a free kick that deceived ex-Fulham keeper Edwin van der Sar.

Player Performance 05/06

League Performance

Percentage of total possible time player was on pitch   ⊕ position in league table at end of month

Month:	Aug	Sep	Oct	Nov	Dec	Jan	Feb	Mar	Apr	May	Total
	100%	100%	98%								
	14	17	15	14	15	13	14	15	13	12	29%
				0%	0%	0%	0%	0%	0%	0%	
Team Pts:	4/12	1/9	4/12	6/9	5/18	9/12	3/9	4/15	9/12	3/6	48/114
Team Gls F:	3	2	5	6	7	5	9	3	6	2	48
Team Gls A:	6	4	5	5	9	3	7	12	5	2	58
Total mins:	360	270	352	0	0	0	0	0	0	0	982
Starts (sub):	4	3	4	0	0	0	0	0	0	0	11
Goals:	1	0	1	0	0	0	0	0	0	0	2
Assists:	0	0	1	0	0	0	0	0	0	0	1
Clean sheets:	2	0	1	0	0	0	0	0	0	0	3
Cards (Y/R):	0	0	0	0	0	0	0	0	0	0	0

League Performance Totals

Goals
- Jensen C: 2
- Team-mates: 45
- Total: 47
- own goals: 1

Assists
- Jensen C: 1
- Team-mates: 46
- Total: 47

Cards
- Jensen C: 0
- Team-mates: 66
- Total: 66

Cup Games

	Apps	Goals	Cards
European	0	0	0
FA Cup	0	0	0
Carling Cup	0	0	0
Total	**0**	**0**	**0**

Career History

Career Milestones

Club Debut:
vs Man City (A), D 1-1, Premiership

14.08.04

First Goal Scored for the Club:
vs Derby (H), W 4-2, FA Cup

12.02.05

Time Spent at the Club:
▶ 2 Seasons

Full International:
▶ Denmark

Premiership Totals

92-06

Appearances	145
Goals	18
Assists	23
Yellow Cards	1
Red Cards	1

Clubs

Year	Club	Apps	Gls
04-06	Fulham	26	3
00-04	Charlton Ath	134	17
98-00	Bolton	108	10
	Lyngby		
	Naestved		

Off the Pitch

Age:
- Jensen C: 29 years, 1 month
- Team: 28 years, 11 months
- League: 26 years, 11 months

Height:
- Jensen C: 5'9"
- Team: 5'11"
- League: 5'11"

Weight:
- Jensen C: 13st 7lb
- Team: 13st 2lb
- League: 12st

14 Papa Bouba Diop
Midfield

Season Review 05/06

It was very much a season of two halves for The Wardrobe, Fulham's indomitable midfield enforcer.

He started the season in his usual commanding way as he and Claus Jensen pulled the strings in the centre of midfield for the Whites. Bouba chipped in with vital goals against Boro and Blackburn towards the end of 2005 before flying out to join his Senegalese colleagues for the African Nations Cup. Having played a friendly for Senegal shortly after the Nations Cup, Bouba picked up an injury which limited his appearances for the Whites in the second half of the campaign.

Player Details:

Date of Birth:	28.01.1978
Place of Birth:	Dakar
Nationality:	Senegalese
Height:	6'4"
Weight:	14st 12lb
Foot:	Right

Player Performance 05/06

League Performance

Percentage of total possible time player was on pitch — position in league table at end of month

Month:	Aug	Sep	Oct	Nov	Dec	Jan	Feb	Mar	Apr	May	Total
% on pitch	75%	100%	100%	100%	26%	11%	6%	0%	75%	100%	53%
League position	14	17	15	14	15	13	14	15	13	12	
Team Pts:	4/12	1/9	4/12	6/9	5/18	9/12	3/9	4/15	9/12	3/6	48/114
Team Gls F:	3	2	5	6	7	5	9	3	6	2	48
Team Gls A:	6	4	5	5	9	3	7	12	5	2	58
Total mins:	270	270	360	270	139	40	15	0	270	180	1,814
Starts (sub):	3	3	4	3	2	1	0 (1)	0	3	2	21 (1)
Goals:	0	0	0	1	1	0	0	0	0	0	2
Assists:	0	0	0	0	0	0	0	0	0	0	0
Clean sheets:	1	0	1	0	1	0	0	0	1	1	5
Cards (Y/R):	1	1	1	0	1	0	0	0	2	0	6

League Performance Totals

Goals
- Diop: 2
- Team-mates: 45
- **Total: 47**
- own goals: 1

Assists
- Diop: 0
- Team-mates: 47
- **Total: 47**

Cards
- Diop: 6
- Team-mates: 60
- **Total: 66**

Cup Games

	Apps	Goals	Cards
European	0	0	0
FA Cup	0	0	0
Carling Cup	1	0	1
Total	**1**	**0**	**1**

Career History

Career Milestones

Club Debut:
vs Man City (A), D 1-1, Premiership
14.08.04

First Goal Scored for the Club:
vs Chelsea (H), L 1-4, Premiership
13.11.04

Time Spent at the Club:
2 Seasons

Full International:
Senegal

Premiership Totals
92-06

Appearances	51
Goals	8
Assists	0
Yellow Cards	13
Red Cards	2

Clubs

Year	Club	Apps	Gls
04-06	Fulham	58	9
	RC Lens		

Off the Pitch

Age:
- Diop: 28 years, 4 months
- Team: 28 years, 11 months
- League: 26 years, 11 months

Height:
- Diop: 6'4"
- Team: 5'11"
- League: 5'11"

Weight:
- Diop: 14st 12lb
- Team: 13st 2lb
- League: 12st

7
Mark Pembridge
Midfield

Season Review 05/06

Pembridge was plagued with early season calf injuries but the tenacious Welshman had no intention of giving up and battled his way back into Chris Coleman's plans by the beginning of March.

Mark slotted straight back in to the side in March and was a welcome addition at a time when the Whites were struggling due to the injuries of Diop and Elliott. His calm demeanour and immense experience was a massive boon to the Whites and the partnership he struck with Michael Brown was one of the factors that aided Fulham in their historic success over west London rivals Chelsea.

Player Details:

Date of Birth:	29.11.1970
Place of Birth:	Merthyr Tydfil
Nationality:	Welsh
Height:	5'6"
Weight:	12st 4lb
Foot:	Left

Player Performance 05/06

League Performance

Percentage of total possible time player was on pitch   ⊖ position in league table at end of month

Month:	Aug	Sep	Oct	Nov	Dec	Jan	Feb	Mar	Apr	May	Total
	14	17	15	14	15	13	14	80% / 15	13 / 20%	12	13%
	0%	0%	0%	0%	0%	0%	0%			0%	
Team Pts:	4/12	1/9	4/12	6/9	5/18	9/12	3/9	4/15	9/12	3/6	48/114
Team Gls F:	3	2	5	6	7	5	9	3	6	2	48
Team Gls A:	6	4	5	5	9	3	7	12	5	2	58
Total mins:	0	0	0	0	0	0	0	360	72	0	432
Starts (sub):	0	0	0	0	0	0	0	4	1	0	5
Goals:	0	0	0	0	0	0	0	0	0	0	0
Assists:	0	0	0	0	0	0	0	0	0	0	0
Clean sheets:	0	0	0	0	0	0	0	2	0	0	2
Cards (Y/R):	0	0	0	0	0	0	0	0	0	0	0

League Performance Totals

Goals

▶ Pembridge: 0
▷ Team-mates: 47
Total: 47
▶ own goals: 1

Assists

▶ Pembridge: 0
▷ Team-mates: 47
Total: 47

Cards

▶ Pembridge: 0
▷ Team-mates: 66
Total: 66

Cup Games

	Apps	Goals	Cards
European	0	0	0
FA Cup	0	0	0
Carling Cup	0	0	0
Total	**0**	**0**	**0**

Career History

Career Milestones

Club Debut:
vs Birmingham (A), D 2-2, Prem.
▶ **14.09.03**

First Goal Scored for the Club:
vs Chelsea (A), L 2-1, Premiership
▶ **20.03.04**

Time Spent at the Club:
▶ **3 Seasons**

Full International:
▶ **Wales**

Premiership Totals

92-06

Appearances	229
Goals	17
Assists	29
Yellow Cards	21
Red Cards	0

Clubs

Year	Club	Apps	Gls
03-06	Fulham	54	2
99-03	Everton	101	4
98-99	SL Benfica		
95-98	Sheff Wed	108	13
92-95	Derby Cty	140	37
89-92	Luton Town	70	6

Off the Pitch

Age:

▶ Pembridge: 35 years, 6 months
▷ Team: 28 years, 11 months
| League: 26 years, 11 months

Height:

▶ Pembridge: 5'6"
▷ Team: 5'11"
| League: 5'11"

Weight:

▶ Pembridge: 12st 4lb
▷ Team: 13st 2lb
| League: 12st

23 Michael Timlin
Midfield

Season Review 05/06

An encouraging season for the Under 21 Republic of Ireland captain, two appearances for the First Team and victory in the Madeira Cup for his national side.

Timlin once again showed that he has made great progress since graduating from the Fulham Academy and recovering from the injuries that had dogged him for the past couple of seaons. Blessed with an excellent array of passing he played the whole 120 minutes against Lincoln City in the Carling Cup. The New Year saw Michael given the chance to gain more First Team experience with two loan spells, firstly with Scunthorpe United and then Doncaster Rovers.

Player Details:

Date of Birth:	19.03.1985
Place of Birth:	Lambeth
Nationality:	Irish
Height:	5'8"
Weight:	11st 2lb
Foot:	Left

Player Performance 05/06

League Performance

Percentage of total possible time player was on pitch — position in league table at end of month

Month:	Aug	Sep	Oct	Nov	Dec	Jan	Feb	Mar	Apr	May	Total
position	14	17	15	14	15	13	14	15	13	12	
	0%	0%	0%	0%	0%	0%	0%	0%	0%	0%	0%
Team Pts:	4/12	1/9	4/12	6/9	5/18	9/12	3/9	4/15	9/12	3/6	48/114
Team Gls F:	3	2	5	6	7	5	9	3	6	2	48
Team Gls A:	6	4	5	5	9	3	7	12	5	2	58
Total mins:	0	0	0	0	0	0	0	0	0	0	
Starts (sub):	0	0	0	0	0	0	0	0	0	0	0
Goals:	0	0	0	0	0	0	0	0	0	0	0
Assists:	0	0	0	0	0	0	0	0	0	0	0
Clean sheets:	0	0	0	0	0	0	0	0	0	0	0
Cards (Y/R):	0	0	0	0	0	0	0	0	0	0	0

League Performance Totals

Goals

Timlin:	0
Team-mates:	47
Total:	**47**
own goals:	1

Assists

Timlin:	0
Team-mates:	47
Total:	**47**

Cards

Timlin:	0
Team-mates:	66
Total:	**66**

Cup Games

	Apps	Goals	Cards
European	0	0	0
FA Cup	1	0	0
Carling Cup	1	0	0
Total	**2**	**0**	**0**

Career History

Career Milestones

Club Debut:
vs Boston Utd (A), W 1-4, League Cup
▶ 22.09.04

First Goal Scored for the Club:
—
▶ —

Time Spent at the Club:
▶ 2 Seasons

Full International:
▶ —

Premiership Totals
92-06

Appearances	0
Goals	0
Assists	0
Yellow Cards	0
Red Cards	0

Clubs

Year	Club	Apps	Gls
06-06	Doncaster	3	0
06-06	Scunthorpe	1	0
04-06	Fulham	3	0

Off the Pitch

Age:

- Timlin: 21 years, 2 months
- Team: 28 years, 11 months
- League: 26 years, 11 months

Height:

- Timlin: 5'8"
- Team: 5'11"
- League: 5'11"

Weight:

- Timlin: 11st 2lb
- Team: 13st 2lb
- League: 12st

4 Steed Malbranque
Midfield

Season Review 05/06

Steed was at his mercurial best throughout 05/06 as he put in a number of man of the match appearances in the Whites midfield and scored some important goals along the way.

The Frenchman broke his season's goalscoring duck in quite spectacular fashion as he bagged a brace against Stuart Pearce's Manchester City. In the return leg, at the City of Manchester Stadium, he scored the 90th minute winner that secured the Whites' first away win of the season. The winners at home against Newcastle and Wigan were further highlights of a characteristically first class season. Steed was also awarded the Performance of The Season Award for his display against Liverpool at the Cottage.

Player Details:

Date of Birth:	06.01.1980
Place of Birth:	Mouscron
Nationality:	French
Height:	5'6"
Weight:	11st 12lb
Foot:	Right/Left

Player Performance 05/06

League Performance

Percentage of total possible time player was on pitch

⊖ position in league table at end of month

Month:	Aug	Sep	Oct	Nov	Dec	Jan	Feb	Mar	Apr	May	Total
	100%	100%	100%	100%	33%	56%	100%	100%	100%	100%	85%
position	14	17	15	14	15	13	14	15	13	12	
Team Pts:	4/12	1/9	4/12	6/9	5/18	9/12	3/9	4/15	9/12	3/6	48/114
Team Gls F:	3	2	5	6	7	5	9	3	6	2	48
Team Gls A:	6	4	5	5	9	3	7	12	5	2	58
Total mins:	360	270	360	270	180	201	270	449	360	180	2,900
Starts (sub):	4	3	4	3	2	2 (2)	3	5	4	2	32 (2)
Goals:	0	0	0	2	0	1	0	0	3	0	6
Assists:	0	1	2	0	0	0	1	1	0	0	5
Clean sheets:	2	0	1	0	1	1	0	2	1	1	9
Cards (Y/R):	1	0	1	0	0	0	0	0	2	0	4

League Performance Totals

Goals

▶ Malbranque: 6
▷ Team-mates: 41
Total: 47
▶ own goals: 1

Assists

▶ Malbranque: 5
▷ Team-mates: 42
Total: 47

Cards

▶ Malbranque: 4
▷ Team-mates: 62
Total: 66

Cup Games

	Apps	Goals	Cards
European	0	0	0
FA Cup	0	0	0
Carling Cup	1	0	0
Total	**1**	**0**	**0**

Career History

Career Milestones

Club Debut:
vs Man Utd (A), L 3-2, Premiership
▶ **19.08.01**

First Goal Scored for the Club:
vs Arsenal (H), L 1-3, Prem.
▶ **15.09.01**

Time Spent at the Club:
▶ **5 Seasons**

Full International:
▶ —

Premiership Totals

92-06

Appearances	172
Goals	32
Assists	41
Yellow Cards	13
Red Cards	0

Clubs

Year	Club	Apps	Gls
01-06	Fulham	211	44
	Lyon		

Off the Pitch

Age:

▶ Malbranque: 26 years, 4 months
▷ Team: 28 years, 11 months
| League: 26 years, 11 months

Height:

▶ Malbranque: 5'6"
▷ Team: 5'11"
| League: 5'11"

Weight:

▶ Malbranque: 11st 12lb
▷ Team: 13st 2lb
| League: 12st

5

Sylvain Legwinski
Midfield

Season Review 05/06

It was a frustrating start to the 05/06 season for Leggy as he picked up a knock in the first match of the campaign against Birmingham.

However, having worked his way back into the First Team set-up the Frenchman was on hand to show a selection of committed displays during Fulham's hectic festive and New Year period.

Player Details:

Date of Birth:	06.10.1973
Place of Birth:	Clermont-Ferrand
Nationality:	French
Height:	6'1"
Weight:	11st 9lb
Foot:	Right

Player Performance 05/06

League Performance

Percentage of total possible time player was on pitch   ⊖ position in league table at end of month

Month:	Aug	Sep	Oct	Nov	Dec	Jan	Feb	Mar	Apr	May	Total
	25%	0%	0%	44%	76%	77%	0%	0%	0%	0%	26%
position	14	17	15	14	15	13	14	15	13	12	
Team Pts:	4/12	1/9	4/12	6/9	5/18	9/12	3/9	4/15	9/12	3/6	48/114
Team Gls F:	3	2	5	6	7	5	9	3	6	2	48
Team Gls A:	6	4	5	5	9	3	7	12	5	2	58
Total mins:	90	0	0	119	408	276	0	0	0	0	893
Starts (sub):	1	0	0	1 (1)	4 (2)	4	0	0	0	0	10 (3)
Goals:	0	0	0	0	0	0	0	0	0	0	0
Assists:	0	0	0	1	0	0	0	0	0	0	1
Clean sheets:	1	0	0	0	0	0	0	0	0	0	1
Cards (Y/R):	1	0	0	0	1	2	0	0	0	0	4

League Performance Totals

Goals

- Legwinski: 0
- Team-mates: 47
- **Total: 47**
- own goals: 1

Assists

- Legwinski: 1
- Team-mates: 46
- **Total: 47**

Cards

- Legwinski: 4
- Team-mates: 62
- **Total: 66**

Cup Games

	Apps	Goals	Cards
European	0	0	0
FA Cup	1	0	0
Carling Cup	1	0	0
Total	**2**	**0**	**0**

Career History

Career Milestones

Club Debut:
vs Derby (H), D 0-0, Premiership

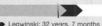 **25.08.01**

Time Spent at the Club:

➤ **5 Seasons**

First Goal Scored for the Club:
vs Derby Cty (H), W 5-2, League Cup

➤ **10.10.01**

Full International:

➤ **—**

Premiership Totals
92-06

Appearances	128
Goals	8
Assists	8
Yellow Cards	25
Red Cards	1

Clubs

Year	Club	Apps	Gls
01-06	Fulham	164	12
	Bordeaux		
	AS Monaco		

Off the Pitch

Age:

- Legwinski: 32 years, 7 months
- Team: 28 years, 11 months
- League: 26 years, 11 months

Height:

- Legwinski: 6'1"
- Team: 5'11"
- League: 5'11"

Weight:

- Legwinski: 11st 9lb
- Team: 13st 2lb
- League: 12st

13 Tomasz Radzinski
Forward

Season Review 05/06

Radzinski started off the season as a regular up front with Brian McBride, but was unlucky as his efforts on goal did everything but hit the back of the net.

As the season progressed Manager Chris Coleman saw the threat of Radz's pace and started deploying him more on the wing. The Canadian's pace and ability to get to the bye-line and deliver quality passes into the area made him a real asset to the Whites' midfield. Radzinski's first League goal of the season came in Fulham's win over West Brom having already notched one in the Carling Cup victory Lincoln.

Player Details:

Date of Birth:	14.12.1973
Place of Birth:	Poznan
Nationality:	Canadian
Height:	5'7"
Weight:	11st 11lb
Foot:	Right/Left

Player Performance 05/06

League Performance

Percentage of total possible time player was on pitch   Ο- position in league table at end of month

Month:	Aug	Sep	Oct	Nov	Dec	Jan	Feb	Mar	Apr	May	Total
	85%	84%	44% (100%)	14 (100%)	15	69% 13	77% 14	44% 15	13	51% 12	67%
	14	17								10%	
Team Pts:	4/12	1/9	4/12	6/9	5/18	9/12	3/9	4/15	9/12	3/6	48/114
Team Gls F:	3	2	5	6	7	5	9	3	6	2	48
Team Gls A:	6	4	5	5	9	3	7	12	5	2	58
Total mins:	307	227	158	270	540	247	209	196	36	92	2,282
Starts (sub):	4	3	1 (2)	3	6	2 (2)	2 (1)	2 (1)	0 (2)	0 (2)	23 (10)
Goals:	0	0	0	0	0	0	1	0	0	1	2
Assists:	1	0	0	1	2	0	2	0	0	0	6
Clean sheets:	1	0	0	0	1	0	0	0	0	0	2
Cards (Y/R):	0	0	0	0	1	0	1	0	1	0	3

League Performance Totals

Goals
- ► Radzinski: 2
- ► Team-mates: 45
- **Total: 47**
- ► own goals: 1

Assists
- ► Radzinski: 6
- ► Team-mates: 41
- **Total: 47**

Cards
- ► Radzinski: 3
- ► Team-mates: 63
- **Total: 66**

Cup Games

	Apps	Goals	Cards
European	0	0	0
FA Cup	1	0	0
Carling Cup	1	1	0
Total	**2**	**1**	**0**

Career History

Career Milestones

Club Debut:
vs Man City (A), D 1-1, Premiership
► **14.08.04**

Time Spent at the Club:
►**2 Seasons**

First Goal Scored for the Club:
vs Boston Utd (A), W 1-4, Lge Cup
► **22.09.04**

Full International:
►**Canada**

Premiership Totals
92-06

Appearances	159
Goals	33
Assists	26
Yellow Cards	7
Red Cards	0

Clubs

Year	Club	Apps	Gls
04-06	Fulham	76	14
01-04	Everton	101	26
	RSC Ancerlecht		
	Germinal Ekeren		

Off the Pitch

Age:
- ► Radzinski: 32 years, 5 months
- ► Team: 28 years, 11 months
- | League: 26 years, 11 months

Height:
- ► Radzinski: 5'7"
- ► Team: 5'11"
- | League: 5'11"

Weight:
- ► Radzinski: 11st 11lb
- ► Team: 13st 2lb
- | League: 12st

10

Heidar Helguson
Forward

Season Review 05/06

A summer signing from Championship side Watford, where he had been an integral part of the North West London side.

The Icelander's early appearances on his return to the Premiership were initially from the bench. He opened his Fulham account in the epic encounter with Lincoln City and this proved to be a taste of what was to come. His first full Premier League appearance came against Chelsea at Stamford Bridge where he scored a cheeky penalty. Helguson enjoyed a rich vein of scoring form, including a brace in the 6-1 demolition of West Brom. He established a strong partnership with fellow frontman Brian McBride, finishing the season with an impressive 10 goals.

Player Details:

Date of Birth:	22.08.1977
Place of Birth:	Akureyi
Nationality:	Icelandic
Height:	5'10"
Weight:	12st 10lb
Foot:	Right/Left

Player Performance 05/06

League Performance

Percentage of total possible time player was on pitch   ⊖ position in league table at end of month

Month:	Aug	Sep	Oct	Nov	Dec	Jan	Feb	Mar	Apr	May	Total
	3%	3%	5%	10%	45%	89%	85%	34%	70%	69%	40%
	14	17	15	14	15	13	14	15	13	12	
Team Pts:	4/12	1/9	4/12	6/9	5/18	9/12	3/9	4/15	9/12	3/6	48/114
Team Gls F:	3	2	5	6	7	5	9	3	6	2	48
Team Gls A:	6	4	5	5	9	3	7	12	5	2	58
Total mins:	9	9	18	26	243	320	230	154	252	124	1,385
Starts (sub):	0 (1)	0 (1)	0 (1)	0 (3)	3 (2)	3 (1)	3	2 (1)	3 (1)	1 (1)	15 (12)
Goals:	0	0	0	0	2	1	4	0	0	1	8
Assists:	0	0	0	0	1	1	1	0	1	1	5
Clean sheets:	0	0	0	0	0	2	0	0	0	0	2
Cards (Y/R):	0	0	0	0	1	1	1	0	0	0	4

League Performance Totals

Goals
- Helguson: 8
- Team-mates: 39
- **Total: 47**
- own goals: 1

Assists
- Helguson: 5
- Team-mates: 42
- **Total: 47**

Cards
- Helguson: 4
- Team-mates: 62
- **Total: 66**

Cup Games

	Apps	Goals	Cards
European	0	0	0
FA Cup	0	0	0
Carling Cup	2	2	0
Total	**2**	**2**	**0**

Career History

Career Milestones

Club Debut:
vs Blackburn (A), L 2-1, Premiership

20.08.05

Time Spent at the Club:
1 Season

First Goal Scored for the Club:
vs Lincoln City (H), W 5-4, Lge Cup
21.09.05

Full International:
Iceland

Premiership Totals

92-06

Appearances	43
Goals	14
Assists	8
Yellow Cards	10
Red Cards	0

Clubs

Year	Club	Apps	Gls
05-06	Fulham	29	10
00-05	Watford	199	64
	Lillestrom		

Off the Pitch

Age:

- Helguson: 28 years, 9 months
- Team: 28 years, 11 months
- League: 26 years, 11 months

Height:
- Helguson: 5'10"
- Team: 5'11"
- League: 5'11"

Weight:
- Helguson: 12st 10lb
- Team: 13st 2lb
- League: 12st

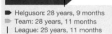

15
Collins John
Forward

Player Details:

Date of Birth:	17.10.1985
Place of Birth:	Zwandru
Nationality:	Dutch
Height:	5'10"
Weight:	12st 10lb
Foot:	Right/Left

Season Review 05/06

After six goals in all competitions last season Fulham's young Dutch striker, Collins John, was looking to make even more progress in 05/06.

The early stages of the season saw the striker being mainly used as a substitute but even his brief appearances suggested that there were goals to come. His first start coincided with his first goal of the season as he opened the scoring in Fulham's narrow defeat to Manchester United at the Cottage. From there he went on to score in the next two games, against Charlton and Liverpool. Other highlights of the season included his brace against Sunderland at the Cottage and his Goal of the Season winner against Middlesbrough at the Riverside.

Player Performance 05/06

League Performance
Percentage of total possible time player was on pitch   ⊖ position in league table at end of month

Month:	Aug	Sep	Oct	Nov	Dec	Jan	Feb	Mar	Apr	May	Total
	22%	21%	91%	95%	53%	34%	20%	60%	25%	48%	48%
	14	17	15	14	15	13	14	15	13	12	
Team Pts:	4/12	1/9	4/12	6/9	5/18	9/12	3/9	4/15	9/12	3/6	48/114
Team Gls F:	3	2	5	6	7	5	9	3	6	2	48
Team Gls A:	6	4	5	5	9	3	7	12	5	2	58
Total mins:	79	58	327	257	285	123	55	268	90	86	1,628
Starts (sub):	0 (3)	0 (3)	4	3	3 (3)	1 (3)	0 (3)	3 (2)	1 (1)	1 (1)	16 (19)
Goals:	0	0	3	1	0	2	2	2	1	0	11
Ass sts:	0	0	0	1	0	1	0	1	0	1	4
Clean sheets:	0	0	1	0	0	0	0	0	0	0	1
Cards (Y/R):	1	1	0	0	1	0	0	1	0	0	4

League Performance Totals

Goals
- John: 11
- Team-mates: 36
- **Total: 47**
- own goals: 1

Assists
- John: 4
- Team-mates: 43
- **Total: 47**

Cards
- John: 4
- Team-mates: 62
- **Total: 66**

Cup Games

	Apps	Goals	Cards
European	0	0	0
FA Cup	1	1	0
Carling Cup	2	0	0
Total	**3**	**1**	**0**

Career History

Career Milestones

Club Debut:
vs Chelsea (A), L 2-1, Premiership
▶ 20.03.04

First Goal Scored for the Club:
vs Leicester (A), W 0-2, Premiership
▶ 10.04.04

Time Spent at the Club:
▶ 2.5 Seasons

Full International:
▶ Holland

Premiership Totals
92-06

Appearances	70
Goals	19
Assists	5
Yellow Cards	7
Red Cards	0

Clubs

Year	Club	Apps	Gls
04-06	Fulham	80	22
	FC Twente		

Off the Pitch

Age:

- John: 20 years, 7 months
- Team: 28 years, 11 months
- League: 26 years, 11 months

Height:

- John: 5'10"
- Team: 5'11"
- League: 5'11"

Weight:

- John: 12st 10lb
- Team: 13st 2lb
- League: 12st

20

Brian McBride
Forward

Season Review 05/06

Fulham's most consistent performer upfront this season and one of the team's hardest working players, Brian McBride's contribution went far beyond his impressive 10 goal haul.

Repeatedly running his socks off and dedicating as much time to his defensive, as well as his attacking duties, the former MLS All-Star repeatedly scored a number of match winning goals – perhaps most notably against Lincoln City in the Carling Cup in the 120th minute. A deserved winner of the Player of the Season award.

Player Details:

Date of Birth:	19.06.1972
Place of Birth:	Arlington Heights
Nationality:	American
Height:	6'
Weight:	12st 13lb
Foot:	Right

Player Performance 05/06

League Performance

Percentage of total possible time player was on pitch

⊖ position in league table at end of month

Month:	Aug	Sep	Oct	Nov	Dec	Jan	Feb	Mar	Apr	May	Total
	90%	91%	29% / 95%	99%	90%	94%	83%	100%	72%		85%
(position)	14	17	15	14	15	13	14	15	13	12	
Team Pts:	4/12	1/9	4/12	6/9	5/18	9/12	3/9	4/15	9/12	3/6	48/114
Team Gls F:	3	2	5	6	7	5	9	3	6	2	48
Team Gls A:	6	4	5	5	9	3	7	12	5	2	58
Total mins:	325	246	106	257	533	323	255	372	360	130	2,907
Starts (sub):	4	3	1 (3)	3	6	4	3	4 (1)	4	2	34 (4)
Goals:	2	1	0	2	3	0	1	0	0	0	9
Assists:	0	0	1	0	1	2	1	0	1	0	6
Clean sheets:	2	0	0	0	1	1	0	2	1	0	7
Cards (Y/R):	0	0	0	0	2	0	0	0	1	0	3

League Performance Totals

Goals

▶ McBride:	9
▷ Team-mates:	38
Total:	**47**
▶ own goals:	1

Assists

▶ McBride:	6
▷ Team-mates:	41
Total:	**47**

Cards

▶ McBride:	3
▷ Team-mates:	63
Total:	**66**

Cup Games

	Apps	Goals	Cards
European	0	0	0
FA Cup	0	0	0
Carling Cup	1	1	0
Total	**1**	**1**	**0**

Career History

Career Milestones

Club Debut:
vs Tottenham (H), W 2-1, Premiership
▶ **31.01.04**

Time Spent at the Club:
▶ **2.5 Seasons**

First Goal Scored for the Club:
vs Tottenham (H), W 2-1, Prem.
▶ **31.01.04**

Full International:
▶ **USA**

Premiership Totals

92-06
Appearances	93
Goals	23
Assists	13
Yellow Cards	3
Red Cards	0

Clubs

Year	Club	Apps	Gls
04-06	Fulham	95	24
03-03	Everton	8	4
00-01	Preston	11	1
	Columbus Crew		

Off the Pitch

Age:

- ▶ McBride: 33 years, 11 months
- ▷ Team: 28 years, 11 months
- | League: 26 years, 11 months

Height:
- ▶ McBride: 6'
- ▷ Team: 5'11"
- | League: 5'11"

Weight:
- ▶ McBride: 12st 13lb
- ▷ Team: 13st 2lb
- | League: 12st

Reserves Review 2005/06

2005/06 was a respectable debut season for Billy McKinlay and Ray Lewington as the new-look Reserve team management duo took Fulham to a solid eighth place finish in the Barclays Premier Reserve League South. However, in as much as results and final positions were important, the Whites were also able to take a lot of satisfaction from the development and emergence of a number of youngsters last season, making it an even more successful campaign.

The first game of the season dealt Fulham a short trip to face Watford and the Whites could not have asked for a better start as Rob Watkins lashed home the ball after Dean Leacock's header had slammed against the bar. Fulham also got their home record off to an impressive start at the end of the month as they overcame a youthful Ipswich side to record back-to-back victories with a 3-1 win. The side boasted a strong line-up on the evening with Helguson, Rosenior and John all making an appearance. Indeed, it was Helguson who opened the scoring before the Whites added two more for a comfortable victory.

Fulham's blistering start came to an unceremonious halt, however, with their second away game of the season at Norwich City. A much changed line-up was punished by the Canaries as Fulham's young Reserve side couldn't maintain their early season run, going down 3-0. Worse was to follow a week later on the road as Spurs ran out 2-0 winners.

The promise of Fulham's youngsters really appeared in the 2-1 victory over Southampton as a virtual Academy side, with the exception of the assured presence of Ian Pearce, dominated a talented Southampton. The goals came courtesy of New Zealand international Chris James and from Wayne Brown. This excellent result was followed up with a more workman-like performance against last season's Reserve League South Champions, Charlton Athletic; 0-0 the eventual outcome.

October saw Fulham pushing teams at the top end of the table. McKinlay and Lewington were utilising an exciting blend of youth and experience to great

effect and the results bore fruit when Rob Milsom, just 18, was drafted in to the First Team for Fulham's Cup victory over Lincoln City. Although the central midfielder didn't get on to the pitch the signs were there for Fulham's newest crop of youngsters. In the League, October started off well with victory over Capital rivals Crystal Palace. One appearance of note was that of new signing Phillippe Christanval, who continued his drive to full match fitness. On the day though it was TJ Moncur and Ismael Ehui who stole the plaudits bagging the crucial goals. Eight days later Fulham were pitted against a young but strong Arsenal side and, although they took the lead early on through Ismael Ehui, it was the Gunners who stormed back, hitting three goals past the returning Jaroslav Drobny.

With the 'keeping crisis continuing, late October and early November saw the inclusion of promising young Portuguese stopper Ricardo Batista for four straight games in the First Team squad. The Reserves picked up an impressive seven points from their three games in November, a 1-1 draw against Leicester City in torrid conditions was followed up by consecutive 3-0 victories against Portsmouth away and Coventry City at Motspur Park. The pick of those six goals was undoubtedly Michael Timlin's exocet at Fratton Park which propelled the Whites up to third in the table.

With the injury list increasing during the hectic festive period for the First Team, Chris Coleman turned to a Reserve ever present, Dean Leacock, to solve his dearth of defensive cover. Leacock played five games in a row, impressing management and fans alike with his no nonsense approach; the Reserve structure had once again shown its worth. December started with dissapointment but ended with the sweetest of victories to enable the Reserve side to see out 2005 in style. Fulham's visit to Southampton saw them sent packing with the biggest defeat of the season as they slumped to a 5-1 loss. However, joy followed despair as the Whites travelled to play bitter rivals Chelsea, a solitary Yinka Casal strike was the difference, giving Fulham the spoils; a scoreline that was eventually matched by the First Team of course! The turn of the New Year saw mixed results as, bizarrely, Fulham lost both of their home games - to Chelsea and Tottenham – while, sandwiched inbetween, a battling victory over Ipswich away was gained. Having beaten Chelsea in their last game, it was a disappointed Billy McKinlay who watched his side succumb 2-1 to the Blues. A slight boost was gained from the 2-0 win over Ipswich but defeat lay just around the corner once again, this time Spurs handed the Whites defeat with a comprehensive 4-0 victory over a much changed side.

On the International front Reserve regular, Michael Timlin, was bestowed with the proud honour of leading out the Ireland Under 21 side in the prestigious Madeira Cup. Captain Timlin eventually lifted the trophy as the men in green beat Portugal, with Ricardo Batista in goal, 2-1 in the Final.

Elsewhere, February was a difficult month for the Whites as they lost three straight games – all by a 1-0 scoreline – to West Ham, Charlton and Crystal Palace. It was a difficult month for Fulham, stripped totally of established players through injury and loan moves, the Whites had to rely totally on a very young squad. Some admirable performances were put in but the goals, and the luck, were missing.

One thing that McKinlay and Lewington's charges learnt last season was resilience and even when they faced defeat they were able to look with confidence to the next match and learn from past mistakes. They bounced back strongly at the beginning of March by beating an Arsenal side competing at the top of the League; it was a Mark Pembridge thunderbolt that separated the sides.

The April run-in saw mixed results for the Whites but some resolute performances from a side trying to better last season's ninth place finish. The first two fixtures of April brought two defeats, a 2-0 reverse against Coventry City and a 1-0 loss in the rearranged fixture against Watford.

With two games left in the season, Fulham had a tricky away match against West Ham before entertaining basement club, Norwich City. The West Ham encounter seemed to be going the way of the previous two games after Niclas Jensen had put through his own net. However, with stoppage time looming, Lewis Smith popped up to score a deserved equaliser for the Whites. The last game of the season saw Fulham looking to make amends for the early season defeat at Carrow Road. The Whites were 2-0 ahead within 15 minutes, playing some of their best football all season. Goals from Ismael Ehui, fresh back from a loan spell with Scunthorpe United, and Lino Goncalves sealed City's fate. Although there were no more goals to add to this fine display, it was a great way to finish a very satisfactory season and, with so many talented youngsters coming through the ranks, the future looks bright for the Whites.

Reserve Fixtures & Results 2005/06

AUGUST 2005			
Mon 15	Watford (A)		W 1-0
Thur 30	Ipswich (H)		W 3-1
SEPTEMBER 2005			
Mon 5	Norwich (A)		L 1-3
Mon 12	Tottenham (A)		L 0-2
Mon 19	Southampton (H)	MP	W 2-1
Tue 27	Charlton (H)	MP	D 0-0
OCTOBER 2005			
Mon 10	C. Palace (H)	MP	W 2-1
Tue 18	Arsenal (H)	MP	L 1-3
NOVEMBER 2005			
Wed 2	Leicester City (A)	-	D 1-1
Wed 16	Portsmouth (A)	--	W 3-0
Wed 23	Coventry City (H)	MP	W 3-0
DECEMBER 2005			
Tue 13	Southampton (A)	-	L 1-5
Mon 19	Chelsea (A)	-	W 1-0
JANUARY 2006			
Wed 4	Chelsea (H)	MP	L 1-2
Mon 16	Ipswich Town (A)	-	W 2-0
Tue 24	Tottenham (H)	MP	L 0-4
FEBRUARY 2006			
Tue 14th	West Ham (H)	MP	L 0-1
Mon 20	Charlton (A)	-	L 0-1
Mon 27	C. Palace (H)	-	L 0-1
MARCH 2006			
Mon 6	Arsenal (A)	-	W 1-0
Tue 14	Leicester C. (H)	MP	L 0-2
Mon 27	Portsmouth (H)	MP	W 1-0
APRIL 2006			
Mon 3	Coventry City (A)	-	L 0-2
Thur 6	Watford (H)	MP	L 0-1
Mon 10	West Ham (A)	-	D 1-1
Tue 18	Norwich (H)	MP	W 2-0

Fulham FC FA Premiership Reserve League Appearances and Goalscorers 2005/06

	FAPRL		CAREER	
	A	G	A	G
Ricardo Batista	3	-	10	-
Wayne Brown	10+3	3	10+3	3
Yinka Casal	9+4	3	9+4	3
Phillippe Christanval	6	-	6	-
Matthew Collins	2+1	-	13+6	1
Lance Cronin	1	-	1	-
Mark Crossley	3	-	15	-
Lewis Cumber	0+1	-	0+1	-
Mark Davidson	12+1	-	13+1	-
Jaroslav Drobny	4	-	4	-
Ismael Ehui	10+2	3	25+10	7
Simon Eliott	1	-	1	-
Ahmad Elrich	4	2	4	2
Liam Fontaine	1	-	26+2	-
Alain Goma	1	-	4+1	1
Lino Goncalves	1+7	1	1+7	1
Jefferson Gowland	0+6	-	0+6	-
Adam Green	11	1	65+7	3
Lee Hall	3+5	-	5+13	3
Heidar Helguson	2+1	3	2+1	3
Bradley Hudson-Odoi	7+7	-	7+7	-
Chris James	17+2	1	21+2	1
Claus Jensen	2	-	4	-
Niclas Jensen	1	-	1	-
Collins John	1	-	6	2
Zatyiah Knght	1	-	24	-
Dean Leacock	12	-	44+5	1
Sylvain Legwinski	11	-	13	-
Gary Mabbutt	2	-	2+2	-
Neale McDermott	4	-	37+10	6
Aouled Miguil	2+3	-	2+4	-
Robert Milsom	24	-	40+4	-
Tom Moncur	15+2	3	15+3	3
Nicholas Murtagh	8+2	-	8+2	-
Elliott Omozusi	14+1	-	17+1	-
Kazeem Orelaja	5+2	-	8+7	-
Andrew Ottley	6+1	-	6+1	-
Ian Pearce	12	-	19	-
Mark Pembridge	4	1	8	1
Darren Pratley	1	-	44+7	1
Zeshan Rehman	5	-	40+7	1
Liam Rosenior	6	-	37+1	1
Saheed Sankoh	10+2	1	10+5	1
Chris Sanna	1	-	1	-
Lewis Smith	0+6	1	0+6	1
Michael Timlin	9	1	38+13	5
Moritz Volz	1	-	1	-
Tony Warner	2	-	2	-
Robert Watkins	8+3	1	48+7	2
Adam Watts	11	-	18	-
Opponent o.g.		1		

Final Reserve League Table – South

		P	Home					Away						GD	Pts
			W	D	L	F	A	W	D	L	F	A		
1	Tottenham	26	10	1	2	25	5	10	2	1	32	8	+44	63
2	Southampton	26	8	2	3	27	9	8	1	4	23	17	+24	51
3	Arsenal	26	6	5	2	29	17	8	2	3	31	17	+26	49
4	Charlton Athletic	26	7	2	4	18	13	6	2	5	19	17	+7	43
5	Coventry City	26	9	0	4	21	10	4	1	8	9	26	-6	40
6	Chelsea	26	6	3	4	19	9	4	6	3	15	15	+10	39
7	Crystal Palace	26	7	2	4	28	15	4	3	6	16	26	+3	38
8	Fulham	26	6	1	6	15	16	5	2	6	11	16	-6	36
9	Ipswich Town	26	7	1	5	27	17	3	0	10	17	37	-10	31
10	West Ham	26	4	4	5	24	21	3	4	6	13	17	-1	29
11	Leicester City	26	3	5	5	22	30	4	2	7	16	27	-19	28
12	Watford	26	3	1	9	12	29	5	2	6	13	22	-26	27
13	Portsmouth	26	4	2	7	18	23	2	2	9	17	31	-19	22
14	Norwich City	26	3	3	7	12	25	1	3	9	7	21	-27	18

www.fulhamfc.com
Follow the action all the way to the net!

Academy

Academy Review 2005/06

By Head of Youth, John Murtough

John Murtough

Every season the Academy's approach is the same, to work as a support system for the First Team squad and management. In that capacity I think we have done well in providing the First Team with potential options throughout 2005/06.

We want to develop these young lads so that they are eventually in a position to be knocking on the door of the First Team squad. From the Under 9s all the way through to the Under 18s it is a case of preparing them for the numerous challenges that will face them and at Fulham we feel we give them a fantastic grounding to go on to achieve their football dreams.

I think the biggest plus point this season has been the amount of exposure that a number of our Academy boys have had by playing in the Reserves. What they have been able to learn from Billy McKinlay and Ray Lewington this term has been incredibly beneficial to their development. I think to get better as a player these lads have to be challenged every day in training and game situations. By receiving such a high level of coaching and having to perform to high standards every day we feel that they are getting just that challenge. Lads like Rob Milsom, Elliot Omozusi, Adam Watts and TJ Moncur are training with the Reserves on a consistent basis now and I think they have reaped the benefits from making that step up. They have been lucky to get an insight in to what is expected of them and, when players from the First Team drop down for whatever reason, then they can learn first hand, the requirements expected from them. As well as that, of course, they can also pick up good training habits

and techniques that the First Team lads have learnt during their careers.

As so many of the older Academy players have progressed into the Reserves this season, it has meant that we have been able to push some of our younger players into Paul Clement's Under 18 side to fill the gaps.

We don't tend to gauge the Academy on results, instead we look at performances and the development of the lads in the right direction. We need to be sure of individual development and constant improvement, as our ultimate goal is to offer quality players to the First Team management. However, in 2005/06 the Academy side itself finished a respectable sixth in the League, which we were satisfied with on the whole. There was a bit of a shaky start early on but it hasn't stopped the lads putting in some great performances during the season.

One of the real positives has been getting a lot of the Under 16 players involved in the Under 18s, players like Lewis Smith, Lewis Cumber, Joe Anderson, Max Noble. This will have given them an idea of what to expect when they make the permanent step up at the beginning of next season.

Although we exited the FA Youth Cup in the Fourth Round, a special mention should be made for one of our best performances of the season against Middlesbrough in the Third Round. Boro won the competition in 2004/05 and you can see how many members of that team have progressed this season in and around the First Team set-up at the Riverside. We played them up there and put in a fantastic team effort on the night to win. Goals from Bradley Hudson-Odoi and Andrew Ottley set us up with a Fourth Round tie against Burnley.

It was a big night for the lads but, unfortunately, they weren't able to emulate the performance of the previous round. Burnley were a strong and physical side and probably deserved to win on the night. The lads took a lot from being involved in the Cup, however, it's a great experience and another one of those building blocks that is so important to the development of their careers. This is the only knock out competition they play and they get a taste for the importance of a one off game, it also gives an insight into the importance of every game the First Team play. They are all must win games and the pressure for the three points from every game is immense.

This season has been a real success for the Academy in terms of the lads gaining International recognition. Elliot Omozusi has played a number of games for England Under 18s this season; most recently in a match against Slovenia where he equipped himself fantastically well in a right back role. An additional bonus in that game was that Adam Watts, a Second Year centre back, came on as a second half substitute. Since Christmas Adam has really pushed on, his attitude has been tremendous and I think this was his reward for the hard work he has put in.

Lino Goncalves has played a number of games for Portugal Under18s this season, and has come on well in the second half of the year. He has knuckled down in the last few months and, as a consequence, has matured as a player and this has seen him get more chances with the Reserves. He grabbed the opportunity of playing with the second string side and actually scored the second in the 2-0 victory over Norwich.

Lower down the age groups there have been call-ups to the International sides as well. Max Noble was called up for the Wales Under 17 side, Neil Etheridge and Callum Hawthorne, both goalkeepers, have also had a chance to show their ability at International level for England Under 16s and Wales Under 17s respectively.

A special mention should be made to TJ Moncur, Rob Milsom and Elliot Omozusi who were offered professional contracts in December. All these lads have shown their potential and it is a fitting reward for their efforts. Rob Milsom has been a shining light this season, he moved up from captaining the Academy side last season to establishing himself in the Reserves and was even made captain by Billy and Ray. He was also involved with the First Team squad for the Carling Cup game against Lincoln City and I think his displays should be the benchmark for the younger lads coming through.

We have taken on 10 new scholars for 2006/07, which is a large intake for us. These lads are really going to form the core of the Under 18 side next year, players like Lewis Smith, who incidentally scored having come on as a substitute against West Ham. The potential is there, it is now just a case of developing them in the hope that they will be ready to make the huge step into Reserve and then ultimately First Team action.

John Murtough, Head of Youth

FA Premier Academy League U18: Group A

		P	W	D	L	F	A	GD	Pts
1	Southampton U18	28	17	5	6	72	35	+37	56
2	Chelsea U18	28	17	5	6	45	21	+24	56
3	West Ham United U18	28	13	6	9	51	41	+10	45
4	Arsenal U18	28	11	5	12	47	47	0	38
5	Norwich City U18	28	10	6	12	31	34	-3	36
6	Fulham U18	28	9	5	14	30	46	-16	32
7	Ipswich Town U18	28	8	7	13	53	64	-11	31
8	Crystal Palace U18	28	8	6	14	54	59	-5	30
9	Charlton Athletic U18	28	8	4	16	36	52	-16	28
10	Millwall U18	28	6	8	14	30	52	-22	26

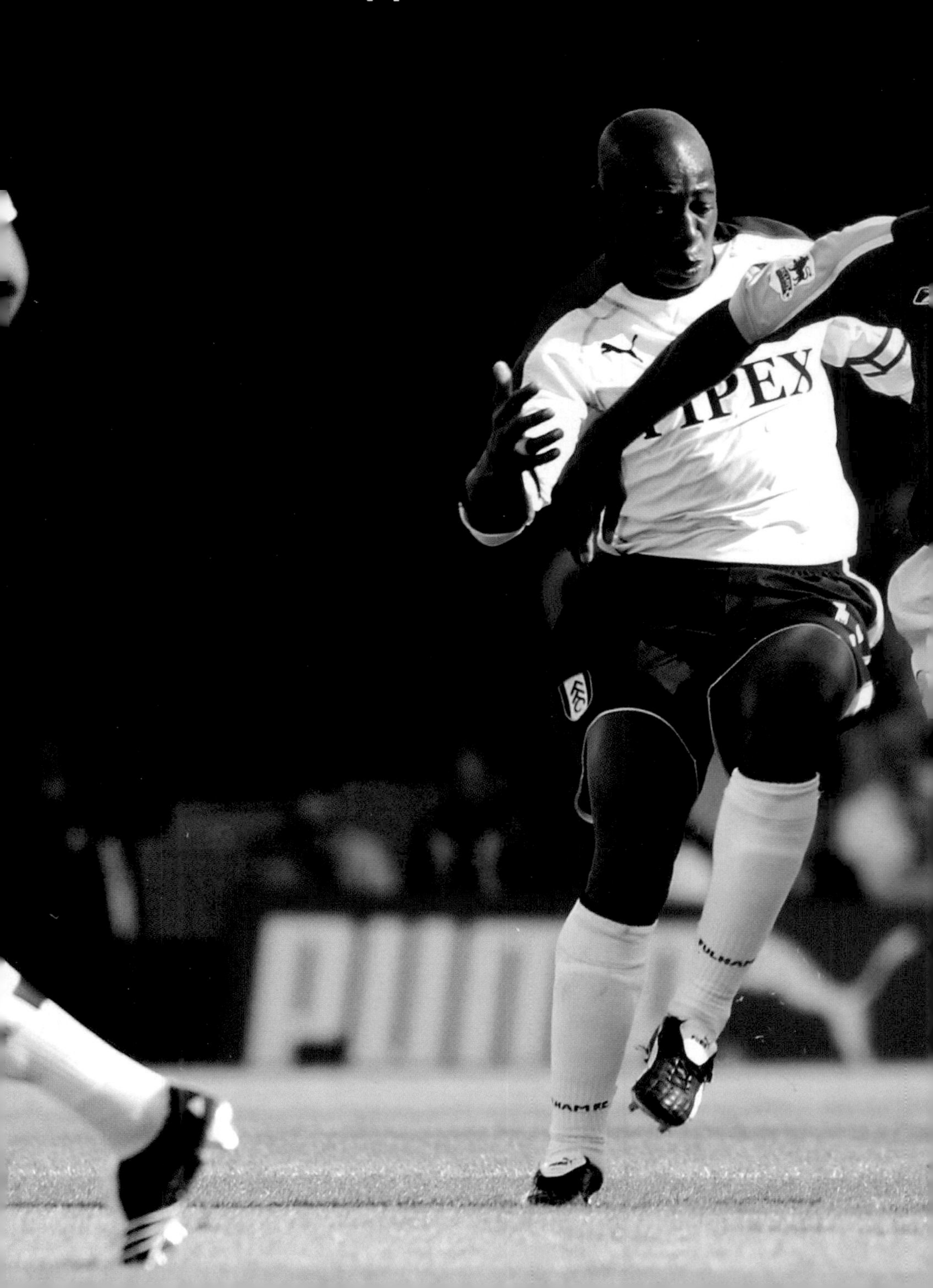
PIPEX
FULHAM

Arsenal

Nickname:	The Gunners	Telephone:	020 7704 4000
Manager:	Arsène Wenger	Ticket Office:	020 7704 4040
Chairman:	Peter Hill-Wood	Club Shop:	020 7704 4120
Website:	www.arsenal.com		

Season Review 05/06

It was a season of mixed fortunes for an Arsenal side that grew up enormously over the course of the campaign.

Reaching the Champions League Final was a terrific achievement, with defeat to Barcelona tempered by Thierry Henry's decision to stay at the club. Prior to that, the Gunners said goodbye to Highbury by clinching fourth place at the expense of Tottenham.

Points / Position

won drawn lost H home A away

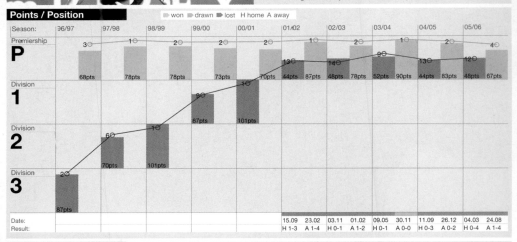

Season:	96/97	97/98	98/99	99/00	00/01	01/02	02/03	03/04	04/05	05/06
Premiership P	3	1	2	2	2	1	2	1	2	4
	68pts	78pts	78pts	73pts	70pts					67pts
Division 1				9	1	13	14	9	13	12
				67pts	101pts	44pts	87pts	48pts	78pts	52pts	90pts	44pts	83pts	48pts
Division 2		6	1							
		70pts	101pts							
Division 3	2									
	87pts									

Date:						15.09	23.02	03.11	01.02	09.05	30.11	11.09	26.12	04.03	24.08
Result:						H 1-3	A 1-4	H 0-1	A 1-2	H 0-1	A 0-0	H 0-3	A 0-2	H 0-4	A 1-4

Prem. Head-to-Head

Facts	O Fulham	Arsenal O
Games		
Points	1	28
Won	0	9
Drawn	1	1
Goals		
For	4	24
Clean Sheets	1	6
Shots on Target	31	79
Disciplinary		
Fouls	123	153
Yellow Cards	14	22
Red Cards	0	0

Goals by Area

O Fulham   O Arsenal

	8
3	16
0	0

Goals Scored by Period

1	2	0	1	0	0
0	15	30	45	60	75	90
4	2	5	2	4	7

Goals by Position

O Fulham   O Arsenal

	forward:	1		forward:	12
	midfield:	3		midfield:	7
	defence:	0		defence:	3
				own goals:	2

Average Attendance

► **20,357**

► 38,011

All-Time Records

Total Premiership Record	O Fulham	Arsenal O
Played	190	544
Points	236	1,013
Won	63	289
Drawn	47	146
Lost	80	109
For	229	911
Against	258	481
Players Used	60	113

All-Time Record vs Fulham						
Competition	Played	Won	Drawn	Lost	For	Against
League	38	27	6	5	86	45
FA Cup	1	1	0	0	3	2
League Cup	0	0	0	0	0	0
Other	0	0	0	0	0	0
Total	39	28	6	5	89	47

Arsenal

Emirates Stadium

Stadium History

The new 60,000-capacity Emirates Stadium has been designed to take Arsenal to a new level both on and off the pitch. Built at a total cost of £390 million, the state-of-the-art facility is located within walking distance of Highbury.

Though everything has been constructed on a grander scale, it is the increased dimensions of the playing surface that will perhaps take most getting used to. Players will now run out onto a pitch measuring 113m by 76m.

Seating Plan

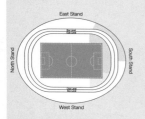

East Stand
North Stand
South Stand
West Stand

Capacity
60,000

- family area
- away fans
- disabled

Stadium Statistics 05/06

Highest attendance (Highbury)
38,359 vs Wigan Athletic 07.05.06

Lowest attendance (Highbury)
37,867 vs Fulham 24.08.05

Average attendance (Highbury)
38,184

How to Get There

Travel Information

Car parking
Parking near the ground is difficult; it is advised to park further away and get the Tube in.

Train & Tube
Arsenal (Piccadilly Line) is the nearest tube station, around 3 minutes walk from the ground. Finsbury Park (Victoria & Piccadilly Lines and GN rail) and Highbury & Islington (Victoria Line, North London Line and Great Northern Line) stations are around a 10 minute walk – these should be slightly less crowded. King's Cross is the main connecting station for overgound rail and many underground lines. From here you can travel to the ground via the Piccadilly Line (to Arsenal) or the Victoria Line (to Highbury & Islington). Alternatively, a short overground rail journey of one stop will take you to Finsbury Park station.

Area Map

Local Map

- A roads
- trunk roads
- route

Aston Villa

Nickname:	The Villans	Telephone:	0121 327 2299
Manager:	David O'Leary	Ticket Office:	0121 327 5353
Chairman:	Doug Ellis	Club Shop:	0121 326 1559
Website:	www.avfc.co.uk		

Season Review 05/06

It was a season of frustration at Villa Park, with many disillusioned fans calling for the heads of Manager David O'Leary and Chairman Doug Ellis.

A 3-0 Carling Cup hammering at League One side Doncaster was the low point of a campaign in which Villa finished just eight points and two places away from relegation to the Championship.

Points / Position

won ■ drawn ■ lost H home A away

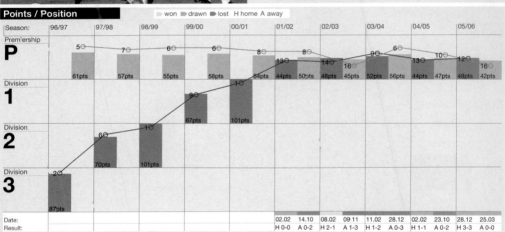

Season:	96/97	97/98	98/99	99/00	00/01	01/02	02/03	03/04	04/05	05/06
Premiership	5 (61pts)	7 (57pts)	6 (55pts)	6 (58pts)	8 (54pts)	8 (44pts)	14/16 (50pts/48pts)	9 (45pts/52pts/56pts)	6/13/10 (44pts/47pts)	12/16 (48pts/42pts)
Division 1				9 (67pts)	1 (101pts)					
Division 2		6 (70pts)	1 (101pts)							
Division 3	2 (87pts)									

Date:						02.02	14.10	08.02	09.11	11.02	28.12	02.02	23.10	28.12	25.03
Result:						H 0-0	A 0-2	H 2-1	A 1-3	H 1-2	A 0-3	H 1-1	A 0-2	H 3-3	A 0-0

Prem. Head-to-Head

Facts	O Fulham	Aston Villa O
Games		
Points	7	19
Won	1	5
Drawn	4	4
Goals		
For	8	17
Clean Sheets	2	5
Shots on Target	42	55
Disciplinary		
Fouls	114	145
Yellow Cards	9	17
Red Cards	1	0

Goals by Area

O Fulham   O Aston Villa

Goals by Position

O Fulham   O Aston Villa

	Fulham		Aston Villa
■ forward:	3	■ forward:	10
■ midfield:	4	■ midfield:	5
■ defence:	1	■ defence:	2

Goals Scored by Period

	0	15	30	45	60	75	90
	3	0	2	1	1	1	
	2	3	2	3	4	3	

Average Attendance

▶ 18,271

▶ 32,165

All-Time Records

Total Premiership Record	O Fulham	Aston Villa O
Played	190	544
Points	236	767
Won	63	203
Drawn	47	158
Lost	80	183
For	229	668
Against	258	632
Players Used	60	120

All-Time Record vs Fulham						
Competition	Played	Won	Drawn	Lost	For	Against
League	44	15	14	15	67	64
FA Cup	2	1	0	1	5	2
League Cup	2	1	1	0	3	1
Other	0	0	0	0	0	0
Total	**48**	**17**	**15**	**16**	**75**	**67**

Aston Villa

Villa Park

Stadium History

Opened in 1897, Villa Park has become an important venue for English football. The ground was used during Euro '96, and has hosted more FA Cup Semi-Finals than any other stadium.

The club recorded its highest Premiership attendance in the final game of the 1993/94 season against Liverpool. The Villa fans turned out to see the terracing in the Holte End for the last time, before it was replaced with seating. More recently, the Trinity Road stand has been redeveloped.

Seating Plan

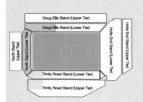

Capacity
42,573

▶ family area
▶ away fans
disabled

Stadium Statistics 05/06

Highest attendance
42,551 vs Liverpool 05.11.05

Lowest attendance
26,422 vs Manchester City 25.04.06

Average attendance
34,111

How to Get There

Travel Information

Car parking
Use local car parks – Aston Villa Events Centre Car Park or at the Aston Hall Road. You are advised not to park in the streets surrounding Villa Park.

Train
New Street Station, Birmingham City Centre – Take taxi to Villa Park (15 minutes away). Or from Birmingham New Street Station change for Aston or Witton.

Bus
From Birmingham City Centre: Catch West Midlands Travel Bus No.7 to Witton.

Area Map

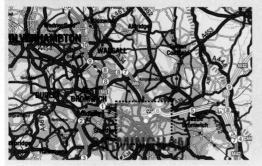

Local Map

A roads
trunk roads
route

157

Blackburn Rovers ○

Nickname:	Rovers	Telephone:	08701 113 232
Manager:	Mark Hughes	Ticket Office:	08701 123 456
Chairman:	John Williams	Club Shop:	0870 042 3875
Website:	www.rovers.co.uk		

Season Review 05/06

Mark Hughes guided Blackburn to sixth place and UEFA Cup qualification in his first full season in charge. Despite operating with a relatively small squad, the Ewood Park outfit also reached the last four in the Carling Cup.

Craig Bellamy proved to be a shrewd acquisition, whilst the likes of Steven Reid and Morten Gamst Pedersen really shone.

Points / Position

won ▶ drawn ▶ lost H home A away

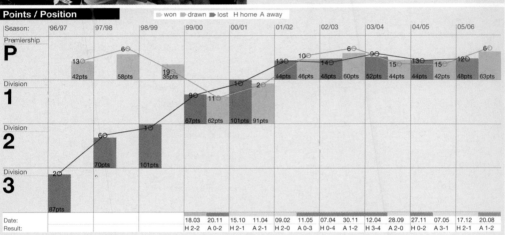

Season:	96/97	97/98	98/99	99/00	00/01	01/02	02/03	03/04	04/05	05/06
Premiership	13 / 42pts	6 / 58pts	19 / 35pts			13 / 44pts	10 / 46pts	6 / 48pts	9 / 60pts	15 / 52pts	13 / 44pts	15 / 42pts	12 / 48pts	6 / 63pts
Division 1				9 / 67pts	11 / 62pts	1 / 101pts	2 / 91pts			
Division 2		6 / 70pts	1 / 101pts							
Division 3	2 / 87pts									

Date:				18.03	20.11	15.10	11.04	09.02	11.05	07.04	30.11	12.04	28.09	27.11	07.05	17.12	20.08
Result:				H 2-2	A 0-2	H 2-1	A 2-1	H 2-0	A 0-3	H 0-4	A 1-2	H 3-4	A 2-0	H 0-2	A 3-1	H 2-1	A 1-2

Prem. Head-to-Head

Facts	○ Fulham	Blackburn ○
Games		
Points	12	18
Won	4	6
Drawn	0	0
Goals		
For	14	19
Clean Sheets	2	3
Shots on Target	51	64
Disciplinary		
Fouls	133	163
Yellow Cards	18	20
Red Cards	2	2

Goals by Area

○ Fulham   ○ Blackburn

Fulham: 3 / 9 / 1   Blackburn: 13 / 3

Goals by Position

○ Fulham   ○ Blackburn

Fulham		Blackburn	
▶ forward:	7	▶ forward:	9
▶ midfield:	7	▶ midfield:	6
▶ defence:	0	▶ defence:	2
		▶ own goals:	2

Goals Scored by Period

	0-15	15-30	30-45	45-60	60-75	75-90
Fulham	1	2	3	6	1	1
Blackburn	3	1	3	5	3	4

Average Attendance

▶ **17,364**

▶ **21,902**

All-Time Records

Total Premiership Record	○ Fulham	Blackburn ○
Played	190	468
Points	236	695
Won	63	190
Drawn	47	125
Lost	80	153
For	229	650
Against	258	553
Players Used	60	124

All-Time Record vs Fulham

Competition	Played	Won	Drawn	Lost	For	Against
League	66	28	16	22	104	95
FA Cup	7	2	3	2	7	6
League Cup	0	0	0	0	0	0
Other	0	0	0	0	0	0
Total	**73**	**30**	**19**	**24**	**111**	**101**

Ewood Park

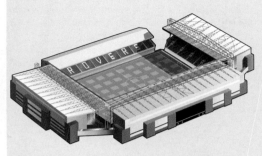

Stadium History

After occupying five different grounds in 15 years, Blackburn finally settled at Ewood Park in 1890. Laurence Cotton took over as chairman in 1905, and by 1913 he had spent thousands of pounds on completely redeveloping the stadium.

Sir Jack Walker followed in his footsteps towards the end of the century, providing the steel needed to build the 'Walkersteel Stand' in 1987, and then taking over as chairman in 1991. Investment followed both on and off the pitch, giving the town a facility to be proud of.

Seating Plan

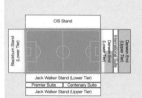

Capacity
31,367

- family area
- away fans
- disabled

Stadium Statistics 05/06

Highest attendance
29,142 vs Liverpool 16.04.06

Lowest attendance
16,953 vs Fulham 20.08.05

Average attendance
21,015

How to Get There

Travel Information

Car parking
Street parking close to Ewood Park is restricted, please use the car parks provided.

Train
Blackburn station is approximately a mile and a half from Ewood Park. Mill Hill station is approximately one mile away from the ground.

Bus
Services 3, 3A, 3B, 46, 346 all go from Blackburn to Darwen, Ewood Park is about a mile and a half along the journey.

Area Map

Local Map

- A roads
- trunk roads
- route

Bolton Wanderers

Nickname:	The Trotters		Telephone:	01204 673 673
Manager:	Sam Allardyce		Ticket Office:	0871 871 2932
Chairman:	Phil Gartside		Club Shop:	01204 673 650
Website:	www.bwfc.co.uk			

Season Review 05/06

It was another encouraging season for Bolton, with a top-half finish and European adventure to boot. Games against the likes of eventual winners Sevilla in the UEFA Cup only served to raise the profile of the club.

A disappointing end to the campaign was attributed in many quarters to the incessant speculation linking boss Sam Allardyce to the England job.

Points / Position

won · drawn · lost H home A away

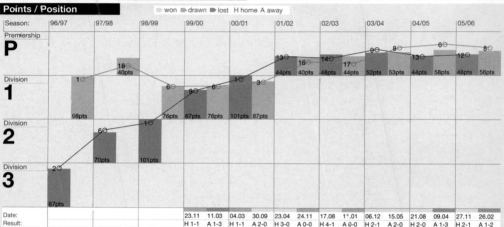

Season:	96/97	97/98	98/99	99/00	00/01	01/02	02/03	03/04	04/05	05/06

Premiership / P / Division 1 / Division 2 / Division 3

| Date: | | | | 23.11 | 11.03 | 04.03 | 30.09 | 23.04 | 24.11 | 17.08 | 11.01 | 06.12 | 15.05 | 21.08 | 09.04 | 27.11 | 26.02 |
| Result: | | | | H 1-1 | A 1-3 | H 1-1 | A 2-0 | H 3-0 | A 0-0 | H 4-1 | A 0-0 | H 2-1 | A 2-0 | H 2-0 | A 1-3 | H 2-1 | A 1-2 |

Prem. Head-to-Head

Facts	○ Fulham	Bolton ○
Games		
Points	20	8
Won	6	2
Drawn	2	2
Goals		
For	17	8
Clean Sheets	5	2
Shots on Target	54	45
Disciplinary		
Fouls	136	125
Yellow Cards	10	14
Red Cards	1	1

Goals by Area

○ Fulham ○ Bolton

3 2
11 6
3 0

Goals Scored by Period

3 2 4 1 2 5
0 15 30 45 60 75 90
2 0 2 2 1 1

Goals by Position

○ Fulham ○ Bolton

forward:	12	forward:	2
midfield:	5	midfield:	4
defence:	0	defence:	0
		own goals:	2

Average Attendance

▶ **17,229**
▶ **24,997**

All-Time Records

Total Premiership Record	○ Fulham	Bolton ○
Played	190	266
Points	236	320
Won	63	81
Drawn	47	77
Lost	80	108
For	229	311
Against	258	386
Players Used	60	109

All-Time Record vs Fulham

Competition	Played	Won	Drawn	Lost	For	Against
League	64	26	16	22	84	86
FA Cup	2	2	0	0	4	1
League Cup	3	1	2	0	6	5
Other	0	0	0	0	0	0
Total	**69**	**29**	**18**	**22**	**94**	**92**

Bolton Wanderers

Reebok Stadium

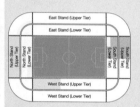

Stadium History

Though leaving Burnden Park at the end of the 1996-97 season was a wrench for Bolton fans, they were delighted to move into the purpose-built £35m Reebok Stadium. The first competitive match at their new home was a 0-0 draw against Everton on September 1st 1997.

Playing in such impressive surroundings has helped attract high-profile stars such as Jay-Jay Okocha and Fernando Hierro to the club, resulting in the ground playing host to European football for the first time in 2005/06.

Seating Plan

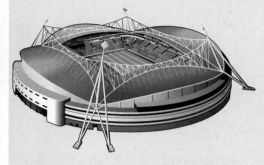

Capacity
28,723

▶ family area
▶ away fans
　 disabled

Stadium Statistics 05/06

Highest attendance
27,718 vs Manchester United 01.04.06

Lowest attendance
22,733 vs Middlesbrough 03.05.06

Average attendance
25,265

How to Get There

Travel Information

Car parking
2,800 spaces at the ground – costs £5. In the surrounding industrial estate cheaper parking options available.

Train
Horwich Parkway railway station serves the stadium, with regular trains from Bolton's main station. Horwich Parkway is only a few minutes walk from the stadium.

Area Map

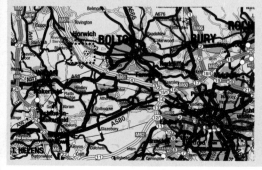

Local Map

▶ A roads
▶ trunk roads
　 route

Charlton Athletic °

Nickname: The Addicks
Manager: Iain Dowie
Chairman: Richard Murray
Website: www.cafc.co.uk

Telephone: 020 8333 4000
Ticket Office: 020 8333 4010
Club Shop: 020 8333 4035

Season Review 05/06

The 2005/06 season will be remembered at Charlton as the last in Alan Curbishley's 15-year reign. A great start saw the Addicks win five of their first six league games, but they ultimately slipped to a respectable 13th place.

Darren Bent arrived from Ipswich with a bang, firing in 18 goals to finish as the leading English marksman in the Premiership.

Points / Position

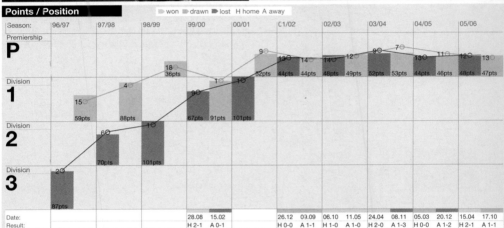

won drawn lost H home A away

Season:	96/97	97/98	98/99	99/00	00/01	01/02	02/03	03/04	04/05	05/06
Date:				28.08	15.02		26.12	03.09	06.10	11.05	24.04	08.11	05.03	20.12	15.04	17.10
Result:				H 2-1	A 0-1		H 0-0	A 1-1	H 1-0	A 1-0	H 2-0	A 1-3	H 0-0	A 1-2	H 2-1	A 1-1

Premiership: 9 (52pts), 13 (44pts), 14 (44pts), 14 (48pts), 12 (49pts), 9 (52pts), 7 (53pts), 13 (44pts), 11 (46pts), 12 (48pts), 13 (47pts)
Division 1: 18 (36pts), 15 (59pts), 4 (88pts), 9 (67pts), 1 (91pts), 1 (101pts)
Division 2: 6 (70pts), 4 (101pts)
Division 3: 2 (87pts)

Prem. Head-to-Head

Facts	O Fulham	Charlton O
Games		
Points	16	10
Won	4	2
Drawn	4	4
Goals		
For	10	8
Clean Sheets	5	2
Shots on Target	48	41
Disciplinary		
Fouls	129	148
Yellow Cards	17	14
Red Cards	0	1

Goals by Area

O Fulham   O Charlton

2	2	
5		6
2		0

Goals by Position

O Fulham   O Charlton

	Fulham	Charlton
forward:	4	3
midfield:	6	3
defence:	0	1
own goals:		1

Goals Scored by Period

	0	15	30	45	60	75	90
	1	3	3	0	1	2	
	1	2	1	1	2	1	

Average Attendance

17,339

25,064

All-Time Records

Total Premiership Record	O Fulham	Charlton O
Played	190	266
Points	236	327
Won	63	85
Drawn	47	72
Lost	80	109
For	229	308
Against	258	382
Players Used	60	74

All-Time Record vs Fulham

Competition	Played	Won	Drawn	Lost	For	Against
League	52	17	17	18	69	62
FA Cup	8	3	2	3	11	13
League Cup	2	1	1	0	5	3
Other	0	0	0	0	0	0
Total	62	21	20	21	85	78

The Valley

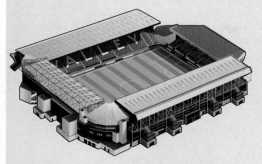

Stadium History

After years of ground sharing and financial problems, Charlton returned to The Valley on December 5th 1992. The move back home owed much to a crusade by supporters, who in 1989 undertook a massive clean-up operation to prepare the ground for redevelopment. It was another two years before planning permission was granted to build on the site, but things have gone from strength to strength since then. Work on the East Stand will raise the capacity to 30,900, with future redevelopment of the South Stand also a possibility.

Seating Plan

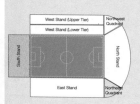

family area
away fans
disabled

Capacity
27,111

Stadium Statistics 05/06

Highest attendance
27,111 vs Chelsea 17.09.05

Lowest attendance
23,453 vs Wigan Athletic 20.08.05

Average attendance
26,195

How to Get There

Travel Information

Car parking
Parking around the ground is limited to 2 hours only.

Train
Connex runs train services to Charlton railway station, which is about a two minute walk from the stadium.

Bus
Extensive network. Routes include the 177, 180, 472, 161, 53 and 54. The M1 service provides an overland link to Charlton train station from the North Greenwich Tube station.

Area Map

Local Map

A roads
trunk roads
route

Chelsea ○

Nickname:	**The Blues**	Telephone:	**0870 300 2322**
Manager:	**José Mourinho**	Ticket Office:	**0870 300 2322**
Chairman:	**Bruce Buck**	Club Shop:	**0870 300 1212**
Website:	**www.chelseafc.com**		

Season Review 05/06

Chelsea dominated the league season from start to finish, though they were less successful in cup competitions. Barcelona, Liverpool and Charlton ensured that José Mourinho had to be content with the Premiership and Community Shield.

John Terry and Frank Lampard were once again star performers, whilst Joe Cole found the consistency to match his abundance of skill.

Points / Position

won drawn lost H home A away

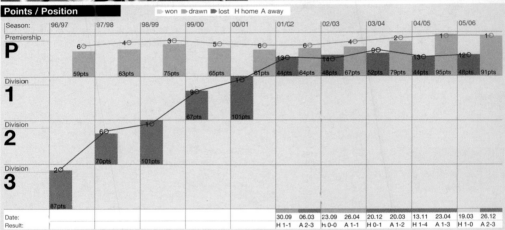

Season:	96/97	97/98	98/99	99/00	00/01	01/02	02/03	03/04	04/05	05/06

Premiership **P**: 6 (59pts), 4 (63pts), 3 (75pts), 5 (65pts), 6 (61pts), 6 (44pts / 64pts), 4 (48pts / 67pts), 2 (52pts / 79pts), 1 (44pts / 95pts), 1 (48pts / 91pts)

Division **1**: 1 (101pts), 9 (67pts)

Division **2**: 6 (70pts), 1 (101pts)

Division **3**: 2 (87pts)

Date:	30.09	06.03	23.09	26.04	20.12	20.03	13.11	23.04	19.03	26.12
Result:	H 1-1	A 2-3	H 0-0	A 1-1	H 0-1	A 1-2	H 1-4	A 1-3	H 1-0	A 2-3

Prem. Head-to-Head

Facts	○ Fulham	Chelsea ○
Games		
Points	6	21
Won	1	6
Drawn	3	3
Goals		
For	10	18
Clean Sheets	2	2
Shots on Target	39	73
Disciplinary		
Fouls	122	126
Yellow Cards	13	19
Red Cards	0	2

Goals by Area

○ Fulham ○ Chelsea

3
5 / 11
2 / 4

Goals Scored by Period

0	15	30	45	60	75	90
0	4	1	3	2	0	
2	5	3	1	4	3	

Goals by Position

○ Fulham ○ Chelsea

forward:	6	forward:	7
midfield:	4	midfield:	7
defence:	0	defence:	3
		own goals:	1

Average Attendance

▶ **19,861**

▶ **41,220**

All-Time Records

Total Premiership Record	○ Fulham	Chelsea ○
Played	190	544
Points	236	930
Won	63	261
Drawn	47	147
Lost	80	136
For	229	848
Against	258	556
Players Used	60	135

All-Time Record vs Fulham

Competition	Played	Won	Drawn	Lost	For	Against
League	54	32	15	7	93	51
FA Cup	6	2	2	2	7	7
League Cup	3	2	1	0	4	2
Other	0	0	0	0	0	0
Total	**63**	**36**	**18**	**9**	**104**	**60**

Stamford Bridge

Stadium History

Stamford Bridge is more than just a football stadium. Alongside it stands 'Chelsea Village', a complex housing, amongst other things, two hotels, five restaurants and a health club.

The ground was initially offered to Fulham, but their decision not to play there led to the formation of Chelsea in 1905. After years of uncertainty, chairman Ken Bates secured the future of the venue in 1992. Since then wholesale changes have taken place, with completion of the West Stand in 2001 resulting in a spectacular facility.

Seating Plan

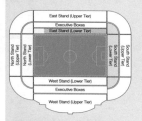

Capacity
42,449

▶ family area
▶ away fans
  disabled

Stadium Statistics 05/06

Highest attendance
42,321 vs Manchester City 25.03.06

Lowest attendance
40,652 vs Birmingham City 31.12.05

Average attendance
41,901

How to Get There

Travel Information

Train
West Brompton is a new station accessible from Clapham Junction.

Tube
The nearest tube station is Fulham Broadway on the District Line.

Bus
Bus numbers 14, 211, 11, 28, 295 and C4.

Area Map

Local Map

Everton

Everton

Nickname:	The Toffees	Telephone:	0870 442 1878
Manager:	David Moyes	Ticket Office:	0870 442 1878
Chairman:	Bill Kenwright	Club Shop:	0870 442 1878
Website:	www.evertonfc.com		

Season Review 05/06

Everton followed up the amazing form of their previous campaign with a mid-table finish. A return to European football brought only heartbreak, as the Toffees fell early in both the Champions League and UEFA Cup.

Nigel Martyn continued to defy his advancing years in goal, whilst James Beattie began to show what he could do at the other end.

Points / Position

won drawn lost H home A away

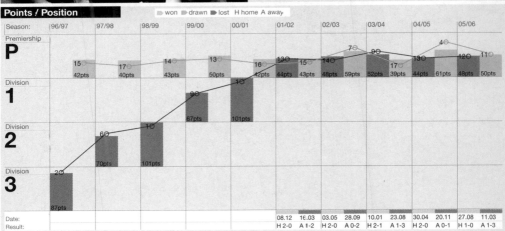

Season:	96/97	97/98	98/99	99/00	00/01	01/02	02/03	03/04	04/05	05/06
Premiership **P**	15 / 42pts	17 / 40pts	14 / 43pts	13 / 50pts	16 / 42pts	13 / 44pts, 15 / 43pts	14 / 48pts, 7 / 59pts	9 / 52pts, 17 / 39pts	4 / 13 / 44pts, 61pts	12 / 48pts, 11 / 50pts
Division **1**				9 / 67pts	1 / 101pts					
Division **2**		6 / 70pts	1 / 101pts							
Division **3**	2 / 87pts									

Date:						08.12	16.03	03.05	28.09	10.01	23.08	30.04	20.11	27.08	11.03
Result:						H 2-0	A 1-2	H 2-0	A 0-2	H 2-1	A 1-3	H 2-0	A 0-1	H 1-0	A 1-3

Prem. Head-to-Head

Facts	○ Fulham	Everton ○
Games		
Points	15	15
Won	5	5
Drawn	0	0
Goals		
For	12	12
Clean Sheets	4	2
Shots on Target	55	51
Disciplinary		
Fouls	159	153
Yellow Cards	19	15
Red Cards	2	3

Goals by Area
○ Fulham   ○ Everton

	4	
6		2
2		6

Goals by Position
○ Fulham   ○ Everton

Fulham	Everton
◗ forward: 8	◗ forward: 6
◗ midfield: 2	◗ midfield: 2
◗ defence: 0	◗ defence: 4
◗ own goals: 2	

Goals Scored by Period

1	0	5	4	1	1
0	15	30	45	60	75	90
4	1	4	1	1	1

Average Attendance

◗ **18,775**

▷ **35,578**

All-Time Records

Total Premiership Record	○ Fulham	Everton ○
Played	190	544
Points	236	677
Won	63	177
Drawn	47	146
Lost	80	221
For	229	651
Against	258	739
Players Used	60	132

All-Time Record vs Fulham

Competition	Played	Won	Drawn	Lost	For	Against
League	36	17	8	11	58	41
FA Cup	7	0	3	4	5	9
League Cup	0	0	0	0	0	0
Other	0	0	0	0	0	0
Total	43	17	11	15	63	50

Everton

Goodison Park

Stadium History

Opened in 1892, Goodison Park achieved the highest average gate during each of the Football League's first 10 seasons. Completion of the Gwladys Street End in 1938 meant that the stadium was the first to house double-decker stands on all four sides.

The Main Stand was replaced in 1970, and Everton were also one of the first clubs to introduce seating in all parts of the ground. Official website users voted a win against Bayern Munich in 1985 as the greatest ever game at the venue.

Seating Plan

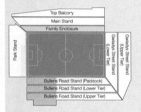

Top Balcony
Main Stand
Family Enclosure
Park Stand
Gwladys Street Stand (Lower Tier)
Gwladys Street Stand (Upper Tier)
Bullens Road Stand (Paddock)
Bullens Road Stand (Lower Tier)
Bullens Road Stand (Upper Tier)

Capacity
40,569

⬛ family area
⬛ away fans
⬛ disabled

Stadium Statistics 05/06

Highest attendance
40,158 vs Liverpool 28.12.05

Lowest attendance
34,333 vs Charlton Athletic 02.01.06

Average attendance
36,860

How to Get There

Travel Information

Train
Lime Street railway station is in the city centre, a couple of miles from Goodison Park. Kirkdale Railway Station is 30 minutes walk from the ground.

Bus
Buses from the city centre 19, 20, F1, F9, F2 and 30.

Area Map

Local Map

⬛ A roads
⬛ trunk roads
⬛ route

Liverpool °

Nickname: **The Reds** Telephone: **0151 263 2361**
Manager: **Rafael Benítez** Ticket Office: **0870 444 4949**
Chairman: **David Moores** Club Shop: **0870 066 7036**
Website: **www.liverpoolfc.tv**

Season Review 05/06

Liverpool added both the UEFA Super Cup and FA Cup to their trophy collection, with captain Steven Gerrard winning the PFA Player of the Year award.

A clear improvement was also evident in the league, as Rafael Benitez's team finished 24 points better off than 12 months previously. In fact, only Champions Chelsea could boast a better defensive record than the Merseysiders.

Points / Position

▶ won ▶ drawn ▶ lost   H home A away

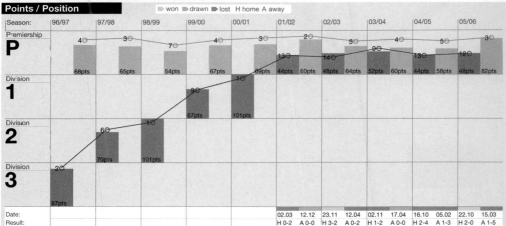

Season:	96/97	97/98	98/99	99/00	00/01	01/02	02/03	03/04	04/05	05/06
Premiership P	4 / 68pts	3 / 65pts	7 / 54pts	4 / 67pts	3 / 69pts	2 / 44pts 80pts	5 / 48pts 64pts	4 / 52pts 60pts	5 / 44pts 58pts	3 / 48pts 82pts
Division 1				9 / 67pts	1 / 101pts					
Division 2		6 / 70pts	1 / 101pts							
Division 3	2 / 87pts									

Date:						02.03	12.12	23.11	12.04	02.11	17.04	16.10	05.02	22.10	15.03
Result:						H 0-2	A 0-0	H 3-2	A 0-2	H 1-2	A 0-0	H 2-4	A 1-3	H 2-0	A 1-5

Prem. Head-to-Head

Facts	○ Fulham	Liverpool ○
Games		
Points	8	20
Won	2	6
Drawn	2	2
Goals		
For	10	20
Clean Sheets	3	4
Shots on Target	41	65
Disciplinary		
Fouls	130	120
Yellow Cards	18	10
Red Cards	2	1

Goals by Area
○ Fulham   ○ Liverpool

	2	6	
6			10
2			4

Goals by Position
○ Fulham   ○ Liverpool

▶ forward: 6   ▶ forward: 12
▶ midfield: 4   ▶ midfield: 4
▶ defence: 0   ▶ defence: 2
  ▶ own goals: 2

Goals Scored by Period

1	5	2	0	1	1
0	15	30	45	60	75	90
2	2	2	2	4	8

Average Attendance

▶ **20,259**
▶ **41,430**

All-Time Records

Total Premiership Record	○ Fulham	Liverpool ○
Played	190	544
Points	236	931
Won	63	265
Drawn	47	136
Lost	80	143
For	229	868
Against	258	552
Players Used	60	108

All-Time Record vs Fulham

Competition	Played	Won	Drawn	Lost	For	Against
League	38	21	11	6	74	40
FA Cup	4	1	1	2	5	9
League Cup	9	7	2	0	30	6
Other	0	0	0	0	0	0
Total	**51**	**29**	**14**	**8**	**109**	**55**

Anfield

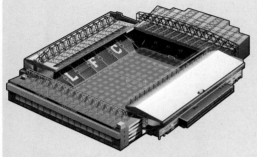

Stadium History

Anfield has been around longer than Liverpool Football Club, originally playing host to Everton. A dispute over rent saw the Toffees move out in 1892, leading to the formation of Liverpool. By 1906 the ground had taken shape, with stands on either side of the pitch and terracing at both ends.

Success on the pitch was matched by improvements to the stadium, which was made all-seater in 1994. To this day, 'The Kop' remains one of the best known places in world football.

Seating Plan

Capacity
45,362

- family area
- away fans
- disabled

Stadium Statistics 05/06

Highest attendance
44,983 vs Tottenham Hotspur 14.01.06

Lowest attendance
42,293 vs Fulham 15.03.06

Average attendance
44,236

How to Get There

Travel Information

Car parking
Limited parking. Only a small number of privately operated car parks are available in the area. Coaches should contact Merseyside Police. Contact Ian Kidd on 0151 777 4766.

Train
Lime Street railway station is in the city centre, two miles from Anfield. Kirkdale Railway Station is 30 minutes walk from the ground.

Area Map

Local Map

A roads
trunk roads
route

Manchester City

★★★

Nickname:	The Citizens	Telephone:	0870 062 1894
Manager:	Stuart Pearce	Ticket Office:	0870 062 1894
Chairman:	John Wardle	Club Shop:	0870 062 1894
Website:	www.mcfc.co.uk		

Season Review 05/06

It was largely a season of disappointment for the blue half of Manchester. Stuart Pearce's team made an encouraging start to the campaign, but lost nine of their final 10 games to slide down the table.

There was still reason for optimism, however, with the continued emergence of talented youngsters such as Micah Richards and Stephen Ireland.

Points / Position

won drawn lost H home A away

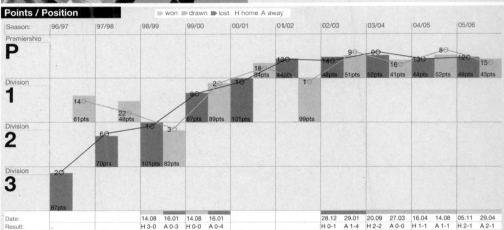

Season:	96/97	97/98	98/99	99/00	00/01	01/02	02/03	03/04	04/05	05/06

Date:			14.08	16.01	14.08	16.01				28.12	29.01	20.09	27.03	16.04	14.08	05.11	29.04
Result:			H 3-0	A 0-3	H 0-0	A 0-4				H 0-1	A 1-4	H 2-2	A 0-0	H 1-1	A 1-1	H 2-1	A 2-1

Prem. Head-to-Head

Facts	Fulham	Man City
Games		
Points	10	10
Won	2	2
Drawn	4	4
Goals		
For	9	11
Clean Sheets	1	2
Shots on Target	33	34
Disciplinary		
Fouls	91	122
Yellow Cards	9	15
Red Cards	0	0

Goals by Area
Fulham   Man City

	2	
6		8
2		1

Goals Scored by Period

2	0	1	1	1	4
0	15	30	45	60	75	90
0	4	0	2	3	2

Goals by Position
Fulham   Man City

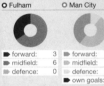

forward:	3	forward:	4
midfield:	6	midfield:	5
defence:	0	defence:	1
		own goals:	1

Average Attendance

19,524

41,234

All-Time Records

Total Premiership Record	Fulham	Man City
Played	190	354
Points	236	410
Won	63	103
Drawn	47	101
Lost	80	150
For	229	413
Against	258	482
Players Used	60	126

All-Time Record vs Fulham

Competition	Played	Won	Drawn	Lost	For	Against
League	42	19	10	13	87	68
FA Cup	3	1	1	1	4	4
League Cup	1	0	0	1	2	3
Other	0	0	0	0	0	0
Total	46	20	11	15	93	75

Manchester City

City of Manchester Stadium

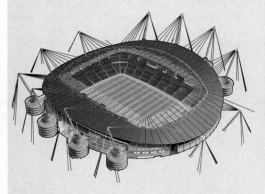

Stadium History

Built to host the 2002 Commonwealth Games, the City of Manchester Stadium was quickly transformed into the home of Manchester City. Having removed the athletics track, the pitch was lowered to make room for an extra tier of seating, while a permanent North Stand was also constructed. A crowd of 46,287 witnessed the first competitive game at the new venue, a 1-1 draw with Portsmouth on August 23rd 2003.

The site also offers 2,000 parking spaces, as well as several restaurants and function rooms.

Seating Plan

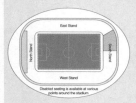

Disabled seating is available at various points around the stadium

Capacity
48,000

▶ family area
▶ away fans
▷ disabled

Stadium Statistics 05/06

Highest attendance
47,192 vs Manchester United 14.01.06

Lowest attendance
40,256 vs Middlesbrough 02.04.06

Average attendance
42,856

How to Get There

Travel Information

Train

Manchester Piccadilly Railway Station is about a mile away from the stadium, which is about a 20 minute walk away. There is currently no Metrolink service to the stadium, so either jump in a taxi or take a bus (numbers 53, 54, 185, 186, 216, 217, 230, 231, 232, 233, 234, 235, 236, 237,X36 and X37 go to Sportcity) from Piccadilly Gardens (which is a five minute walk from the railway station going straight down the approach from it, look for bus stops situated near to the 'Moon Under Water' pub).

Area Map

Local Map

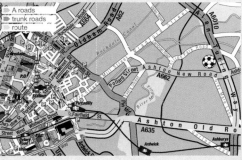

A roads
trunk roads
route

Manchester United

Nickname:	The Red Devils	Telephone:	0870 442 1994
Manager:	Sir Alex Ferguson	Ticket Office:	0870 442 1994
Owner:	Malcolm Glazer	Club Shop:	0870 111 8107
Website:	www.manutd.com		

Season Review 05/06

A Carling Cup triumph and second place in the Premiership would be seen as success at most clubs, but not at Manchester United. In fact, Sir Alex Ferguson's charges never genuinely threatened Chelsea's grip on the title.

The performances of Wayne Rooney continued to win him admirers across the globe. Off the pitch, the club was contentiously taken over by the Glazer family.

Points / Position

won ▶ drawn ▶ lost H home A away

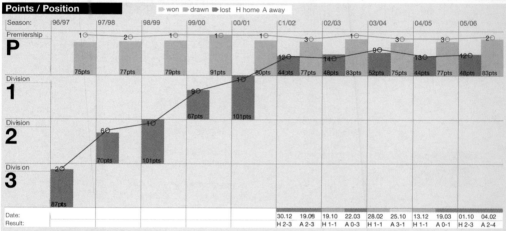

Season:	96/97	97/98	98/99	99/00	00/01	01/02	02/03	03/04	04/05	05/06
Premiership P	1	2	1	1	1	3	1	3	3	2
	75pts	77pts	79pts	91pts	80pts	44pts 77pts	48pts 83pts	52pts 75pts	44pts 77pts	48pts 83pts
Division 1				9	1					
				67pts	101pts					
Division 2		6	1							
		70pts	101pts							
Division 3	2									
	87pts									

Date:						30.12	19.05	19.10	22.03	28.02	25.10	13.12	19.03	01.10	04.02
Result:						H 2-3	A 2-3	H 1-1	A 0-3	H 1-1	A 3-1	H 1-1	A 0-1	H 2-3	A 2-4

Prem. Head-to-Head

Facts	○ Fulham	Man Utd ○
Games		
Points	6	21
Won	1	6
Drawn	3	3
Goals		
For	14	21
Clean Sheets	0	2
Shots on Target	55	82
Disciplinary		
Fouls	147	124
Yellow Cards	13	20
Red Cards	0	0

Goals by Area

○ Fulham   ○ Man Utd

	4		2	
7				15
3				4

Goals Scored by Period

3	2	3	1	2	3
0	15	30	45	60	75	90
4	4	6	3	2	2

Goals by Position

○ Fulham   ○ Man Utd

▶ forward:	7	▶ forward:	13
▶ midfield:	7	▶ midfield:	7
▶ defence:	0	▶ defence:	0
		▶ own goals:	1

Average Attendance

▶ **20,274**

▶ **67,754**

All-Time Records

Total Premiership Record	○ Fulham	Man Utd ○
Played	190	544
Points	236	1,143
Won	63	339
Drawn	47	126
Lost	80	79
For	229	1,057
Against	258	489
Players Used	60	99

All-Time Record vs Fulham

Competition	Played	Won	Drawn	Lost	For	Against
League	52	29	13	10	99	61
FA Cup	9	6	2	1	17	11
League Cup	0	0	0	0	0	0
Other	0	0	0	0	0	0
Total	61	35	15	11	116	72

Manchester United

Old Trafford

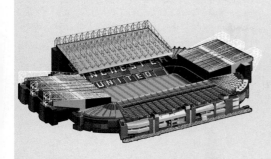

Stadium History

Currently the biggest stadium in English football, Old Trafford has grown in tandem with the success achieved on the pitch by Manchester United. Work to raise the capacity to 45,000 was completed in 1994, but it soon became apparent that more seating was required.

Since then the club has gone from strength to strength, attracting supporters from all over the world. In order to cope with an ever-increasing demand for tickets, the capacity was raised to just in excess of 73,000 during the 2005/06 season.

Seating Plan

Capacity
76,000

- family area
- away fans
- disabled

Stadium Statistics 05/06

Highest attendance
73,006 vs Charlton Athletic 07.05.06

Lowest attendance
67,684 vs Portsmouth 03.12.05

Average attendance
68,764

How to Get There

Travel Information

Car parking
No on street parking allowed, residential parking permits only.

Train
Train service from Piccadilly/Oxford Road Stations to the ground.

Metrolink
Nearest Metrolink stations are Old Trafford and Trafford Bar.

Bus
Regular service from Manchester Chorlton Street Station.

Area Map

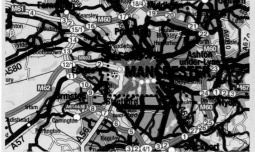

Local Map

- A roads
- trunk roads
- route

Middlesbrough ○

Nickname:	Boro	Telephone:	0870 421 1986
Manager:	Gareth Southgate	Ticket Office:	0870 421 1986
Chairman:	Steve Gibson	Club Shop:	0870 421 1986
Website:	www.mfc.co.uk		

Season Review 05/06

An unforgettable season at the Riverside saw Middlesbrough struggle in the league but thrive in cup competitions. Victories against FC Basle and Steaua Bucharest resulted in a UEFA Cup Final appearance, whilst an FA Cup Semi-Final was also reached.

Following weeks of intense speculation, manager Steve McClaren was finally unveiled as the successor to Sven-Goran Eriksson as England boss in May.

Points / Position

won ■ drawn ■ lost H home A away

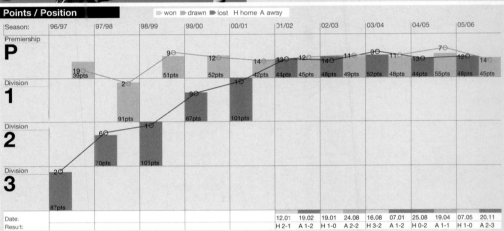

Season:	96/97	97/98	98/99	99/00	00/01	01/02	02/03	03/04	04/05	05/06

Premiership P — 19 39pts, 9, 12 51pts, 14 52pts, 13 42pts, 12 44pts, 14 45pts, 11 48pts, 9 49pts, 11 52pts, 13 48pts, 7 44pts, 12 55pts, 14 48pts, 45pts

Division 1 — 2, 9 91pts, 1 67pts, 101pts

Division 2 — 6, 1, 70pts, 101pts

Division 3 — 2, 87pts

Date:						12.01	19.02	19.01	24.08	16.08	07.01	25.08	19.04	07.05	20.11
Result:						H 2-1	A 1-2	H 1-0	A 2-2	H 3-2	A 1-2	H 0-2	A 1-1	H 1-0	A 2-3

Prem. Head-to-Head

Facts	○ Fulham	Boro ○
Games		
Points	14	14
Won	4	4
Drawn	2	2
Goals		
For	14	15
Clean Sheets	2	1
Shots on Target	53	51
Disciplinary		
Fouls	133	126
Yellow Cards	9	13
Red Cards	0	0

Goals by Area
○ Fulham   ○ Middlesbrough

6

8   7

0   2

Goals Scored by Period

1	1	3	2	2	5
0	15	30	45	60	75	90
3	1	1	2	2	6

Goals by Position
○ Fulham   ○ Middlesbrough

forward:	10	forward:	11
midfield:	4	midfield:	3
defence:	0	defence:	1

Average Attendance

▶ **17,593**

▶ 28,188

All-Time Records

Total Premiership Record	○ Fulham	Boro ○
Played	190	422
Points	236	516
Won	63	131
Drawn	47	123
Lost	80	168
For	229	506
Against	258	582
Players Used	60	132

All-Time Record vs Fulham

Competition	Played	Won	Drawn	Lost	For	Against
League	50	23	7	20	84	69
FA Cup	0	0	0	0	0	0
League Cup	0	0	0	0	0	0
Other	0	0	0	0	0	0
Total	50	23	7	20	84	69

Riverside Stadium

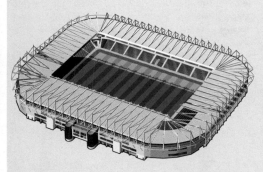

Stadium History

Constructed in just 32 weeks, the Riverside Stadium breathed new life into Middlesbrough. Chelsea were beaten 2-0 on August 26th 1995 in the first competitive match at the new ground, following the move from Ayresome Park.

The fans had been responsible for naming their new home, and saw the capacity increase by 5,000 in the summer of 1998. When it was opened, the stadium was the first in the country to be built in line with the safety requirements set out in the Taylor report.

Seating Plan

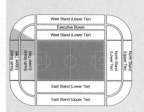

Capacity
35,100

family area
away fans
disabled

Stadium Statistics 05/06

Highest attendance
31,908 vs Liverpool 13.08.05

Lowest attendance
25,971 vs Bolton Wanderers 26.03.06

Average attendance
28,463

How to Get There

Travel Information

Train
Middlesbrough station is located on Albert Road, ten minutes walk from the ground.

Bus
From town centre.

Area Map

Local Map

Newcastle United

Nickname:	The Magpies	Telephone:	0191 201 8400
Manager:	Glenn Roeder	Ticket Office:	0191 261 1571
Chairman:	Freddy Shepherd	Club Shop:	0191 201 8426
Website:	www.nufc.co.uk		

Season Review 05/06

Glenn Roeder was the toast of Tyneside as he led Newcastle from a position of adversity to InterToto Cup qualification. The team collected 32 points from 15 games under the former West Ham boss, thus earning him the job on a permanent basis.

Alan Shearer finally hung up his boots, bowing out of competitive action with a goal in the 4-1 triumph at arch-rivals Sunderland.

Points / Position

won drawn lost H home A away

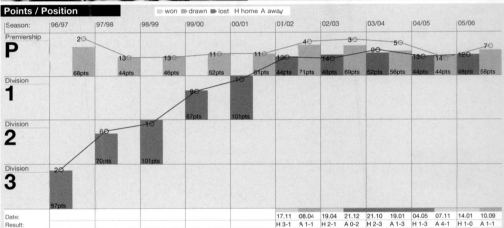

Season:	96/97	97/98	98/99	99/00	00/01	01/02	02/03	03/04	04/05	05/06

Premiership P — 2 (68pts), 13 (44pts), 13 (46pts), 11 (52pts), 11 (51pts), 4 (71pts), 3 (69pts), 5 (56pts), 14 (44pts), 7 (58pts)

Division 1 — 9 (67pts), 1 (101pts), 13 (48pts), 9 (52pts), 13 (44pts), 12 (48pts)

Division 2 — 6 (70pts), 1 (101pts)

Division 3 — 2 (97pts)

Date:					17.11	08.04	19.04	21.12	21.10	19.01	04.05	07.11	14.01	10.09
Result:					H 3-1	A 1-1	H 2-1	A 0-2	H 2-3	A 1-3	H 1-3	A 4-1	H 1-0	A 1-1

Prem. Head-to-Head

Facts	○ Fulham	Newcastle ○
Games		
Points	14	14
Won	4	4
Drawn	2	2
Goals		
For	16	16
Clean Sheets	1	1
Shots on Target	50	74
Disciplinary		
Fouls	118	138
Yellow Cards	10	16
Red Cards	1	2

Goals by Area

○ Fulham ○ Newcastle

5, 9, 8, 5, 3

Goals Scored by Period

0	15	30	45	60	75	90
3	3	0	0	6	4	
3	2	2	3	4	2	

Goals by Position

○ Fulham ○ Newcastle

	Fulham		Newcastle
▶ forward:	7	▶ forward:	7
▶ midfield:	9	▶ midfield:	8
▶ defence:	0	▶ defence:	1

Average Attendance

▶ 19,308

▶ 51,005

All-Time Records

Total Premiership Record	○ Fulham	Newcastle ○
Played	190	502
Points	236	786
Won	63	218
Drawn	47	132
Lost	80	152
For	229	761
Against	258	606
Players Used	60	125

All-Time Record vs Fulham

Competition	Played	Won	Drawn	Lost	For	Against
League	48	17	12	19	83	83
FA Cup	4	4	0	0	20	4
League Cup	3	1	0	2	4	4
Other	0	0	0	0	0	0
Total	**55**	**22**	**12**	**21**	**107**	**91**

St James' Park

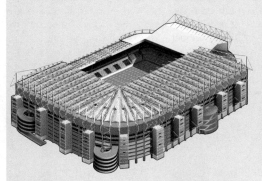

Stadium History

The oldest stadium in the North East, St James' Park houses some of the most devoted supporters in the country. A capacity in excess of 50,000 is still not enough to meet the demand for tickets.

The 1990s saw plans for a new £65m stadium shelved, as the club opted instead to spend £40m on upgrading the Sir John Hall and Milburn stands. The work was completed in August 2000, leaving Newcastle with a fantastic arena and visiting fans reaching for their binoculars.

Seating Plan

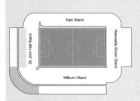

Capacity
52,327

- family area
- away fans
- disabled

Stadium Statistics 05/06

Highest attendance
52,327 vs Manchester United 28.08.05

Lowest attendance
50,451 vs Charlton Athletic 22.02.06

Average attendance
52,032

How to Get There

Travel Information

Train
Newcastle is on the East Coast Main Line route, served by GNR and Virgin railways.

Bus
Gallowgate or Haymarket bus stations.

Metro
St James Metro is adjacent to the ground. Haymarket, Monument and Central Station are all a very short walk from St James' Park.

Area Map

Local Map

- A roads
- trunk roads
- route

Portsmouth

Nickname:	Pompey	Telephone:	02392 731 204
Manager:	Harry Redknapp	Ticket Office:	0871 230 1898
Chairman:	Milan Mandaric	Club Shop:	02392 778 552
Website:	www.pompeyfc.co.uk		

Season Review 05/06

Portsmouth seemed destined to be relegated for much of the season, but were saved by a combination of Alexandre Gaydamak's millions and the nous of returning manager Harry Redknapp.

Having picked up just 18 points from their first 28 games, an astonishing turnaround in form saw the South Coast club collect a further 20 to beat the drop with a match to spare.

Points / Position

won drawn lost H home A away

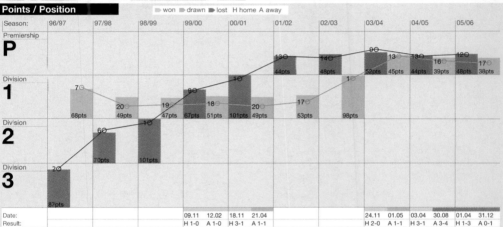

Season:	96/97	97/98	98/99	99/00	00/01	01/02	02/03	03/04	04/05	05/06

Premiership P — 13 44pts, 14 48pts, 9 52pts, 13 45pts, 13 44pts, 16 39pts, 12 48pts, 17 38pts

Division 1 — 7 68pts, 20 49pts, 19 47pts, 9 67pts, 10 51pts, 18 101pts, 20 49pts, 17 53pts, 1 98pts

Division 2 — 6 70pts, 1 101pts

Division 3 — 2 87pts

| Date: | | | | 09.11 | 12.02 | 18.11 | 21.04 | | | 24.11 | 01.05 | 03.04 | 30.08 | 01.04 | 31.12 |
| Result: | | | | H 1-0 | A 1-0 | H 3-1 | A 1-1 | | | H 2-0 | A 1-1 | H 3-1 | A 3-4 | H 1-3 | A 0-1 |

Prem. Head-to-Head

Facts	○ Fulham	Portsmouth ○
Games		
Points	7	10
Won	2	3
Drawn	1	1
Goals		
For	10	10
Clean Sheets	1	1
Shots on Target	31	39
Disciplinary		
Fouls	69	84
Yellow Cards	13	10
Red Cards	1	1

Goals by Area

○ Fulham   ○ Portsmouth

6 — 1 — 7
2 — 2

Goals Scored by Period

	0	15	30	45	60	75	90
	1	1	3	0	2	3	
	1	4	2	0	2	1	

Goals by Position

○ Fulham   ○ Portsmouth

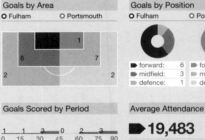

	Fulham		Portsmouth
forward:	6	forward:	6
midfield:	3	midfield:	4
defence:	1	defence:	0

Average Attendance

➤ **19,483**
➤ 19,631

All-Time Records

Total Premiership Record	○ Fulham	Portsmouth ○
Played	190	114
Points	236	122
Won	63	32
Drawn	47	26
Lost	80	56
For	229	127
Against	258	175
Players Used	60	64

All-Time Record vs Fulham

Competition	Played	Won	Drawn	Lost	For	Against
League	44	20	14	10	70	50
FA Cup	3	2	1	0	3	0
League Cup	0	0	0	0	0	0
Other	0	0	0	0	0	0
Total	47	22	15	10	73	50

Portsmouth

Fratton Park

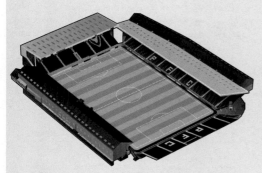

Stadium History

What Fratton Park lacks in terms of numbers, it more than makes up for by way of atmosphere. The ground was the first to host a league match under floodlights, when Newcastle were the visitors in 1956.

Attempts to find a new home during the late 1980s and early 1990s were unsuccessful, with the conversion to an all-seater stadium in 1997 resulting in a reduced capacity. Plans are currently in place to rotate the pitch and build some new and improved stands.

Seating Plan

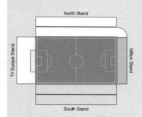

Capacity
20,288

- family area
- away fans
- disabled

Stadium Statistics 05/06

Highest attendance
20,240 vs Liverpool 07.05.06

Lowest attendance
19,030 vs Charlton Athletic 22.10.05

Average attendance
19,839

How to Get There

Travel Information

Car parking
There is a large car park behind the TY Europe Stand which costs £5. Otherwise street parking.

Train
Once at Fratton Station continue down Goldsmiths Avenue for approximately half a mile and Frogmore Road is on your left. Fratton Park is situated at the bottom.

Bus
Numbers 13, 17 and 18.

Area Map

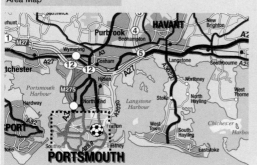

Local Map

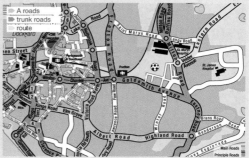

Reading

Nickname:	**The Royals**
Manager:	**Steve Coppell**
Chairman:	**John Madejski**
Website:	**www.readingfc.co.uk**

Telephone:	**0118 968 1100**
Ticket Office:	**0870 999 1871**
Club Shop:	**0118 968 1234**

Season Review 05/06

Reading were an unstoppable force as they blazed a trail towards promotion to the top-flight. The 106 points amassed by the Royals were a record for the second-tier of English football, whilst 99 goals were also scored along the way.

Manager Steve Coppell engendered a real spirit of togetherness amongst his troops, with no one player more important than the team.

Points / Position

won drawn lost H home A away

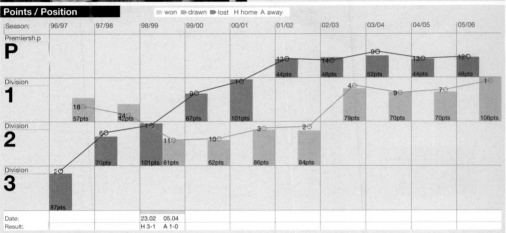

Date:			23.02	05.04					
Result:			H 3-1	A 1-0					

Prem. Head-to-Head

Facts	OFulham	Reading O
Games		
Points	0	0
Won	0	0
Drawn	0	0
Goals		
For	0	0
Clean Sheets	0	0
Shots on Target	0	0
Disciplinary		
Fouls	0	0
Yellow Cards	0	0
Red Cards	0	0

Goals by Area

O Fulham   O Reading

0	0
0	0
0	0

Goals by Position

O Fulham   O Reading

	Fulham		Reading
forward:	0	forward:	0
midfield:	0	midfield:	0
defence:	0	defence:	0

Goals Scored by Period

0	0	0	0	0	0
0	15	30	45	60	75	90
0	0	0	0	0	0

Average Attendance

All-Time Records

Total Premiership Record	OFulham	Reading O
Played	190	0
Points	236	0
Won	63	0
Drawn	47	0
Lost	80	0
For	229	0
Against	258	0
Players Used	60	0

All-Time Record vs Fulham

Competition	Played	Won	Drawn	Lost	For	Against
League	28	10	7	11	33	37
FA Cup	4	0	2	2	1	3
League Cup	5	1	3	1	6	5
Other	0	0	0	0	0	0
Total	**37**	**11**	**12**	**14**	**40**	**45**

Madejski Stadium

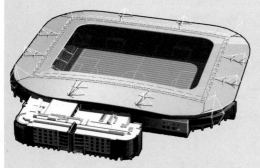

Stadium History

Built at a cost of more than £50m on the site of a former household waste dump, the Madejski Stadium is an impressive modern facility. The complex also plays host to an indoor training centre and both the Royal Berkshire Conference Centre and Millennium Madejski Hotel.

The ground opened its doors in 1998, and has since played host to several Under-21 internationals. Top-class Rugby Union is also on offer, with London Irish playing their home matches at the stadium.

Seating Plan

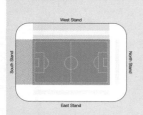

West Stand
South Stand
North Stand
East Stand

Capacity
24,200

- family area
- away fans
- disabled

Stadium Statistics 05/06

Highest attendance
23,845 vs Southampton 10.02.06

Lowest attendance
14,027 vs Burnley 29.08.05

Average attendance
20,207

How to Get There

Travel Information

Car parking
There are spaces at Shinfield Park, HP Invent and the nearby Greyhound Stadium.

Train
Reading Station is a bus ride away from the ground.

Bus
Number 79 'Football Special' bus runs from near the railway station at a cost of £2.50 return.

Area Map

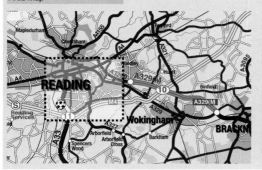

Local Map

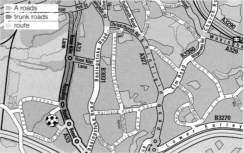

- A roads
- trunk roads
- route

Sheffield United

Nickname:	The Blades	Telephone: 0870 787 1960
Manager:	Neil Warnock	Ticket Office: 0870 787 1799
Chairman:	Derek Dooley	Club Shop: 0870 442 8705
Website:	www.sufc.co.uk	

Season Review 05/06

Having been in the top-two for most of the season, few could argue that Sheffield United deserved to win promotion. Ten wins from the opening 11 games of the campaign laid the foundations for success.

Manager Neil Warnock continued to court controversy on the touchline, getting into a war of words with Norwich's Nigel Worthington and being sent to the stands against Leeds.

Points / Position

▶ won ▶ drawn ▶ lost H home A away

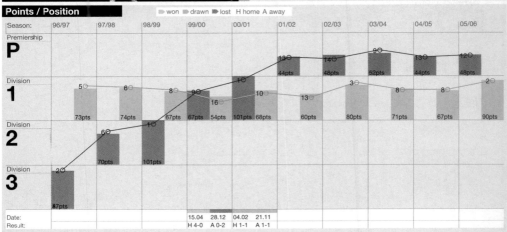

Season:	96/97	97/98	98/99	99/00	00/01	01/02	02/03	03/04	04/05	05/06

Premiership
P — 13 44pts / 14 48pts / 9 52pts / 13 44pts / 12 48pts

Division 1 — 5 73pts / 6 74pts / 8 67pts / 9 67pts 16 54pts / 1 101pts 10 68pts / 13 60pts / 3 80pts / 8 71pts / 8 67pts / 2 90pts

Division 2 — 6 70pts / 1 101pts

Division 3 — 2 87pts

Date:				15.04	28.12	04.02	21.11			
Result:				H 4-0	A 0-2	H 1-1	A 1-1			

Prem. Head-to-Head

Facts	O Fulham	Sheff Utd O
Games		
Points	0	0
Won	0	0
Drawn	0	0
Goals		
For	0	0
Clean Sheets	0	0
Shots on Target	0	0
Disciplinary		
Fouls	0	0
Yellow Cards	0	0
Red Cards	0	0

Goals by Area
O Fulham   O Sheff Utd

0   0
0   0
0   0

Goals Scored by Period
0   0   0   0   0   0
0   15 30 45 60 75 90
0   0   0   0   0   0

Goals by Position
O Fulham   O Sheff Utd

▶ forward: 0	▶ forward: 0
▶ midfield: 0	▶ midfield: 0
▶ defence: 0	▶ defence: 0

Average Attendance

All-Time Records

Total Premiership Record

	O Fulham	Sheff Utd O
Played	190	84
Points	236	94
Won	63	22
Drawn	47	28
Lost	80	34
For	229	96
Against	258	113
Players Used	60	34

All-Time Record vs Fulham

Competition	Played	Won	Drawn	Lost	For	Against
League	52	22	12	18	78	82
FA Cup	5	4	1	0	11	4
League Cup	3	2	1	0	8	1
Other	0	0	0	0	0	0
Total	**60**	**28**	**14**	**18**	**97**	**87**

Sheffield United

Bramall Lane

Stadium History

Sheffield Club and Hallam contested the first football match at Bramall Lane in December 1862. The ground had begun life as a venue for cricket, and the sport continued to be played there until 1973.

The Sheffield United of today were formed in 1889, and it wasn't until the building of the South Stand in 1975 that their stadium became four-sided. Only The Oval shares the distinction of hosting an FA Cup Final. England football international and an England cricket test.

Seating Plan

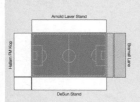

Capacity
30,558

- family area
- away fans
- disabled

Stadium Statistics 05/06

Highest attendance
30,558 vs Sheffield Wednesday 03.12.05

Lowest attendance
17,739 vs Coventry City 27.08.05

Average attendance
23,650

How to Get There

Travel Information

Car parking
No official spaces for away fans, though street parking is available.

Train
Bramall Lane is around one mile from Sheffield Midland Station.

Bus
Number 13 from Arundel Gate goes to Bramall Lane.

Area Map

Local Map

Tottenham Hotspur

Nickname:	Spurs	Telephone:	0870 420 5000
Manager:	Martin Jol	Ticket Office:	0870 420 5000
Chairman:	Daniel Levy	Club Shop:	020 8365 5042
Website:	www.tottenhamhotspur.com		

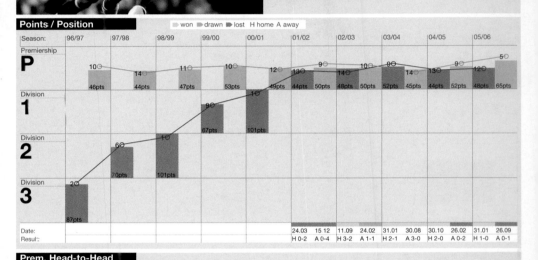

Season Review 05/06

Despite being pipped to Champions League qualification by their great rivals Arsenal on the final day of the season, Spurs could still look back on a campaign in which they made tremendous progress.

Manager Martin Jol was unafraid to put his faith in youth, allowing the likes of Aaron Lennon and Michael Dawson to shine.

Points / Position

won drawn lost H home A away

Season:	96/97	97/98	98/99	99/00	00/01	01/02	02/03	03/04	04/05	05/06
Premiership **P**	10 / 46pts	14 / 44pts	11 / 47pts	10 / 53pts	12 / 49pts	13 / 44pts, 9 / 50pts	10 / 48pts, 14 / 50pts	9 / 52pts, 14 / 45pts	13 / 44pts, 9 / 52pts	12 / 48pts, 5 / 65pts
Division **1**					1 / 101pts	9 / 67pts				
Division **2**		6 / 70pts	1 / 101pts							
Division **3**	2 / 87pts									

Date:						24.03	15.12	11.09	24.02	31.01	30.08	30.10	26.02	31.01	26.09
Result:						H 0-2	A 0-4	H 3-2	A 1-1	H 2-1	A 3-0	H 2-0	A 0-2	H 1-0	A 0-1

Prem. Head-to-Head

Facts	Fulham	Tottenham
Games		
Points	16	13
Won	5	4
Drawn	1	1
Goals		
For	12	13
Clean Sheets	3	4
Shots on Target	56	50
Disciplinary		
Fouls	115	125
Yellow Cards	14	11
Red Cards	1	2

Goals by Area
Fulham   Tottenham

6   3
9   7
1   3

Goals by Position
Fulham   Tottenham

	Fulham	Tottenham
forward:	4	9
midfield:	6	3
defence:	1	1
own goals:	1	

Goals Scored by Period

	0	15	30	45	60	75	90
	1	1	2	0	5	3	
	1	3	5	0	1	3	

Average Attendance

18,413

35,098

All-Time Records

Total Premiership Record	Fulham	Tottenham
Played	190	544
Points	236	728
Won	63	195
Drawn	47	143
Lost	80	206
For	229	716
Against	258	732
Players Used	60	139

All-Time Record vs Fulham						
Competition	Played	Won	Drawn	Lost	For	Against
League	54	26	19	9	91	61
FA Cup	4	3	1	0	6	1
League Cup	3	2	0	1	4	4
Other	0	0	0	0	0	0
Total	**61**	**31**	**20**	**10**	**101**	**66**

Tottenham Hotspur

White Hart Lane

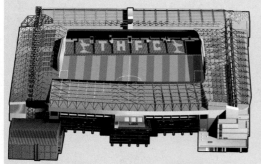

Stadium History

Tottenham moved to White Hart Lane, or the High Road Ground as it was known then, back in 1899. Within five years the ground had a capacity of 32,000, and it had reached 50,000 by 1911. Development of the East Stand was completed in 1934, providing the stadium with enough room to house around 80,000 spectators.

Improved safety regulations, including a switch to all-seater stadia, have seen the capacity dramatically reduced since then, but the stadium is still one to be proud of.

Seating Plan

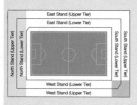

Capacity
36,247

- family area
- away fans
- disabled

Stadium Statistics 05/06

Highest attendance
36,247 vs Everton 15.10.05

Lowest attendance
35,427 vs Fulham 26.09.05

Average attendance
36,073

How to Get There

Travel Information

Car parking
Limited parking available near the ground. Car parks near the ground are pricey. Free parking in residential areas 10 minutes away.

Train
White Hart Lane, Seven Sisters or Northumberland Park.

Tube
Seven Sisters (then long walk).

Bus
259, 279, 149.

Area Map

Local Map

Watford

Nickname: **The Hornets**
Manager: **Adrian Boothroyd**
Chairman: **Graham Simpson**
Website: **www.watfordfc.co.uk**

Telephone: **0870 111 1881**
Ticket Office: **0870 111 1881**
Club Shop: **01923 496 005**

Season Review 05/06

Watford were the surprise package of the Championship, finishing third and going on to gain promotion through the Play-Offs.

Success was built around a belief instilled in his players by ultra-confident young boss Aidy Boothroyd. The likes of Marlon King and Matthew Spring were given a new lease of life, whilst Ashley Young and Jay DeMerit blossomed into stars.

Points / Position

won drawn lost H home A away

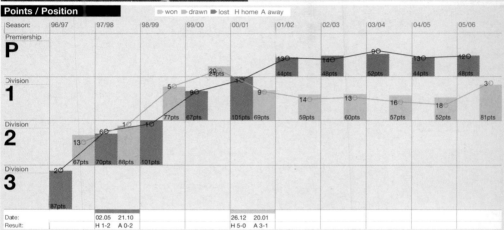

Season:	96/97	97/98	98/99	99/00	00/01	01/02	02/03	03/04	04/05	05/06

| Date: | | 02.05 | 21.10 | | | 26.12 | 20.01 | | | |
| Result: | | H 1-2 | A 0-2 | | | H 5-0 | A 3-1 | | | |

Prem. Head-to-Head

Facts	O Fulham	Watford O
Games		
Points	0	0
Won	0	0
Drawn	0	0
Goals		
For	0	0
Clean Sheets	0	0
Shots on Target	0	0
Disciplinary		
Fouls	0	0
Yellow Cards	0	0
Red Cards	0	0

Goals by Area

O Fulham   O Watford

Goals by Position

O Fulham   O Watford

	Fulham	Watford
forward:	0	0
midfield:	0	0
defence:	0	0

Goals Scored by Period

0	0	0	0	0	0
0	15	30	45	60	75	90
0	0	0	0	0	0

Average Attendance

All-Time Records

Total Premiership Record	O Fulham	Watford O
Played	190	38
Points	236	24
Won	63	6
Drawn	47	6
Lost	80	26
For	229	35
Against	258	77
Players Used	60	32

All-Time Record vs Fulham

Competition	Played	Won	Drawn	Lost	For	Against
League	16	5	3	8	23	39
FA Cup	6	2	3	1	8	6
League Cup	0	0	0	0	0	0
Other	1	0	0	1	0	1
Total	**23**	**7**	**6**	**10**	**31**	**46**

Vicarage Road

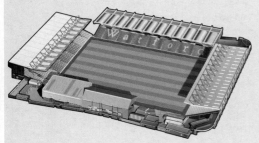

Stadium History

Watford moved to Vicarage Road in 1922, with the ground being officially opened by Colonel Charles Healey. Much has changed since that opening match against Millwall, with only the section of the Main, or East, Stand on the Occupation Road side of the stadium still in existence today.

The Vicarage Road Stand and The Rookery were both constructed during the 1990s, while The Rous Stand was built in 1986. Top-flight Rugby Union outfit Saracens also call the ground their home.

Seating Plan

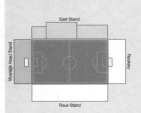

East Stand

Vicarage Road Stand

Rookery

Rous Stand

family area
away fans
disabled

Capacity
22,100

Stadium Statistics 05/06

Highest attendance
19,842 vs Coventry City 11.02.06

Lowest attendance
11,722 vs Crewe Alexandra 28.01.06

Average attendance
15,449

How to Get There

Travel Information

Car parking
Due to restrictions around the ground, Church Car Park in the town centre is a good option.

Train
The nearest station is Watford High Street.

Tube
The nearest station is Watford on the Metropclitan line (10-15 minute walk).

Bus
Services run from Watford Junction Bus Station.

Area Map

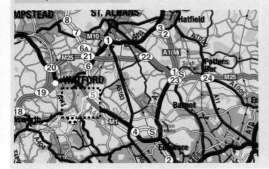

Local Map

A roads
trunk roads
route

West Ham United ○

Nickname:	The Hammers	Telephone:	020 8548 2748
Manager:	Alan Pardew	Ticket Office:	0870 112 2700
Chairman:	Terence Brown	Club Shop:	020 8548 2730
Website:	www.whufc.com		

Season Review 05/06

West Ham enjoyed a memorable return to the top-flight, finishing ninth and reaching the FA Cup Final. The Hammers came within four minutes of lifting the trophy, but were ultimately undone by some magic from Liverpool's Steven Gerrard.

Manager Alan Pardew won over his many critics with a stylish brand of attacking football firmly in keeping with the traditions of the club.

Points / Position

won drawn lost H home A away

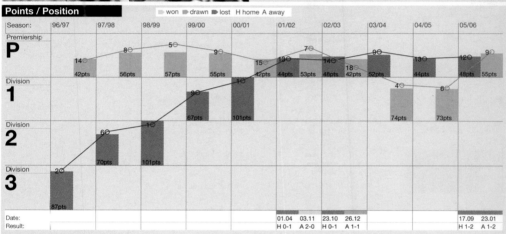

Season:	96/97	97/98	98/99	99/00	00/01	01/02	02/03	03/04	04/05	05/06

Premiership **P**

14 — 42pts; 8 — 56pts; 5 — 57pts; 9 — 55pts; 15 — 42pts; 13 — 44pts; 7 — 53pts; 14 — 48pts; 18 — 42pts; 9 — 52pts; 13 — 44pts; 12 — 48pts; 9 — 55pts

Division **1**

9 — 67pts; 1 — 101pts; 4 — 74pts; 8 — 73pts

Division **2**

6 — 70pts; 1 — 101pts

Division **3**

2 — 87pts

Date:						01.04	03.11	23.10	26.12					17.09	23.01
Result:						H 0-1	A 2-0	H 0-1	A 1-1					H 1-2	A 1-2

Prem. Head-to-Head

Facts	○ Fulham	West Ham ○
Games		
Points	4	13
Won	1	4
Drawn	1	1
Goals		
For	5	7
Clean Sheets	1	2
Shots on Target	28	28
Disciplinary		
Fouls	83	77
Yellow Cards	11	10
Red Cards	1	1

Goals by Area

○ Fulham   ○ West Ham

2

2   4

1   1

Goals Scored by Period

	0	0	1	2	2	0
	0	15	30	45	60	75	90
	0	2	1	2	1	1

Goals by Position

○ Fulham   ○ West Ham

▶ forward:	2	▶ forward:	3
▶ midfield:	3	▶ midfield:	2
▶ defence:	0	▶ defence:	1
		● own goals:	1

Average Attendance

▶ **19,060**

▶ **30,351**

All-Time Records

Total Premiership Record	○ Fulham	West Ham ○
Played	190	426
Points	236	555
Won	63	148
Drawn	47	111
Lost	80	167
For	229	514
Against	258	590
Players Used	60	142

All-Time Record vs Fulham

Competition	Played	Won	Drawn	Lost	For	Against
League	68	30	14	24	109	101
FA Cup	6	2	2	2	6	7
League Cup	1	0	0	1	1	2
Other	0	0	0	0	0	0
Total	**75**	**32**	**16**	**27**	**116**	**110**

West Ham United

Boleyn Ground

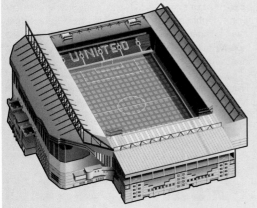

Stadium History

West Ham took up residence at the Boleyn Ground in 1904, beating rivals Millwall 3-0 in the first game played at their new home. The ground has since become renowned for housing good football, and has developed into a modern sporting venue.

In January 1994, the lower tier of the new Bobby Moore Stand was opened. One year later, completion of the Centenary Stand meant that the Boleyn had become an all-seater stadium. Further work has taken place in recent years, thus increasing the capacity.

Seating Plan

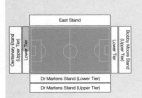

Capacity
35,647

- family area
- away fans
- disabled

Stadium Statistics 05/06

Highest attendance
34,970 vs Tottenham Hotspur 07.05.06

Lowest attendance
29,582 vs Aston Villa 12.09.05

Average attendance
33,742

How to Get There

Travel Information

Car parking
Near the ground is difficult; residents scheme is in operation. Some places can be found over 15 minutes walk away.

Tube
Upton Park station on the District Line is a short walk away.

Bus
Numbers 5, 15, 58, 104, 115, 147, 330 & 376.

Area Map

Local Map

Wigan Athletic ○

Nickname:	**The Latics**
Manager:	**Paul Jewell**
Chairman:	**Dave Whelan**
Website	**www.wiganlatics.co.uk**

Telephone:	**01942 774 000**
Ticket Office:	**0870 112 2552**
Club Shop:	**01942 216 945**

Season Review 05/06

Wigan surprised pundits and supporters alike by finishing in the top half of the table. A trip to Cardiff in the Carling Cup Final also served to highlight just how far the club had come in such a short space of time.

The platform for success was built early in the season, with Paul Jewell's men amassing 25 points from their first 11 Premiership matches.

Points / Position

■ won ■ drawn ■ lost H home A away

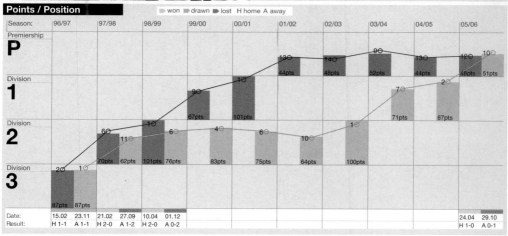

Season:	96/97	97/98	98/99	99/00	00/01	01/02	02/03	03/04	04/05	05/06
Date:	15.02	23.11	21.02	27.09	10.04	01.12			24.04	29.10
Result:	H 1-1	A 1-1	H 2-0	A 1-2	H 2-0	A 0-2			H 1-0	A 0-1

Prem. Head-to-Head

Facts	○ Fulham	Wigan ○
Games		
Points	3	3
Won	1	1
Drawn	0	0
Goals		
For	1	1
Clean Sheets	1	1
Shots on Target	7	16
Disciplinary		
Fouls	18	20
Yellow Cards	5	3
Red Cards	0	0

Goals by Area
○ Fulham   ○ Wigan

	0	
1		1
0		0

Goals Scored by Period

0	0	1	0	0	0
0	15	30	45	60	75	90
0	0	0	0	0	1

Goals by Position
○ Fulham   ○ Wigan

▶ forward:	0	▶ forward:	0
▶ midfield:	1	▶ midfield:	0
▷ defence:	0	▷ defence:	1

Average Attendance

▶ **17,149**
▶ **17,266**

All-Time Records

Total Premiership Record	○ Fulham	Wigan ○
Played	190	38
Points	236	51
Won	63	15
Drawn	47	6
Lost	80	17
For	229	45
Against	258	52
Players Used	60	25

All-Time Record vs Fulham

Competition	Played	Won	Drawn	Lost	For	Against
League	26	7	7	12	25	36
FA Cup	0	0	0	0	0	0
League Cup	2	2	0	0	3	1
Other	0	0	0	0	0	0
Total	**28**	**9**	**7**	**12**	**28**	**37**

Wigan Athletic

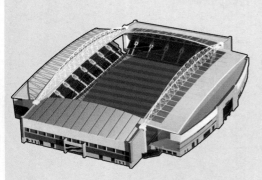

Stadium History

Opened in August 1999, the JJB Stadium is home to both football and rugby league. A 3-0 win against Scunthorpe gave Wigan a great start to life in their new surroundings. Built at an overall cost of £30m, the ground floor of the West Stand even contains a purpose-built Police Station with cells.

Chairman Dave Whelan can be rightly proud of his investment, and would have been delighted to see promotion to the Premiership secured on home soil. Playing top-flight football in 2005/06 resulted in a dramatic improvement in attendances.

Seating Plan

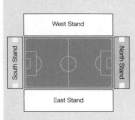

West Stand
South Stand
North Stand
East Stand

Capacity
25,023

- family area
- away fans
- disabled

Stadium Statistics 05/06

Highest attendance
25,023 vs Liverpool 11.02.06

Lowest attendance
16,641 vs Middlesbrough 18.09.05

Average attendance
20,609

How to Get There

Travel Information

Car parking
There is a huge amount of parking located on and around the Retail Park and Stadium itself. You should have no problems if you arrive in plenty of time.

Train
Wigan Wallgate Station is just ten minutes walk from the JJB Stadium. Follow the signposts.

Bus
There are no particular bus routes as the Bus Station is only a ten minute walk from the Stadium.

Area Map

Local Map

pipex

Fulham FC Manager Chris Coleman and deputy Steve Kean celebrate the Pipex signing with CEO Mike Read.

Mike Read, CEO of Pipex, talks about Pipex's first season as Fulham FC's official shirt sponsor:

"We're absolutely delighted to be involved with Fulham FC".

What a season it has been. Great wins against Liverpool, Newcastle, Spurs and Chelsea have been some of the highlights. Of course, it was also the season in which we said goodbye to Fulham legend Johnny Haynes, who'll be missed by everyone involved in the Club.

We're here for all Fulham fans - whether it's keeping up to date with all the transfer gossip on the football websites, downloading football games or building and hosting your own website dedicated to your Fulham heroes.

The new season promises to be a cracker and we're already excited about being associated with Fulham FC again next year.

Pipex provided 6,000 Fulham fans with a helping hand to support the team

Pipex teamed up with Fiat to give Fulham fan Alan Fisher a new Grande Punto.

Boca, Boa and Liam entertained 30 lucky Fulham fans at their Pipex 'An Audience with.....'

Pipex produced the giant Johnny Haynes shirt in tribute to the Maestro